THE
ROYAL BASTARDS
OF MEDIEVAL
ENGLAND

THE
ROYAL BASTARDS
OF MEDIEVAL
ENGLAND

CHRIS GIVEN-WILSON
AND
ALICE CURTEIS

Routledge & Kegan Paul
London, Boston, Melbourne and Henley

First published in 1984
by Routledge & Kegan Paul plc
39 Store Street, London WC1E 7DD, England
9 Park Street, Boston, Mass. 02108, USA
464 St Kilda Road, Melbourne,
Victoria 3004, Australia, and
Broadway House, Newtown Road
Henley-on-Thames, Oxon RG9 1EN, England

Set in Sabon Roman
by Input Typesetting Ltd, London SW19 8DR
and printed in Great Britain
by
Robert Hartnoll Ltd, Bodmin, Cornwall

Library of Congress Cataloging in Publication Data

Given-Wilson, Chris.
The royal bastards of medieval England.

Bibliography: p.
Includes index.
1. Great Britain – Kings and rulers – Children –
Biography. 2. Illegitimate children – Great Britain –
Biography. 3. Great Britain – History – Medieval period,
1066–1485 – Biography. 4. Illegitimacy – England –
History. I. Curteis, Alice. II. Title.
DA177.G58   1984   942'.009'92 [B]   83–23690

British Library CIP Data available

ISBN 0–7102–0025–0

FOR RACHEL AND HANNAH

CONTENTS

Acknowledgments   ix

Part I Introduction 1
  1 The English royal family in the Middle Ages 3
  2 Marriage and divorce 20
  3 Sex, love and illegitimacy 37

Part II Royal bastards 1066–1216 55
  4 Henry I's bastards 60
  5 Robert of Gloucester 74
  6 Gervais of Blois 94
  7 Henry II's bastards 97
  8 Geoffrey 'Plantagenet' 103
  9 The bastards of Richard I and King John 126

Part III Royal bastards in late medieval England 133
  10 Sir John de Southeray 138
  11 Sir Roger de Clarendon 143
  12 Katherine Swynford and the Beauforts 147
  13 Allegations of bastardy in the fifteenth-century royal family 154
  14 Yorkist royal bastards 160
  15 Arthur Plantagenet 162

Postscript: The Tudors 174
Appendix: The Bastards of the English kings 1066–1485 178
Note on sources 180
Index of names and places 182
Subject index 194

ILLUSTRATIONS

List of Plates   *between pages 116 and 117*
1 An impotence trial (Walters Art Gallery, Baltimore)
2 Charter of Henry I, 1121 (British Library)
3 (a) Tomb and effigy of William Longsword
   (b) Seal of William Longsword
4 Effigy of King John (photograph by A. F. Kersting)
5 Joan Skerne (reproduced by permission of the vicar and
   churchwardens of All Saints' Church, Kingston-upon-
   Thames)
6 (a) Arms of Roger de Clarendon (line drawing by Robert
   Briggs)
   (b) Arms of John Beaufort before legitimation (line
   drawing by Robert Briggs)
   (c) Arms of John Beaufort after legitimation (line drawing
   by Robert Briggs)
7 Edward IV (reproduced by gracious permission of Her
   Majesty The Queen)
8 Arms of Arthur Plantagenet (Society of Antiquaries of
   London)

Tables   *page*
1 Selective table of English kings 978–1189   x
2 The children of Henry II   xi
3 Selective table of English kings 1327–1509   xii
4 Date-chart of English kings 1066–1485   5
5 The marriages of Joan, the 'Fair Maid of Kent'   16
6 The bastards of Henry I   63
7 Henry I's bastards and the Bréteuil inheritance   66
8 Marriage connections of the English royal house
   and the Breton dukes   69
9 Inter-relation of the English, Castilian and
   Portuguese royal families (selective)   139
10 The children of John of Gaunt   148

Map
Territorial connections of Henry I's bastards in France
(p. 70)

ACKNOWLEDGMENTS

This book has been a long time in the making, and along the way we have received much advice and help from many people; in particular we would like to thank Beatrice Given-Wilson, Tony Mount, Mike Tobert, and Andrew Wheatcroft, all of whom read parts of the book in draft and offered useful comments; Michael Prestwich, Bill Jessop and Tony Goodman, who provided valuable information; Robert Briggs and Peter Adamson, who helped greatly with the illustrations; and both Michele FitzHerbert and Rachel Curteis, who gave of their time to save ours. Finally, we can both say with absolute truthfulness that without our respective partners this book would never have been written.

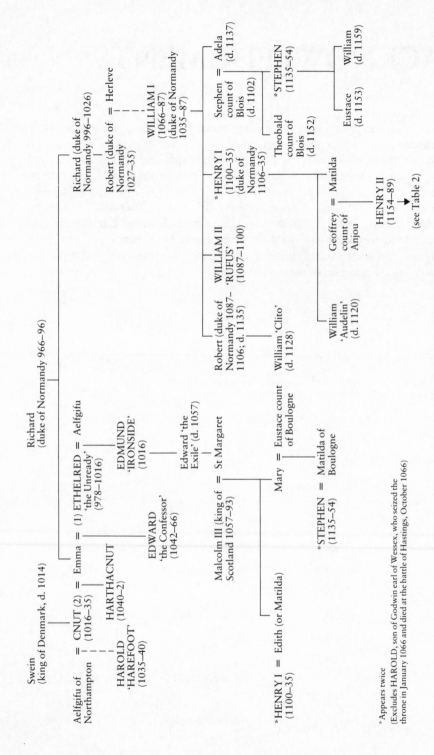

Table 1 Selective table of English kings 978–1189

Swein
(king of Denmark, d. 1014)

Aelfgifu of Northampton = CNUT (2) = Emma = (1) ETHELRED 'the Unready' (978–1016)

Richard (duke of Normandy 966–96)

HAROLD 'HAREFOOT' (1035–40)

HARTHACNUT (1040–2)

EDMUND 'IRONSIDE' (1016)

EDWARD 'the Confessor' (1042–66)

Edward 'the Exile' (d. 1057)

Malcolm III (king of Scotland 1057–93) = St Margaret

Richard (duke of Normandy 996–1026)

Robert (duke of Normandy 1027–35) = Herleve

WILLIAM I (1066–87) (duke of Normandy 1035–87)

Robert (duke of Normandy 1087–1106; d. 1135)

WILLIAM II 'RUFUS' (1087–1100)

*HENRY I (1100–35) (duke of Normandy 1106–35)

Adela (d. 1137) = Stephen count of Blois (d. 1102)

William 'Clito' (d. 1128)

*HENRY I (1100–35) = Edith (or Matilda)

Mary = Eustace count of Boulogne

*STEPHEN (1135–54) = Matilda of Boulogne

Theobald count of Blois (d. 1152)

*STEPHEN (1135–54)

Eustace (d. 1153)

William (d. 1159)

William 'Audelin' (d. 1120)

Geoffrey count of Anjou = Matilda

HENRY II (1154–89) → (see Table 2)

*Appears twice

(Excludes HAROLD, son of Godwin earl of Wessex, who seized the throne in January 1066 and died at the battle of Hastings, October 1066)

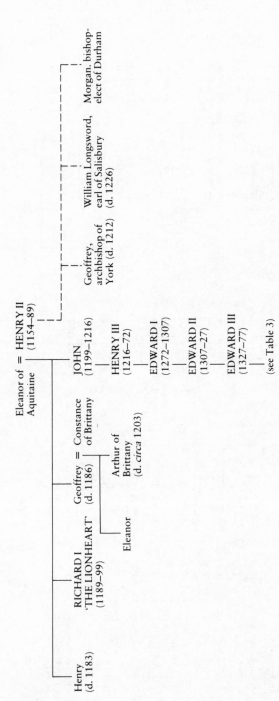

Table 2 The children of Henry II

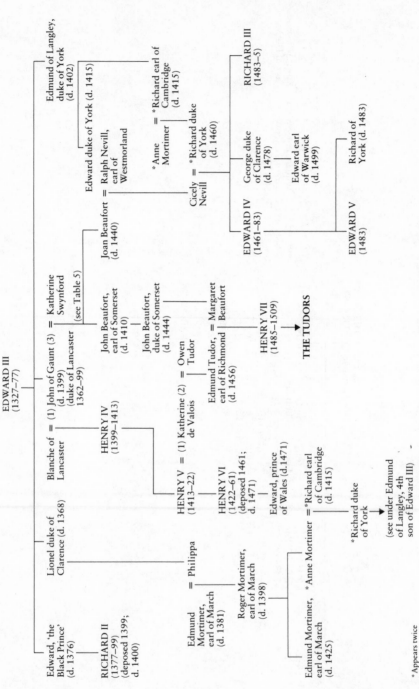

Table 3 Selective table of English kings 1327–1509

EDWARD III (1327–77)

Edward, 'the Black Prince' (d. 1376)

RICHARD II (1377–99) (deposed 1399; d. 1400)

Lionel duke of Clarence (d. 1368)

= Philippa

Edmund Mortimer, earl of March (d. 1381)

Roger Mortimer, earl of March (d. 1398)

Edmund Mortimer, earl of March (d. 1425)

*Anne Mortimer = *Richard earl of Cambridge (d. 1415)

*Richard duke of York
(see under Edmund of Langley, 4th son of Edward III)

Blanche of = (1) John of Gaunt (3) = Katherine Swynford
Lancaster   (d. 1399)   (see Table 5)
                 (duke of Lancaster
                 1362–99)

HENRY IV (1399–1413)

HENRY V = (1) Katherine (2) = Owen Tudor
(1413–22)   de Valois

HENRY VI (1422–61) (deposed 1461; d. 1471)

Edward, prince of Wales (d. 1471)

John Beaufort, earl of Somerset (d. 1410)

John Beaufort, duke of Somerset (d. 1444)

Margaret Beaufort

Edmund Tudor, = Margaret
earl of Richmond   Beaufort
(d. 1456)

HENRY VII (1485–1509)

THE TUDORS

Joan Beaufort (d. 1440)

Edmund of Langley, duke of York (d. 1402)

Edward duke of York (d. 1415)

= Ralph Nevill, earl of Westmorland

Cicely = *Richard duke
Nevill   of York
          (d. 1460)

EDWARD IV (1461–83)

EDWARD V (1483)

Richard of York (d. 1483)

George duke of Clarence (d. 1478)

Edward earl of Warwick (d. 1499)

*Richard earl of Cambridge (d. 1415)

RICHARD III (1483–5)

* Appears twice

PART I

INTRODUCTION

Edmund: *Thou, Nature, art my goddess; to thy law*
My services are bound. Wherefore should I
Stand in the plague of custom, and permit
The curiosity of nations to deprive me,
For that I am some twelve or fourteen moonshines
Lag of a brother? Why bastard? Wherefore base?
When my dimensions are as well compact,
My mind as generous, and my shape as true,
As honest madam's issue? Why brand they us
With base? With baseness? bastardy? base, base?
Who in the lusty stealth of nature take
More composition and fierce quality
Than doth, within a dull, stale, tired bed,
Go to th' creating a whole tribe of fops,
Got 'tween asleep and wake? Well then,
Legitimate Edgar, I must have your land:
Our father's love is to the bastard Edmund
As to th' legitimate. Fine word, 'legitimate'!
Well, my legitimate, if this letter speed,
And my invention thrive, Edmund the base
Shall top th' legitimate—: I grow, I prosper;
Now, gods, stand up for bastards!

Shakespeare, *King Lear*, Act 1, Scene 2

CHAPTER 1

THE ENGLISH ROYAL FAMILY IN THE MIDDLE AGES

On Sunday 22 June 1483, Londoners from all over the city gathered at St Paul's Cross. Dr Ralph Shaw (or Shaa), the brother of the mayor, a preacher renowned for his scholarship and eloquence, was to give a sermon, and rumour had it that this would be no ordinary sermon.

London was full of rumours. Eleven weeks had passed since the death of King Edward IV. His heir was his son, Edward V, but the new king was only twelve, and the intervening weeks had witnessed a struggle for power between the various factions aspiring to control the government during his minority. The central figure in this power-struggle was Richard duke of Gloucester, Edward IV's younger brother and thus uncle to the young king; on his deathbed, Edward IV had committed to Gloucester the Protectorship of the kingdom and of his young heir, but Gloucester's power was vigorously challenged by the Woodville faction, led by Edward IV's widow, Elizabeth Woodville, now the queen mother. Gloucester swiftly arrested several leading members of the Woodville faction, seized the person of the king, and lodged him in the state apartments of the Tower of London, ostensibly to await coronation. Elizabeth Woodville took sanctuary in Westminster Abbey, from where she began plotting Gloucester's downfall. But Gloucester got wind of the plot: at a council meeting in the Tower on 13 June he arrested his dead brother's closest friend, William Lord Hastings, and had him beheaded immediately. On 16 June he forced Elizabeth Woodville to hand over her second son, the ten-year-old Richard of York, who was promptly lodged in the Tower with his brother. The coronation was postponed. Parliament had been summoned to meet on 25 June, but now the writs summoning the members to Westminster were cancelled. Throughout the capital, it was beginning to be whispered that the duke of Gloucester's ambitions extended beyond the Protectorship – that they extended to the crown of England itself. Dr Shaw was known to be one of his closest supporters.

Gloucester and his principal accomplice, Henry duke of Buckingham, were among Shaw's audience (although apparently they arrived late). The learned preacher took a biblical text for his sermon, 'bastard slips shall not take root'. He began by praising Gloucester's acknowledged virtues, remarking that he was a man worthy both in birth and character to sit upon the throne of England. Then he dropped his bombshell: Edward IV's sons, Shaw declared, were illegitimate. His marriage to Elizabeth Woodville had been invalid, because at the time when he married her, he had already made a 'precontract of marriage' to another woman, Lady Eleanor Butler, daughter of the earl of Shrewsbury. This precontract automatically invalidated his marriage to Elizabeth, and equally automatically bastardised any children begotten by him upon her. In the succession to the throne, therefore, they counted for nothing: the duke of Gloucester was the rightful heir to the throne.

The sequel to Dr Shaw's sermon is part of the folklore of English history. Two days later, the duke of Buckingham repeated these allegations in a famous speech at the Guildhall: although he spoke 'so well, and so eloquently, and with such an angelic countenance', few people believed him. Nevertheless, on 25 June an assembly of the estates of the realm at Westminster formally requested Gloucester to assume the crown, and on 6 July he was crowned as King Richard III. Edward IV's 'bastards', the princes in the Tower, were never seen in public again: some time during the next few months they were secretly murdered, probably on Richard's orders. But Richard III did not enjoy his kingship long. Two years and two months later he was defeated and slain at Bosworth Field, and the man who defeated him that day, Henry Tudor, established a dynasty which was to rule England for over a century.

The battle of Bosworth Field is still widely regarded as marking the end of the medieval period in English political history, and in many ways the events of 1483–85 – the usurpation of Richard III, the manner in which it was achieved, and the accession of Henry Tudor – provide a telling climax to that history. From one point of view, they were national tragedies; from another, little more than family squabbles. They highlight two themes which run through that history: firstly, the uncertainty over the succession to the English throne in the Middle Ages, which meant that might often prevailed against an ill-defined right in determining who should be king; secondly, the internecine family feuding to which that uncertainty gave rise, setting son against father, wife against husband, and cousin against cousin in a dismal series of rebellions, conspiracies and sometimes even civil wars. The usurpations of 1483 and 1485 also demonstrate clearly a third aspect of that history: royal promiscuity, and its political consequences. For Edward IV was a notorious womaniser, and there is little doubt that this fact made the story of his 'precontract of marriage' to Eleanor Butler much more believable; while Henry Tudor, the founder of a famous dynasty, was descended on one side from the legitimated bastard of one of Edward III's sons, and on the other from a Welsh clerk who had secretly married a former queen of England. With his accession, the concept of legitimacy in determining the succession to the English throne reached its low point.

The royal family in medieval England was not a happy family. Between 1066 and 1485, the period with which we are here concerned, eighteen kings reigned over England (see Table 4). Five of these eighteen – Edward II, Richard II, Henry VI, Edward V and Richard III – were deposed and/or murdered. A further seven – William I, William II, Henry I, Henry II,

Table 4 Date-chart of English Kings 1066–1485

	Born	Reigned	
WILLIAM I ('The Conqueror' or 'the Bastard')	c.1027–8	1066–87	
WILLIAM II ('Rufus')	c.1056–60	1087–1100	
HENRY I	1068	1100–35	
STEPHEN	c.1097–1100	1135–54	
HENRY II	1133	1154–89	
RICHARD I ('the Lionheart')	1157	1189–99	
JOHN	1167	1199–1216	
HENRY III	1207	1216–72	
EDWARD I	1239	1272–1307	
EDWARD II	1284	1307–27	(deposed Jan. 1327; murdered 21 Sept. 1327 at Berkeley castle)
EDWARD III	1312	1327–77	
RICHARD II	1367	1377–99	(deposed Sept. 1399; murdered? Feb. 1400 at Pontefract castle)
HENRY IV	1367	1399–1413	
HENRY V	1387	1413–22	
HENRY VI	1421	1422–61 and 1470–71	(deposed March 1461; reinstated Sept. 1470–April 1471; murdered in the Tower of London, 21 May 1471)
EDWARD IV	1442	1461–83	(deposed Sept. 1470–April 1471)
EDWARD V	1470	1483 (April-June)	(murdered in the Tower of London? July 1483)
RICHARD III	1452	1483–5	(killed at Bosworth Field, 22 Aug. 1485)

Richard I, Henry III and Edward IV – were confronted with rebellions which were either led or supported by their sons, their brothers, or their wives. A further three – Stephen, John and Henry IV – were widely regarded as having usurped the throne in place of a cousin or a nephew. Of the eighteen kings of medieval England, only three – Edward I, Edward III and Henry V – both succeeded to the throne without serious challenge, and lived out their reigns without serious opposition from within their own families. Family solidarity was a quality conspicuously lacking in the medieval English royal family.

The reasons for this family strife were many. Personalities were always important. So were the accidents of birth and death, such as the tragic drowning of William Audelin, the only legitimate son of Henry I, in the wreck of the White Ship in 1120. Yet uncertainty over the succession was undoubtedly a major factor, for the succession to the throne was never defined by law, and what therefore constituted a 'legitimate' king was always open to question. In the eleventh and twelfth centuries, the custom of primogeniture was gradually establishing itself throughout Western European society; yet if one looks at the succession to the English throne between 1066 and 1216, it is striking that on only one occasion during this period when the throne changed hands did it pass from a father to his eldest surviving son, and that was from Henry II to Richard I 'the Lionheart' in 1189. On two other occasions the eldest (legitimate) son was deliberately passed over: William the Conqueror divided his lands, leaving Normandy to his first son, Robert, and England to William 'Rufus', his second son; while in 1153 Stephen was forced to disinherit both his sons from the throne. On a further two occasions primogenitary custom was ignored, namely when Henry I's daughter Matilda was rejected by the barons in 1135, despite the fact that Henry had thrice compelled them to swear oaths recognising her as his successor, and again when John became king in 1199 in preference to his nephew Arthur of Brittany (see Tables 1 and 2).

For nearly two hundred years after 1216 the succession was more stable, with primogenitary custom consistently followed right through until the end of the fourteenth century, but the deposition of the childless Richard II in 1399 and the subsequent usurpation of Henry IV, who was not the primogenitary heir, reopened the whole question of the succession. Every king of England in the fifteenth century was faced by either a rebellion or a conspiracy led by men who claimed that he had no right to the throne which he occupied. When civil war – the Wars of the Roses – flared up in the 1450s, the dynastic question naturally became one of the central issues. Thus when Richard III and Henry Tudor met at Bosworth Field on 22 August 1485, they claimed to be the 'Yorkist' and 'Lancastrian' heirs to the throne respectively (Table 3).

If it was uncertainty over the succession which provided the backdrop to this unhappy family history, personal relations also played their part. Medieval kings – or at least the vast majority of them – did not marry for love. They married for politics. They married to acquire lands, or to cement political alliances. Many of them never even had a say in the choosing of their wives. They married women who were old enough to be their mothers or young enough to be their daughters, women with whom they could hardly carry on a conversation because they spoke a different language, women whom often they had never met until the day of the wedding. Love, personal compatibility, the mutual consent of the partners – those private bonds which nowadays we think of as the proper ingredients of a successful marriage – were irrelevant. Of course there were some who broke the rules: Edward IV, for instance. In the spring of 1464, aged twenty-one and as yet unmarried, Edward met Elizabeth Woodville, a beautiful widow five years his senior. He fell in love with her and tried to seduce her, but – or so the story goes – she refused to give in to the King's entreaties unless he promised to marry her. So Edward, hopelessly in love, secretly married Elizabeth. When the news broke a few months later it was greeted with anger and amazement by the king's advisors. It was not just that the king had married secretly: what was much more important, and much more foolish, was that by giving his hand to the woman he loved Edward had forgone the opportunity to make a marriage which was in the political or diplomatic interests of the kingdom he ruled. By following the dictates of his heart, he had failed in his duty to his country. This was the crux of the matter: for those of sufficient political importance, marriage was far too serious a matter to be left to the bride and groom.

Nor was it easy to escape from a marriage which turned out to be a personal disaster. King John was the only medieval king of England to divorce and remarry, although both Henry II and Edward II apparently considered divorce, and in the light of their marital relationships this is not surprising. Eleanor of Aquitaine, the wife of Henry II, was rumoured to have been unfaithful to her first husband (King Louis VII of France); in 1173 she and her three eldest sons conspired to rebel against Henry, whereupon Henry promptly imprisoned her, and kept her in prison for the remaining sixteen years of his reign. Isabella, the 'she-wolf of France', the wife of Edward II, went one better. Relations between her and Edward, who was almost certainly homosexual, had never been easy, and in 1326 she personally led the revolution which deposed her husband. Whether she was also responsible for his hideous murder at Berkeley castle in the following year is difficult to say, but the political consequences of an unhappy marriage have never been more clearly manifested. In fact the Middle Ages witnessed profound changes in attitudes towards marriage. From the eleventh century onwards, the Catholic church began to argue much more forcefully for a more 'Christian' view of marriage, emphasising the mutual consent of the partners, the indissolubility of the marriage bond, and so forth. At the lower levels of society the church's teaching had considerable influence, but among the aristocracy and royalty marriages continued to be made with an almost total lack of regard for personal considerations.

Not surprisingly, therefore, kings had mistresses. If they could not marry the women they loved, they could at least have affairs with them. At least ten of the eighteen kings who ruled England in the period 1066–1485 can be shown to have taken mistresses, although the names of these mistresses are not always known. They break neatly into two groups of five – although naturally this division is at least partially dictated by the survival of the evidence. For the first five, the evidence suggests no more than the occasional affair. King Stephen (1135–54) acknowledged one bastard son, Gervais, whom he made abbot of Westminster. We know the name of Gervais's mother – she was a Norman woman called Dameta – but we know precious little else about her. Richard I 'the Lionheart' (1189–99) also acknowledged a bastard son, Philip, but there is no clue as to who Philip's mother was. One or two remarks by chroniclers, however, suggest that King Richard was quite well known in his day as a womaniser. The same was said of Edward I (1272–1307), who may also have had a bastard son, called John de Botetourt, although the attribution of royal paternity to Botetourt is far from conclusive. Despite his homosexual inclinations, Edward II (1307–27) fathered a bastard son called Adam, but again we have no evidence as to who his mother was. Finally, Richard III (1483–5), one of the great villains of Shakespearian myth, acknowledged at least two bastards, a son called John whom he made captain of Calais, and a daughter, Katherine, whom he married to the earl of Huntingdon. Richard III may well have fathered more than two bastards, but the identity of their mothers remains a mystery.

With the remaining five kings we are on much firmer ground: Henry I, Henry II, King John, Edward III and Edward IV were all notorious libertines in their own day. Between them they fathered at least thirty-six, and probably many more, royal bastards. We know the names of several of their mistresses, and in some cases we know a lot more than just their names. The most remarkable of these kings was Henry I, the youngest son of William the Conqueror, who ruled England from 1100 to 1135. Henry's illegitimate offspring numbered twenty for sure, and very probably another three; how many more there were who died young, or who for some reason never chanced to be mentioned in the surviving records, or whom the king was unwilling to acknowledge as his, we shall never know; but it is not difficult to imagine that the true figure may well have reached fifty or more. Even if one credits Henry with just the twenty or so whom he acknowledged, however, that still makes him the most prolific begetter of bastards of all the kings, medieval or later, who have sat on the English throne. Charles II, the most celebrated womaniser among the later English kings, only managed sixteen.

Several of Henry I's bastards were probably the result of casual liaisons on the part of the king, but this was certainly not the case with all of them. His mistress Sybil Corbet, for instance, the daughter of Sir Robert Corbet, was probably the mother of at least five of the king's spurious brood; another mistress, Ansfride, the widow of one of the king's knights, mothered at least two, and probably three, of them. With both of these women, particularly Sybil Corbet, Henry must have carried on a relationship over a period of several years. It is this sort of woman, the woman who succeeded not only in catching the king's eye but in keeping it, who has inevitably been remembered as the archetypal royal mistress, but it is as well to remember that they were few and far between. Henry II, the unpredictable but very able grandson of Henry I, who was king of England from 1154 to 1189, had such a mistress: she was Rosamund Clifford, 'Fair Rosamund', who was the daughter of Sir Walter Clifford. Rosamund was the great love of Henry II's life, but so many legends have grown up around the story of her relationship with the king that it is not always easy to disentangle fact from fiction. She probably became Henry's mistress in about 1173 when he was forty and she still little more than a girl, but three years later she suddenly died and Henry was left heart-broken.

Her name will forever be associated with the series of alternately delightful and gruesome stories that have become part of the Fair Rosamund myth: that the king built a bower for her near Woodstock, hidden away within a labyrinth so that only he could reach her, but that the jealous Queen Eleanor discovered her husband's mistress by following a silken thread which had become attached to Henry's foot and, on finding the poor girl alone, put her to death (there are a number of more or less unpleasant variations concerning the manner of Rosamund's death). Unfortunately – for it is a charming story – there was no bower, no labyrinth, no silken clue, no murder. Rosamund died of some mysterious illness and was buried by her grieving lover at Godstow nunnery at Oxford. Fifteen years later, after Henry too had died, Bishop Hugh of Lincoln ordered that Rosamund's tomb be moved out of the church at Godstow, 'for', he declared, 'she was a harlot'. Such was the eventual – and pitifully unromantic – fate of perhaps the best-remembered royal mistress in medieval England.

Rosamund was undoubtedly Henry II's favourite mistress, but she was not his only one. He was the father of at least three illegitimate children, and it is very unlikely that Rosamund was the mother of any of them. Two of his bastard sons entered the church: Morgan, the son of a woman called Nest Bloet who was the wife of a North Country knight, became provost of Beverley minster and bishop-elect of Durham. Geoffrey 'Plantagenet', the most famous of Henry's bastards and one of the most controversial figures in the medieval church, was a very able but unbelievably stubborn man: he became royal chancellor under Henry and was eventually elevated to the archbishopric of York, in which capacity he quarrelled violently with both of Henry II's legitimate sons, Richard I and King John. Henry's third acknowledged bastard was William Longsword, who became earl of Salisbury. He is the only one of the king's bastards who might have been the son of Rosamund, but it does not seem likely that he was. Indeed, it is unlikely that any of these three were born of the same mother and, judging by Henry II's reputation as a seducer of women, this need come as no surprise. It was even rumoured that he had seduced Princess Alice, the daughter of the French king, who was betrothed to Henry's own son Richard, and who had been placed in the English king's care until she was old enough to marry his son. Whether or not the rumour was true, there is plenty of other evidence that Henry deserved his reputation.

Henry's youngest son, John, king of England from 1199 to 1216 (Plate 4), acquired a reputation much like his father's. His tally of known bastards reached seven – again this is probably a conservative estimate – but unlike Henry he does not seem to have formed lasting attachments with any of his mistresses. Thus although we know the names of some of the women who shared the royal bed with this traditionally 'bad' king, we know very little else about them. However, the same is certainly not true of Edward III (1327–77). Edward's reputation for womanising is not based, like John's, on the accusation that he indulged his fancies with a constant stream of woman, but that he kept as his mistress for over a dozen years one of the most notorious and hated women in English history. Alice Perrers, the greedy, highly ambitious and very shrewd daughter of a Hertfordshire knight, became Edward's mistress when he was already past his fiftieth birthday and remained with him until his death at the age of sixty-four. She used her influence with Edward not only to amass a fortune of staggering proportions, but also to meddle in political affairs at the highest level. Edward, growing senile by now, was infatuated with her, and was prepared to do almost anything to please her. She was the only royal mistress in medieval England who really became a national scandal. After Edward's death in June 1377, she was tried publicly in parliament for corruption, convicted and sentenced to exile and forfeiture of all her lands and goods.

A little over a century after Edward III's death another royal mistress was to find herself subjected to much the same sort of public humiliation as Alice Perrers suffered. This was Elizabeth Shore (often, but incorrectly, called Jane), the celebrated 'merry concubine' of King Edward IV (1461–83)(Plate 7). Edward IV's reputation as an adulterer was second to none. Almost all the contemporary chroniclers remarked on it. 'He pursued with no discrimination the married and the unmarried, the noble and the lowly,' remarked one: 'however, he took none by force. He overcame all by money and promises, and having conquered them, he dismissed them.' Elizabeth Shore, however, he did not dismiss. She was the only one of Edward's many mistresses whom the king kept for more than a year or two and, like Alice Perrers with her own King Edward, she remained with him until his death. Like Alice too, she paid the price for it. She too had her goods confiscated, was twice imprisoned, and was forced by Richard III to perform a humiliating public penance by carrying a lighted taper through the streets of London in solemn procession – the standard punishment for a common adulteress. In fairness to Elizabeth, however, she had little else in common with the grasping Alice Perrers. She seems in fact to have been a thoroughly charming woman – as well as an exceptionally beautiful one – and her public chastisement at the hands of Richard III was not the result of any public outcry against her misdeeds, but because she became implicated in a plot to prevent Richard's seizure of the throne.

Apart from the fact that each of them begot several bastards, these five kings had little in common. It would be difficult to imagine two English kings less alike than the cold, stern Henry I, a man of few words but inestimable cunning, feared throughout his dominions for his awesome temper and savage cruelty, and the ostentatious, pleasure-loving Edward IV, an approachable and amiable man, yet one who also had reserves of will-power and a genius for financial administration hidden behind the façade of easy-going indolence. Henry II and John, father and son, shared many of the same qualities: both were thoroughly able administrators; both immensely energetic kings, both devious and often faithless. Edward III, however, was cast in a quite different mould: a man who revelled in the formal pomp and ceremony of court life, who delighted in the grand gestures of sovereignty, a warm and cheerful yet fiercely ambitious character, Edward had an innate ability for kingship as well as the personal charm to win men over to his way of thinking. What is interesting is that four of the five – King John is the exception – were strikingly successful kings. This is not to suggest, of course, that to be a successful king it was necessarily an advantage to be a womaniser: William the Conqueror, the victor of Hastings, and Henry V, the victor of Agincourt, would both rank high on achievement in any list of English kings, yet both were singled out for the purity of their personal lives. Nevertheless the successful reigns of Henry I, Henry II, Edward III and Edward IV do at least suggest that their contemporaries did not think any the less of them for their amorous propensities. It was only when a royal mistress achieved the sort of influence over her lover which allowed her to sway political decisions that court gossip turned to genuine disapproval. Only Alice Perrers falls into this category.

What sort of women became royal mistresses in medieval England? For a king, it might be thought, the opportunities were almost endless: there must always have been plenty of women who were prepared to share the royal bed for a night, or for several nights, or even years if required, in return for the sort of gratitude which a king could bestow. Yet even for a king there were certain social conventions which he would be well advised not to ignore. Foreign princesses, for instance, or the daughters of the English aristocracy – especially if they were heiresses – were definitely beyond the pale. This is why Henry II's seduction of Princess Alice of France – if indeed it occurred – was noted with such disapproval. Yet King John was accused of lusting after the high-born women of his kingdom too: it was not just that he took mistresses, remarked one contemporary, but that he would insist on pursuing the wives and daughters of his great lords. Nothing was better calculated to make enemies in precisely those circles where John most needed friends.

Later kings were also to be accused of trying to seduce the wives or daughters of their great nobles. It was rumoured, for instance, that Edward III had made overtures to the countess of Salisbury while playing chess with her, and when she refused to go along with him he proceeded to rape her. Edward IV was accused – though only after his death – of having an affair with Eleanor Butler, daughter of the earl of Shrewsbury. But it is difficult to know how much truth there was in either of these stories, for both were designed for use as propaganda against the respective kings. Thomas More recounts a story about Edward IV: the king, said More, would jest that he had three concubines, one the merriest in his kingdom, the second the wiliest, and the third 'the holiest harlot in the realm', who never left off praying in church except to make visits to the royal bed-chamber. The merriest, said More, was Elizabeth Shore; the other two, he went on, 'were somewhat greater personages' and should remain nameless. Thomas More's reticence is understandable, for even if kings did sometimes take the wives and daughters of their great nobles as their mistresses, it was not advisable to make a habit of it.

If the highest-born in the land were excluded from the king's purview by social convention, the low-born were probably excluded as much as anything else by a lack of opportunity. 'Low-born' is of course a relative term. A court gossip might regard, for instance, a serving-lady in the royal household as 'low-born', but it was very unlikely that she would have come from peasant stock. Kings very rarely mixed with the peasantry, and although chroniclers sometimes referred to royal mistresses as 'base-born', or 'of humble parentage', this certainly should not be taken too literally. Of course it is quite possible that a king might have a casual affair with a peasant girl – there is an old tradition that Henry II did so once on a hunting expedition – but it was unthinkable that anything more permanent might come of it and, barring the odd whiff of scandal on the part of a court chronicler, it is very unlikely that anyone would bother to record the fact.

Most of the women who became royal mistresses in the Middle Ages were from one of two backgrounds: either they were the wives or daughters of the lesser landowning class – those who later came to be known as the country gentry – or they were sprung from the civic bourgeoisie. Of Henry I's mistresses, Ansfride was the widow of a knight; Edith, who bore only one bastard by the king, was the daughter of a Northumberland baron; while Sybil Corbet's father was Sir Robert Corbet. Henry II's Rosamund was the daughter of the Shropshire knight Walter Clifford, while his other known mistress, Nest Bloet, was the wife of Sir Ralph Bloet. The mother of Henry II's best-known bastard, Geoffrey 'Plantagenet', was described by one contemporary as 'base-born', but in fact she was probably the daughter of a knight too. Alice Perrers was the daughter of Sir Richard Perrers of Hertfordshire, and she first met the king because she became lady-in-waiting to Edward's queen, Philippa of Hainault. Of Edward IV's mistresses, Elizabeth Shore was the daughter of one wealthy London merchant and the wife of another, while Edward's other known mistress, Elizabeth Wayte (or Lucy), was the daughter of a minor Hampshire landowner. Edward IV was renowned for seducing the wives and daughters of the rather stolid and very prosperous London merchants. 'For here the king resided most', jibed the duke of Buckingham, 'and here therefore he fornicated most.' The good citizens, it seems, were not overly amused. Yet it is hardly surprising that royal mistresses usually came from one of these two backgrounds. They were, so to speak, 'safe': not too low-born, not too high-born. Their future marriage prospects were unlikely to be affected by the knowledge of a royal liaison, as might be the case with a great heiress; whereas unlike genuinely low-born women, they at least had the opportunity to meet the king.

The way that a medieval king treated his mistresses depended on a number of factors: the personality of the king, his attitude towards the woman concerned, the length of time for which the relationship lasted, and so forth. One point which is very striking, though, is that none of these medieval kings were prepared to indulge their mistresses in the way that, for instance, Charles II did. Charles granted titles, landed estates and riches in abundance to his famous series of mistresses. He had their portraits painted by the most eminent artists at his court. For as long as they retained his affections, they were his queens in all but name. Henry VIII did the same with Anne Boleyn: before he married her, while he was still legally married to Katharine of Aragon, he created Anne marquess of Pembroke

13

in her own right (not marchioness, as often stated) and settled £1,000 worth of land on her. In medieval England royal mistresses were less fortunate. None of them received titles. Few of them were granted land – although Alice Perrers is again the notable exception: she amassed an enormous landed estate, partly by gift from the king, partly by dint of her own shrewd business ability. Indeed, in many ways she is more in the tradition of the famous French royal mistresses of the sixteenth to eighteenth centuries, or the mistresses of Charles II, than she is typical of royal mistresses of medieval England. Elizabeth Shore too may have enriched herself during the time that she enjoyed Edward IV's favour, but in general the mistresses of the medieval English kings do not seem to have enjoyed the same prestige as their later counterparts. To what extent they were given jewels, fine clothes and gifts in cash by their royal lovers is largely obscured from us by the lack of surviving evidence. We know that King John once sent a chaplet of roses from his justiciar's garden to one of his mistresses; another of his mistresses, the otherwise unknown 'damoiselle Susanna', was given a splendid robe by John; Henry II granted a manor to Sir Walter Clifford, Rosamund's father, 'because of his love for Rosamund', and there is a tradition that he had a beautiful bejewelled casket made for Rosamund herself. It is difficult to believe that mistresses would go entirely unrewarded by their royal lovers, but it is highly unlikely that any apart from Alice Perrers acquired fortunes as a result of their liaisons.

One way in which a king might set up his mistresses was by arranging good marriages for them. Henry I did this for both Sybil Corbet and the less well known Edith: Sybil he married to Herbert fitzHerbert, son and heir of the chamberlain of the king's household, while Edith was married to Sir Robert d'Oilli, constable of Oxford castle. Both of these were definitely good matches for the ladies concerned. Edward III too found a suitable husband for Alice Perrers: he was Sir William Windsor, knight of the king's household and governor of Ireland. Other kings, however, were accused of treating their mistresses rather less sympathetically once they had tired of them. Of Richard the Lionheart, for instance, one contemporary said that 'he carried off the wives, daughters and kinswomen of his freemen by force and made them his concubines; and when he had sated his lust on them, he handed them over to his knights for whoring'. This was written by a chronicler who had little love for Richard and may contain more than a grain of exaggeration, but three centuries later much the same accusation was to be levelled at Edward IV: 'it was said that he had been most insolent to numerous women after he had seduced them, for as soon as he had grown weary of dalliance, he gave up the ladies much against their will to the other courtiers.' The language is less violent, but the message is the same: an unscrupulous or unfeeling king might have little compunction in gratifying his courtiers with the crumbs that fell from his own table.

14

If this was a risk which might have to be accepted by the sort of woman who enjoyed only a brief liaison with her king, those who established more lasting relationships with a monarch faced a very different sort of problem. A royal mistress's position at court usually depended entirely on the king who loved her; when he died and that support was removed, how would she be treated? Both Alice Perrers and Elizabeth Shore discovered to their cost that those who had pretended to be their friends while the king was still alive could rapidly turn into enemies once he was dead. No doubt jealousy and a desire for revenge against a woman who had had it all her own way for too long had much to do with the punishment inflicted on both Alice and Elizabeth, but in these two cases there was another factor: the political influence which a mistress exercised over a king. In the case of Alice Perrers, this political influence is undeniable: the detailed charges which were brought against her in the parliament which followed Edward III's death have a ring of truth about them, and it is virtually certain that she had been interfering in the government of Ireland in an attempt to protect her husband's position there. With Elizabeth Shore it is less easy to be certain: remarks were certainly made after Edward IV's death to the effect that she had used her favour with the king to influence the course of justice, but there was no public outcry against her as there had been a century earlier against Alice. It is most unlikely that she meddled in politics to the extent that Alice had done. Once again, Alice stands out as the exception rather than the rule as far as the medieval English kings are concerned.

If adultery by kings was considered quite normal, adultery by queens was not. When the mother of a future king was known – or thought – to have lovers, awkward questions might be asked. The only medieval English queen who is known to have been an adulteress was Isabella, wife of Edward II. Eleanor of Aquitaine may have been an adulteress too, but her indiscretions occurred before her marriage to Henry II. There were also rumours about Henry VI's wife, Margaret of Anjou, but these were probably political smears. However, the woman whose marital career best illustrates the problems which could result from a dubious reputation is Joan, the 'Fair Maid of Kent'.

Born in 1328, Joan was the daughter of Edmund earl of Kent, and reputed to be exceptionally beautiful. Early in 1341 she married William Montacute, son of the earl of Salisbury. Six years later, however, Montacute's steward Sir Thomas Holland challenged the validity of her marriage, claiming that he himself had secretly married Joan in the spring of 1340, and that the reason why she had not revealed this when her marriage to Montacute was arranged was that she was afraid of what her kinsfolk would say. Despite Montacute's attempts to hold her in solitary confine-

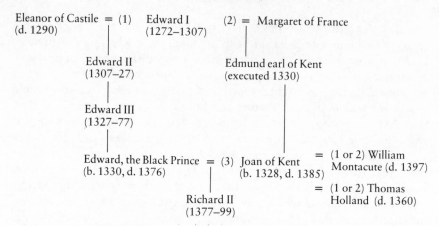

Table 5 The marriages of Joan, the 'Fair Maid of Kent'

ment, Joan was eventually called to give evidence, and she supported Holland's story: thus in 1349 the pope granted her a divorce from Montacute – whose 'lawful spouse' she had been for eight years – and 'reinstated' her as Holland's wife. The story may have been true, but there are some highly suspicious circumstances. Why did Joan and Holland wait six years before revealing their secret? It is hard to believe the most recent explanation for their delay, namely that it was only in 1347 that Holland acquired the funds to enable him to pursue his case at law. Holland only became Montacute's steward in 1344, three years after Montacute had married Joan: is it possible that they began an affair in or after 1344, as a result of which they invented the story about their prior marriage in order to get Montacute out of the way? It is true that various friends were prepared to give evidence that they had witnessed the marriage of Joan and Holland in 1340, but in the nature of things these must have been close friends indeed, and their evidence can hardly be regarded as unimpeachable.

Holland died in 1360, leaving two sons by Joan, and within a year she was married again, to the Black Prince, the heir to the English crown. Edward III, the Black Prince's father, is said to have disapproved strongly of the match, and the archbishop of Canterbury warned the Black Prince before he married Joan that some people might challenge the legitimacy of their issue. At least one chronicler thought that Joan had really been divorced from Montacute because of her adultery with Holland. The point is that Montacute was still alive in 1361 – in fact he lived until 1397. If, therefore, the story of Joan's secret marriage to Holland was untrue, in the eyes of God she was still legally married to Montacute, which made her marriage to the Black Prince invalid and any issue resulting from it illegitimate. Richard II was issue of that marriage. When Richard was taken through the streets of London at the time of his deposition in 1399, the

16

crowd are said to have called out that he was a 'wicked bastard'. His supplanter, Henry IV, apparently levelled the same accusation at him. This may have been no more than an opportune political smear: once it became clear that Richard was going to be deposed, any evidence which could justify that deposition might be brought into play. Yet what is surprising is that the Black Prince should have married a woman with a history like Joan's (one chronicler referred to her sarcastically as 'the virgin of Kent'). She found it difficult to shake off her reputation: at the time of Richard's birth at Bordeaux in 1367, it was rumoured that he was not the son of the Black Prince at all, but had been begotten by a French clerk who had been Joan's lover.

Whether or not Richard II was a bastard will never be known for sure. What is certain is that there were considerable numbers of royal bastards in medieval England. Forty-one illegitimate children of the English kings in the period 1066–1485 can be identified with near certainty. Including doubtful attributions the figure is past the fifty mark. There must have been many more whose names have disappeared entirely. In the absence of effective contraceptive techniques extramarital affairs led inevitably to the birth of illegitimate children. In England the twelfth century was the great age of royal bastards: Henry I alone fathered at least twenty royal bastards, Henry II at least three and King John at least seven. They were usually openly acknowledged and generously treated. Of the bastard sons, several became earls, one became archbishop of York, another abbot of Westminster. Being illegitimate, they were almost entirely dependent on the king's favour and could usually be counted among his most loyal supporters. Bastard daughters were often used to cement political alliances by marriage. Henry I married his illegitimate daughters into several of the aristocratic families of France; one of them married the king of Scotland; one of John's bastard daughters married the prince of North Wales. In the thirteenth and fourteenth centuries both the number of royal bastards and the status accorded to them declined, but in the fifteenth and early sixteenth centuries they were once again more numerous and at the same time they again began to rise to high office.

However, royal bastards could also create problems, not perhaps for the king who fathered them, but for his successors. When the rules governing the succession were ill-defined might not a royal bastard be considered as a possible candidate for the throne? In the eleventh century two men of illegitimate birth became kings of England: Harold 'Harefoot', the son of King Cnut by his concubine Aelfgifu of Northampton, and William the Conqueror, known to his contemporaries as William the Bastard (see Table I). In later centuries other royal bastards seem either to have considered themselves, or to have been considered by others, as possible candidates for the throne, although none of them succeeded in winning it. Perhaps the most remarkable man – in terms of his ancestry – to succeed to the English throne was Henry Tudor (see Table 3).

Henry was not himself illegitimate. His mother, however, was Lady Margaret Beaufort, granddaughter of John Beaufort, and John was the eldest of four children (the Beauforts) born to Edward III's son John of Gaunt and his mistress Katherine Swynford. True, Gaunt did eventually marry Katherine, and after their marriage both the pope and the king agreed formally to legitimate the Beauforts (in 1397), but ten years later, when Henry IV officially confirmed that legitimation, he specifically excluded the Beauforts from the order of succession. Henry Tudor's father, Edmund Tudor, earl of Richmond, came from even more dubious stock. When King Henry V died in 1422 he left a widow, the young Katherine de Valois, daughter of Charles VI of France. As queen mother Katherine lived in relative obscurity for fifteen years, and it was not until after her death in 1437 that it was discovered that during her 'retirement' she had secretly married one of the clerks of her household, a Welshman called Owen Tudor, and had borne three children by him. Owen came from a humble Anglesey family, and initially the court was outraged at his 'presumption in mixing his blood with that of the noble race of kings'. Nevertheless Henry VI agreed to recognise Owen's sons (who were, after all, his half-brothers) and to bring them up at court. The two elder sons, Jasper and Edmund, became earls of Pembroke and Richmond respectively in 1453. In 1456 Edmund, half-brother to one king, issue of a highly irregular union between a queen mother and a Welsh clerk, married Margaret Beaufort, granddaughter of the legitimated bastard of a king's son, who had been half-brother to another king. Their sole issue, born a year later, was Henry Tudor, king of England from 1485 to 1509, one of the most successful of all English kings.

Naturally, the English kings were not the only rulers of medieval Europe to indulge in extramarital affairs. Even Edward IV appears relatively self-restrained by comparison with two of his most illustrious contemporaries. Philip the Good, duke of Burgundy, count of Holland, Flanders and Artois (1419–67), was said to have a mistress in every town in his vast dominions, and he acknowledged at least fifteen illegitimate children, most famous of whom was Anthony, the 'Great Bastard of Burgundy'. Francesco Sforza, duke of Milan (1450–66), who was himself the illegitimate son of a mercenary and who married the illegitimate daughter of the duke who preceded him, fathered at least thirty-seven children, almost all illegitimate, although this is said to be a 'conservative estimate'. In Sicily in both the twelfth and the thirteenth centuries, and in Spain and Portugal in the fourteenth century, royal bastards succeeded to the throne in preference to their legitimate siblings. Royal blood was royal blood, no matter the vessel through which it was transmitted, and in the Middle Ages nobody would have needed to be reminded of this fact.

In the days when monarchs ruled as well as reigned, and when personal privacy was more difficult to come by than it is now, it was not easy for kings and queens to separate their private lives from their public lives. The royal family was the political heart of the kingdom, and when relations between its members were strained, the political repercussions could be immense. The history of the royal family in medieval England demonstrates this point clearly. Against the background of this often fraught family history, the royal bastard could assume an undue degree of importance. Yet it is important to remember that attitudes to matters such as marriage, adultery and illegitimacy seldom remain static for long, and the Middle Ages were no exception to this rule. Throughout this period, changes in both the law and social attitudes were gradually taking place, and before looking at the careers of the medieval English royal bastards, these changes need to be taken into account.

CHAPTER 2

MARRIAGE AND DIVORCE

'Consider of what importance to society the chastity of women is,' remarked Dr Johnson. 'Upon that all the property in the world depends. We hang a thief for stealing a sheep, but the unchastity of a woman transfers sheep, and farm, and all from the right owner.' In twentieth-century Western society it is not fashionable to equate too closely the act of marriage with the passage of property. Marriage is first and foremost a sacrament, an expression of love between a man and a woman; the crucial condition on which it depends is the mutual consent of the marriage partners and of them alone, and in theory it remains indissoluble 'until death us do part'. One of the primary reasons for the act of marriage is often seen as the creation of a family, and most families nowadays are very much child-centred units.

The modern view of marriage in Western society would have appealed to the medieval church. The emphasis on the mutual and exclusive consent of the marriage partners, on theoretical indissolubility, and on the creation of the family unit, were cornerstones of the ecclesiastical view of marriage in medieval Europe. To gain acceptance for these views, churchmen had to fight long and hard against entrenched and often radically different ideas on the function of marriage in the lay world, and the fact that these views gained such widespread acceptance is a measure of the church's triumph. The crucial period, the period during which the church really formulated and began successfully to promulgate its ideas on marriage, came in the late eleventh and the twelfth centuries. Of course there had to be compromise. Marriage, particularly in the upper echelons of society, was too politically important a subject to be left to churchmen, and in practice political and material considerations have continued to play a very large part in marital arrangements, and not only among royalty and aristocracy, right up to the present day. Yet, as the French historian Georges Duby has said, 'the entire history of marriage in Western Christendom amounts to a gradual process of acculturation, in which the ecclesiastical model slowly gained the upper hand'. In the twentieth century, it is true, we may be witnessing the first signs of a reversal of that trend. It is instructive, therefore, to begin by looking at lay ideas on marriage in the Middle Ages.

LAYMEN AND MARRIAGE

Laymen in medieval Europe saw marriage as the key to both property transfer and political alliance. The house – or *domus*, to use the medieval term – was the fundamental social unit. The word *domus* meant much more than man, wife and children: it was the line, the stock, traversing generations, the symbol of wealth and power. If the son of one house married the daughter of another house, it was a visible sign of alliance between the two houses. Harold Godwinson, the last king of Anglo-Saxon England, only repudiated his charmingly named mistress, Edith Swan's Neck, after he seized the throne in 1066, in order to gain the support of the northern earls Edwin and Morcar by marrying their sister (also called Edith). This political aspect of marriage explains why betrothal was so important in the Middle Ages: the betrothal indicated that the diplomatic agreements which underlay the union had been concluded. Betrothals often occurred years ahead of the actual marriage, which might be delayed by such factors as age or difficulty of communications. Betrothal or marriage by proxy was also commonplace. In 1402, Henry IV was betrothed by proxy to Joan, duchess of Brittany: Joan was represented by her envoy, Anthony Ricze, on whose finger Henry actually placed the wedding ring, and who then spoke the words of marriage on Joan's behalf, taking Henry as 'her' husband. Not until the following year was the wedding ceremony performed at Winchester.

Marriage for purposes of political alliance could not wait on age: to cement the Anglo-French peace made at Paris in 1303, it was agreed that Edward, prince of Wales (the future Edward II) should marry Isabella, the French king's daughter. Edward was nineteen at the time, but Isabella was only seven. A century later, when Richard II and Charles VI of France concluded a truce at Calais in 1396, the twenty-nine-year-old King Richard himself married a French princess, another Isabella, this time aged eight. Child-marriages, or child-betrothals, were common in the Middle Ages, particularly among royalty and aristocracy. Although officially frowned upon by the church, they were widely regarded as a political necessity. Officially, the church declared that a marriage contracted by a child under the age of seven was invalid, while a marriage contracted by a child between seven and the age of puberty (fourteen for boys, twelve for girls) might be disclaimed by the child on reaching puberty; yet even the papacy recognised that these rules could be ignored in cases of urgent need, such as the desire for peace.

Marriage, then, was a contract between two houses – or kingdoms. Sometimes these contracts were verbal, but among the landowning classes it became increasingly common to draw up written contracts of marriage, detailing the territorial and financial arrangements which accompanied the

21

marriage. This is the origin of the word 'wedding': the medieval wedding was the formal exchange of 'weds', the solemn tokens of a civil contract. Where the royal families of two different kingdoms were involved, the 'weds' would usually be incorporated in a treaty of peace or alliance. Edward III's marriage contract to Philippa of Hainault (the original of which was sold at Sotheby's for £16,000 in April 1981) included a treaty of alliance between his mother, Isabella, and Philippa's father, Count William of Hainault, by which Count William agreed to provide the troops with which Isabella invaded England and deposed her husband, Edward II. In return, it was agreed that Count William would receive £10,000 if the marriage did not take place. Where noble houses were concerned, the contract would often be hedged around with conditions, time limits, and so forth. In 1354, the houses of Arundel and March agreed that Edmund, son of the earl of March, should marry Alice, daughter of the earl of Arundel,

> for which marriage the earl of Arundel is bound to pay to the earl of March 3,000 marks [£2,000; 1 mark = 13s. 4d.] at St. Paul's church, London, to wit, on the day of the making of this contract, 1,000 marks, at the time when the children are married, namely when they are aged seven years, 1,000 marks, and when they are at the age of fourteen years, so that their marriage be accomplished, 1,000 marks. . . . And if the earl of March, Edmund, or Alice, or one of them die before the age of seven years, then the earl of March shall be bound to repay the 1,000 marks received on the day of the making of this contract. . . . And if the marriage take place at the age of seven and then fail by the death of the earl of March or by default on one side or the other, before the age of fourteen, or if Alice die without issue by Edmund before the age of fourteen, then the earl of March shall be bound to repay to the earl of Arundel all the money received from him for that marriage within two years. . . .

Before the fourteenth century, the gift from the bride's father, or dowry, was more usually in the form of property (known as the *maritagium*). If she was widowed while still childless, the *maritagium* reverted to the bride – and thus in effect to the house from which she came. In the later Middle Ages it became more common for the bride's father to make a gift of money (known as the marriage-portion) to the couple. The amount of the *maritagium* or marriage-portion was usually the main question to be settled in a marriage contract. The other important question to be settled was the extent of the property (or cash) which the bridegroom would inherit from, or be granted by, his father.

The control of property transfer and the establishment of political alliances were therefore two of the main functions of marriage in the eyes of medieval laymen. A third was the begetting of heirs. It was a man's duty to perpetuate the line from which he came, to provide a son to inherit the estates, bear the family arms, and increase the wealth and influence of the house. It was this emphasis on the *domus* that led to the adoption of primogeniture in Western European society: when the eldest son alone inherited, the chances of fragmentation of estates, leading to the dissipation of wealth and power, were greatly reduced. In the eleventh century, primogeniture was far from accepted – as witness William the Conqueror's division of Normandy and England between his sons Robert Curthose and William Rufus. By the thirteenth century, primogeniture was much more common: it was increasingly accepted that a man should pass on to his heir whatever he had received from his father; what he himself had acquired was often passed on to the eldest son too, although it might also be used for the endowment of younger sons or daughters. Primogeniture, when widely accepted and enforced, did bring a degree of order and stability in its wake. The problem was not so much in accepting the principle as in carrying it through. Some kings or queens were either impotent or barren; infant mortality was high; heirs were killed in battle, or died of what were then incurable diseases. Sons were precious commodities, much more so than daughters, and it was advisable to have more than one of them, in case of accidents (such as the White Ship). The kings of France went to great lengths to secure the succession: it was largely because Eleanor of Aquitaine had only produced two daughters in fifteen years of marriage that Louis VII divorced her in 1152 – even so, it took Louis two more marriages to be rewarded with a son. When Edward IV of England was reproached by his mother for marrying Elizabeth Woodville, he is said to have replied,

> and whereas you object that she hath been a wife and is now a widow, and hath already children, why, by God's blessed lady, I that am a bachelor have some [illegitimate] children too, and so for our better comfort each of us hath proof that neither of us is like to be barren.

The point was well made: the chances, of course, were that most marriages would be fertile, but for those that were not, much of the point of the marriage would be lost.

Lay views on marriage must be seen within the context of feudal society. It was in the eleventh, twelfth and thirteenth centuries that Western European society was most highly feudalised, but even in the fourteenth and fifteenth centuries, when some of the basic principles of feudal society no longer applied, men still continued to express their relationships in feudal terms (lord, vassal, wardship, and so forth), and the ownership and transfer of land remained of paramount importance. In such a society there was no possibility of a free 'marriage market'. Control of marriages was written into feudal law: kings had the right to regulate their lords' marriages, and lords had the right to regulate their tenants' marriages. It was an accepted fact of life that marriages, particularly of important heiresses, were bought, sold, exchanged and distributed as valuable and vital commodities. The moral justification for this was that a man had the right to prevent his lands passing into the hands of his enemies. This arose because, technically (after 1066, at least) no one in England truly *owned* land except the king. Feudal custom dictated that land was granted out by the king to his great lords, to be held from the king in return for service – for instance, the provision of a certain number of knights to fight in the king's army for a certain period each year. Lords who had been granted land by the king might in turn grant out (subinfeudate) parts of it to other men, again in return for service, and so on down the scale. Thus was the hierarchical structure of feudal society established. Therefore when a king sold or granted out the marriage of the heiress of one of his lords, or when he granted or withheld permission for the lord to marry his son or daughter into another house, he was in theory regulating the transfer of his own property; when a lord did the same with the heir or heiress of one of his tenants, he was regulating the transfer of property which he held by personal contract with the king.

Naturally this feudal control of marriages was not always enforced to the hilt. In many cases it must have acted more in the nature of a veto of unsuitable matches rather than the imposition of suitable ones. Yet it is clear that the latter was also common. In his coronation charter of 1100 Henry I promised that

> if the wife of one of my tenants shall survive her husband, she shall
> have her dower and marriage-portion, and I will not give her in
> marriage unless she herself consents. . . . And I require that my barons
> shall act likewise towards the widows of their men.

Of course he did not keep his promise – it was too valuable a right for any feudal lord to relinquish. Widows, and heirs and heiresses who were under age at the time of their father's death, were especially vulnerable to the system. In Magna Carta King John made the same promise, adding that women in the king's gift would not in future be disparaged (married to men of inferior social status). Yet is is abundantly clear that the system continued unabated right through the Middle Ages – and well beyond them. Once again there was good theoretical justification for the practice. Widows and minors were outside the social structure: they had no *domus*, or at least a less powerful *domus*, to protect them. It was up to the king or lord to protect them (from abduction, for instance), to take them into his wardship, and make arrangements for their future. The opportunities for profit were too tempting, however, and the system was consistently abused.

The principles which dominated laymen's views of marriage in medieval times can now be enumerated, remembering always that these principles were of greater importance to the landowning classes than to their humbler contemporaries. Firstly, the consent of the marriage partners themselves was virtually negligible: pressure came from the family, and pressure came from the feudal lord, so that most young men or women had little or no say in choosing a marriage partner. Secondly, there were a lot of child-marriages: politics could not wait, and there was another strong incentive to marry one's children when they were young, because that way, if a man died suddenly, his children's marriages did not fall into the hands of his feudal lord. Thirdly, divorce (or, more correctly, annulment) must be available, in case a wife proved barren; it must, of course, be done tactfully, with the least possible disturbance of the political arrangements accompanying the original marriage, but nevertheless the option must be there. Monogamy was indeed preferable, for that reduced the chances of conflict over the inheritance, but, in the eyes of many, monogamy really meant 'serial monogamy', that is, a series of wives, but only one at a time, with the option to repudiate her in favour of another if it was found to be desirable. Fourthly, marriage within both family groups and social groups was common. Marriage to a first or second cousin might reunite parts of a fragmented inheritance, and it would equally strengthen the *domus*. Marriage between social equals was also of cardinal importance, partly for reasons of snobbery, and partly because wealth naturally attracted wealth. Inevitably, this led to a considerable degree of inbreeding. Fifthly, adultery and fornication were tolerated among men, but among women they were not: the bride, the carrier of property, must be a virgin until the day she married, and after her marriage she must be faithful to her husband. There must be no doubt about the paternity of the heir.

Before the eleventh century, these principles were largely reflected in practice. In Roman law, marriage was almost entirely a personal matter. It was easily made, with no public ceremony required, and easily dissolved, by simple repudiation of a wife or remarriage. Bigamy was not even listed as an offence by Roman legal writers, presumably because a new marriage was held automatically to annul the previous one. The Merovingian kings of Dark Age Europe were polygamous, while their successors, the Carolingians, seem to have practised serial monogamy: the great Frankish king Charlemagne (768–814), for instance, made four marriages which were blessed by the church, in addition to which he kept at least five concubines. With the influx of Scandinavians in the ninth and tenth centuries, little seems to have changed. Concubinage and repudiation of wives were common, formal marriage was widely considered unnecessary, and as a result the status of women seems to have declined. In the tenth century the expression *uxor more Danico* (wife by Danish custom) meant much the same as what the twentieth century would call a 'common law wife'. Against such a background, and before primogeniture became common, any king's son (or brother, or nephew) might justifiably put forward a claim to the throne, while any one of a former king's wives would naturally muster all the means at her disposal to try to ensure that she became a queen mother rather than a discarded royal widow. Until the mid-eleventh century, ecclesiastical attempts to impose stricter control over marriage customs were largely ineffective. The laymen had it virtually all their own way. From about 1050, however, the papacy took on a new lease of life. Under the guidance of a series of reforming popes, the medieval church began to grow dramatically in power and prestige, and one of the areas in which it made its influence felt was in the regulation of Christian marriage.

CHURCHMEN AND MARRIAGE

Before 1050, the Roman church hardly had a coherent attitude towards marriage. During the late eleventh and the twelfth centuries a number of ecclesiastical lawyers (canonists), vigorously supported by the papacy, formulated and propagated a series of church laws on marriage; simultaneously, they emphasised the vital point that since marriage was a holy act, jurisdiction over marriage cases pertained exclusively to the church courts. By the early thirteenth century, it was widely – almost universally – accepted that marriage disputes could only be heard in church courts. This meant that the church now had the opportunity to enforce its own ideas on marriage and divorce. In 1234 Pope Gregory IX published his *Decretals*, the whole of the fourth book of which is given over to an exposition of the canon law of marriage. After this, it was no longer a question of formulating new doctrine on marriage: the Catholic law of marriage hardly changed between 1234 and the Council of Trent in the mid-sixteenth century. The remainder of the Middle Ages was spent in gradually trying to widen acceptance of these views among the laity, to that 'gradual process of acculturation' mentioned by Duby.

The achievement of the twelfth-century canonists is remarkable when one considers the importance of marriage to laymen (particularly to the aristocracy) and the radically different views on marriage which they held. Two canonists were pre-eminent: Master Gratian of Bologna, whose *Decretum* (or 'Concord of Discordant Canons') was first issued around 1140, and Master Peter the Lombard, whose *Liber Sententiarum* (the 'Sentences') was completed in Paris in about 1150. Alexander III (1159–81), Innocent III (1198–1216) and Gregory IX (1227–41) were the popes who really took the ideas of Gratian, Peter the Lombard and their fellow canonists and tried to enforce them throughout Christendom. They challenged the lay view of marriage on three main fronts: consent, consanguinity and indissolubility.

'It is evident', declared Gratian, 'that no woman should be coupled to anyone except by her free will'. It is difficult to say how or why he reached this conclusion, for there was little in pre-twelfth-century canon law to support such a doctrine, and much in early Christian teaching to suggest that a woman did not have the right to refuse a marriage partner chosen for her by her parents. His was a doctrine which flew in the face of feudal and parental authority. Yet it became one of the cornerstones of canon law on marriage, and soon the church was teaching not only that the consent of the man and the woman was the vital prerequisite for any marriage, but also that the consent of any other person – parent, lord or whoever – was unnecessary. Among the aristocracy and royalty, it is only in modern times that this idea has really gained acceptance: parentally arranged marriages have remained common among the upper classes right through to the twentieth century. For those social groupings below the landholding class, however, the doctrine of consent seems to have gained ground fairly rapidly from the twelfth century onwards. Even for the elite, the doctrine of consent did have one crucial result: if a man and a woman did flout the wishes of their parents or guardians and get married, perhaps secretly, and if it was then proven in a church court that they had both consented to the marriage, the marriage remained valid in the eyes of the church, and thus, since church jurisdiction over marriage cases was established, the laity must accept it as well. Both points are well illustrated in episodes occurring in the Paston Letters, a collection of letters centring on a landholding family in fifteenth-century East Anglia.

The Pastons, in common with most of their contemporaries, had little regard for their children's personal choice in arranging their marriages. When the teenager Elizabeth Paston refused a match proposed by her parents, she was locked away in her room, allowed no visitors, and beaten 'once or twice a week' to persuade her to submit. She remained immovable, however, and was eventually successful: the marriage she so abhorred (to Stephen Scrope) never took place. Her sister Margery, at the age of seventeen, secretly married the family bailiff, Richard Calle. Her irate parents abused her greatly, even throwing her out of the family home for good, but there was nothing they could do about it. Margery and Richard remained married. English law did what it could to protect feudal rights too. The Statute of Merton (1236) declared that under-age heirs or heiresses who married without the consent of their guardians were punishable at law, usually by payment of a fine. Yet there was by now no way of getting round the basic point: the marriage, once contracted, was valid. If the couple were prepared to put up with the wrath of their kinsfolk and/or the

27

punishment imposed in the lord's court, they could marry whomsoever they wanted. One had to be courageous (or madly in love), but it was possible.

The church's doctrine of consent inevitably created as many problems as it tried to solve. How was 'consent' to be defined? More importantly in many cases, how was it to be proved? It was a problem which permeated to the highest level of society: when Richard II's mother, Joan of Kent, claimed that she had secretly married Sir Thomas Holland several years before she publicly married William Montacute, who was to say whether or not she was speaking the truth? Ultimately the pope, who granted her a divorce from Montacute in 1349, had only the word of Joan, Holland, and a handful of not impartial witnesses to go on. The problem of secret, or clandestine, marriages, as they were called, so vividly highlighted for Englishmen by Edward IV's adventures, was one which troubled both clergy and laity throught the Middle Ages.

In one sense churchmen and laymen were in agreement on the problem of clandestine marriages: in theory, both sides agreed that the act of marriage should be accompanied by as much publicity as possible. From the lay point of view, it was important that heirs must be seen to be legitimate, and that political alliance and property transfer be conducted in the public eye; from the church point of view, publicity acted as a check on concubinage and bigamy. There were two main ways in which the church tried to make marriages more public; by having the banns read out from the pulpit before the day of the wedding, and by performing the actual ceremony of marriage *in facie ecclesie* – in the face of the church, as the saying went (either at the church door or in the church itself). In 1200 the archbishop of Canterbury, Hubert Walter, proclaimed that banns should be read, and couples blessed, in church. In 1215 Pope Innocent III repeated these exhortations at the Fourth Lateran Council, and throughout the rest of the Middle Ages the same two points were made again and again, from the pulpit, in diocesan statutes, and in papal decrees. Yet how could these proclamations be squared with the emphasis placed by the church on consent? Canon law, as developed by Gratian and Peter Lombard and adopted by the twelfth-century papacy, declared that the consent of the couple alone was necessary. Once mutual consent had been given, in the eyes of God a valid marriage had taken place. To deny this was to remove one of the foundation-stones of the church's law on marriage. It was a problem to which the medieval church never found an answer: the clandestine marriage remained a valid marriage in the eyes of the church throughout the Middle Ages.

In fact most people found it increasingly advisable to make public marriages, for the lay courts were just as vigorously opposed to clandestine marriages as the church was. In a famous law case of 1306 a man was not allowed his inheritance because his parents had not married in church, and thus the (lay) court did not accept that he was his father's legitimate son; dower (a widow's entitlement to a proportion – usually a third – of her husband's property) was sometimes refused to women who had not married publicly. Thus in some cases the common-law courts did seem to be making a distinction between a valid marriage *per se* (as defined by a church court), and a valid marriage for purposes of inheritance, which naturally dampened enthusiasm for clandestine marriages. Yet not until the Council of Trent's decree *Tametsi* in 1563, which required the presence of a parish priest for a valid marriage, did the Catholic church finally set itself against clandestine marriage. By this time, however, England no longer adhered to Rome: not until 1843 did English common law declare it essential to have a priest or ordained clergyman present to validate a marriage (this rule has since been modified to cope with registry office marriages). In 1483, one of the arguments used by Richard III to invalidate Edward IV and Elizabeth Woodville's marriage was that it was made 'privily and secretly, without the giving out of banns, in a private chamber, a profane place, and not openly in the face of the church'. He was making a highly complex problem sound deceptively simple.

The continued acceptance by the church of the validity of clandestine marriages contributed more than any other factor to the instability of medieval marriage customs. The problem lay in defining 'mutual consent'. A perfectly valid marriage might be challenged by a previous sexual partner of either husband or wife declaring that a clandestine marriage had existed. Equally, a married person wanting to dissolve his or her marriage and remarry might claim that he or she had previously married the new, preferred, lover. Was that what Joan of Kent did? Joan and Holland claimed that they had been married by *verba de praesenti* – words of present tense. This was how the church defined mutual consent. A distinction was made between present consent and future consent (*verba de futuro*). Words of present consent spoken by the two partners, such as 'I here take thee as my wife/husband', automatically created a permanent and indissoluble marriage; words of future consent, for instance, 'I promise that I will take you as my wife/husband', did not create a marriage – this was merely betrothal, the intention to marry at a future date, and thus revocable. If, however, words of future consent were followed by consummation of the marriage (by sexual intercourse), that too was held to create a permanent marriage. Obviously this created endless problems. People had to be careful about what they said and did. If, for instance, Edward IV had said in a careless moment to Eleanor Butler, 'if you sleep with me, I will take you as my wife', and had then slept with her, in the eyes of the church he was married to her from the moment they had sexual intercourse. Frederick Maitland, the great legal historian, who regarded medieval canon law on marriage as 'a maze of flighty fancies and misapplied logic', remarked pertinently that 'of all the people in the world, lovers are the least likely to distinguish precisely between the present and future tenses' – a fair point.

The upshot of all this was certainly a fair degree of confusion. The doctrine of consent, combined with the toleration of clandestine marriage, meant in practice that the married state was considerably more unstable and more casual than the church hoped it might be. As a result most historians have regarded the medieval church courts as incompetent to uphold the ideals of Christian marriage. Yet it was to safeguard a vital principle that these laws were made: marriage must be an act of mutual consent between bride and bridegroom. The freedom of marriage enjoyed by Christians today is a direct result of the stand taken by the medieval church.

The second main area in which lay and ecclesiastical views on marriage tended to conflict was in dealing with the problem of consanguinity, or incest. The word 'incest' is nowadays usually used to describe relationships in the first degree, for instance between brother and sister. In the Middle Ages it was used much more widely. Before 1215, marriages in the seventh degree (between sixth cousins) were regarded as incestuous; after 1215, this was reduced to the fourth degree (third cousins). Added to straightforward incest were affinity and spiritual ties. Affinity meant, for instance, that a man could not marry the third cousin of a woman with whom he had once had sexual relations, or the third cousin of a woman with whom he had once exchanged *verba de futuro*. Spiritual ties extended to relationships such as godparent: to take an extreme example, a man could not marry the widow who had previously stood godmother to a child by his first wife. When the Black Prince married Joan of Kent in 1361 he needed a dispensation from the pope on two grounds, firstly because they were second cousins once removed, and secondly because he had stood godfather to Joan's child by her first marriage to Thomas Holland.

To the upper classes, the principle was an important one. Medieval aristocracies were never static: there was always social mobility, always marriageable new blood entering the ranks of the nobility from below. At the same time, there was always a large nucleus of aristocratic families whose nobility was well established, families who had been there or thereabouts for several generations. Given the desire to marry into a family of equal status, given also the material advantages often associated with marrying close relatives (strengthening of kinship ties, or recovery of recently divided properties), there was bound to be a considerable amount of aristocratic inbreeding. Here, then, was fertile ground for dispute. The avowed intention of the church's consanguinity laws was not to prevent genetic problems, but to 'expand the dominion of love', to bring more people and more families within ties of friendship and kinship with each other. Sadly, the aristocracy showed little desire to be friendly. Inbreeding was a vital element in their view of the function of marriage.

It was an issue on which there had to be compromise, and so there was. What happened was that, in theory, the laity accepted the church's principle that marriage within the forbidden degrees was not permissible: the church, on the other hand, accepted that dispensations could be granted for such marriages, and in practice these dispensations were obtainable without great difficulty (at least by the wealthy, for they usually had to be accompanied by some form of payment). No doubt this compromise was more acceptable to laymen than to churchmen, but it did mean that the church retained at least nominal control over consanguineous marriages. The church has come in for a lot of criticism as a result of this compromise. Certainly the consanguinity laws seem to have been more effectively applied at the lower social levels, and it was to forestall such criticism that Innocent III reduced the prohibited degrees from seven to four at the Fourth Lateran Council of 1215. The problem with the seventh degree was that it was so often beyond living memory: there are few people nowadays who know who their sixth cousins are, and although oral memory was no doubt more tenacious in the days before widespread literacy, it must often have been impossible to discover, let alone prove in a court of law, whether a bride and bridegroom were within the prohibited degrees. The reduction to the fourth degree in fact represented a tightening-up of the consanguinity laws: from this time onwards the church courts demanded a higher degree of proof for claims of consanguinity (twelve-man juries were often empanelled). The consanguinity laws had another important result: they gave kings a further means of control over their subjects' marriages. If an intending couple who were too closely related requested a dispensation from the pope, but the king did not support the request, the pope would not usually offend the king by granting it.

However, it was not in the making of marriages so much as in the breaking of them that the consanguinity laws really acquired their notoriety. If a pope could grant a dispensation, he could also revoke it – again on payment of a suitable sum. When a man decided that he needed a new wife, his course of action was relatively clear-cut: pointing out that he had required a dispensation for his original marriage, and that, whatever the terms of the dispensation, he and his wife were still within the prohibited degrees, he humbly begged the pope's forgiveness for the former error of his ways and, declaring that his conscience forbade him to prolong this incestuous union further, requested that it be annulled forthwith. Unless there were serious objections from interested parties, it was usual for the pope to comply. This brings us on to the third main area of conflict between church and lay ideas on marriage, the question of repudiation and divorce.

INTRODUCTION

DIVORCE

Divorce as we know it – the civil annulment of a civil contract – did not exist in the Middle Ages. Medieval divorce took two forms. Firstly, divorce *a mensa et thoro* (divorce from bed and board), which was equivalent to judicial separation: legally, the couple remained married, any children born to them remained legitimate, and they were prohibited from remarrying, but they were allowed to live apart. There were three grounds on which divorce *a mensa et thoro* could be granted: adultery, cruelty, and heresy (often called 'spiritual fornication'). Few such cases appear in the records of the courts: most separations were presumably private affairs. Secondly, and much more importantly, there was annulment of the original marriage. This was effectively a declaration by the church that the original marriage had never been valid: it was, so to speak, erased from the history books as if it had never occurred. It usually allowed partners to remarry, and was thus naturally more popular than judicial separation. There was one major drawback, however: if the marriage had never been valid, could the children born of it be considered legitimate? This was a question over which there was much dispute.

To laymen in general, and to the propertied classes in particular, it was essential that divorce should be available. Partly this was because of the sort of political and reproductive pressures already mentioned, and partly it was because there persisted the idea that lay people should have the freedom simply to stop cohabiting with one particular person and start cohabiting with another if they wished to. The doctrine 'till death us do part' has always had its share of unbelievers. Before the mid-eleventh century, this presented no serious problems: in lay society generally, repudiation of wives was considered to be permissible on moral or practical grounds. It was important to do it tactfully, but as long as the political and social obstacles to the divorce were negotiated successfully, few men need worry about the religious ones. Once the church began to concern itself seriously with marriage customs, this situation changed. In the eyes of the church, marriage was a sacrament, an unequivocal declaration of intent which could only be broken by the death of one or other partner. The doctrine of indissolubility, like the doctrine of consent, became one of the cornerstones of the church's view on marriage.

In theory, this doctrine of indissolubility of marriage was maintained. This is why 'divorce' developed as it did: one could not dissolve a valid marriage, therefore one had to find reasons why it had never been valid in the first place. Gradually there developed several grounds on which marriages could be declared invalid, of which the most important were consanguinity and precontract. Both these aspects of marriage law have already been dealt with. Divorce on grounds of precontract was Joan of Kent's

32

type of divorce, where it was claimed that a marriage was invalid because one of the partners had previously contracted a marriage with a third party. Edward IV was, in effect, divorced posthumously on grounds of precontract. Taken in conjunction with the church's toleration of clandestine marriages, it is clear that divorce by precontract might offer many people an escape-route from undesirable marriages. One major problem with divorce by precontract was that one was then legally married to the person with whom one had precontracted. Divorce on grounds of consanguinity was more popular by far with the nobility, in that it left the parties to the divorce free to marry again afterwards. There can be no doubt that, at least among the upper classes, the system was greatly abused: it was almost an incentive to make an incestuous marriage, since a man knew that he would have little trouble in obtaining an annulment if his wife failed in any way to live up to his expectations. The reduction of the prohibited degrees from seven to four in 1215 did put a check on the chicanery involved to some extent: no longer did men find it easy to invent false genealogies stretching back six generations, citing spurious common ancestors whom no one could be expected to remember. Yet even to the fourth degree, most members of the upper classes who wanted divorces do not seem to have encountered great difficulties in discovering an impediment of some sort.

There were other grounds on which annulments could be granted, but none of them were remotely as frequent as consanguinity and precontract. Impotence was one – nearly always male impotence. There was clearly a contradiction in church doctrine here: if impotence was alleged and proven, the official reason for annulment was non-consummation of the marriage, rendering it invalid. Yet canon law did not state that consummation was necessary to make a marriage valid, as long as the appropriate words had been exchanged. Nevertheless, annulment was granted for impotence, largely, one presumes, for humanitarian reasons: Edward IV's mistress Elizabeth Shore had her marriage annulled in 1476 on the grounds of her husband's impotence, and because she declared that she wished to have children. To prove impotence was often difficult, however, as well as embarrassing, as is demonstrated by a rather pathetic extract from the register of the diocese of York in 1433, concerning a man called John alleged by his wife to be impotent. One by one several women 'inspected' him. The evidence of the first was that

the same witness exposed her naked breasts, and with her hands
warmed at the said fire, she held and rubbed the penis and testicles
of the said John, and stirred him up in so far as she could to show his
virility and potency, admonishing him for shame that he should then and
there prove and render himself a man. And, she says, examined and

33

diligently questioned, that the whole time aforesaid, the said penis was scarcely three inches long . . . remaining without any increase or decrease.

Seven women tried this in turn, with the same result; then they cursed John for his failure and walked out. Divorce was granted. Plate 1 shows a medieval illustrator's impression of an impotence trial: it is hardly surprising that few actions were brought on grounds of impotence.

Lack of consent could also lead to annulment, but again this was difficult of proof: what degree of compulsion by, for instance, parents, amounted to lack of consent? In view of the emphasis which the church placed on mutual consent, it was important that this should be accepted as a valid reason for annulment, but in practice it was rarely used. Allied to lack of consent was the problem of the under-age marriage, but here again there were very few cases. There were also a few other rather obscure grounds on which an annulment could be obtained, but these are statistically negligible.

It has recently been argued that the church courts in England were not 'divorce mills', and that only a small proportion of the cases which they heard relating to marriage problems were concerned with divorce. The majority dealt with the enforcement of marriage contracts, reflecting both the instability created by the toleration of clandestine marriages, and the extent to which marriage was seen as a business contract at that time. If one excludes precontract cases from the sum of cases relating to divorce, and counts them instead as cases relating to the enforcement of marriage contracts, then it is true that divorce cases form only a small proportion of the marriage cases heard in medieval church courts. Yet this seems somewhat unrealistic, for one of the main problems encountered by the courts was the use of the precontract, combined with an alleged clandestine marriage, to exchange an old wife or husband for a new one. In many cases, therefore, precontract cases were in effect divorce cases. Royalty and aristocracy, however, hardly ever took their disputes to the church court; they preferred to deal privately with the bishop, or with the pope himself. And there is no doubt that among the upper classes, formal annulment was proportionately far more common than among more humble folk. The importance to the landowning classes of begetting heirs was one reason why this was so. The fact that they were more likely to make consanguineous marriages in the first place was another. The fact that they could afford both dispensations and annulments was a third.

It was on grounds of consanguinity that King John divorced his wife, and he was the only king of medieval England to do so (although both Henry II and Edward II apparently considered doing so). John never seems to have had much affection for his first wife, and when after ten years of marriage she had still not provided him with an heir, he probably had little compunction in discarding her. In view of the frequency of divorce among the upper classes, it is in some ways surprising that only one king of medieval England divorced his wife. Yet marriage at the kingly level was of such immense political importance that for a king to divorce his wife – especially if she was a foreign princess, as so many of them were – was a remedy to be used only in desperation. And once a queen had produced an heir to the throne, her position was virtually unassailable, for what would be the status of the heir if his parents' marriage was subsequently annulled? Henry VIII, of course, made up for all his medieval predecessors. Henry was unlucky: in normal circumstances, there would probably have been little difficulty in obtaining his divorce from Katharine of Aragon (on grounds of undoubted affinity – she had formerly married Henry's elder brother, Arthur). Katharine, however, was the aunt of the Holy Roman Emperor, Charles V, and in the late 1520s the papacy was effectively under Charles's control. So Henry VIII was denied his divorce by Rome. The consequences of that denial, as is well known, were momentous.

CONCLUSIONS

With regard to the upper classes, it is in many ways true that attitudes towards the function and practice of marriage had not changed greatly between 1050 and 1500. Yet the achievements of the church, if sometimes only dimly perceptible, were in fact far from negligible. It was not only lay attitudes to marriage that the church concerned itself with. In the eleventh century, clerical marriage was rife throughout Western Europe. In the late twelfth century, the chronicler Gerald of Wales could speak of 'the houses and hovels of parish priests filled with bossy mistresses, creaking cradles, newborn babes and squawking brats'. The papacy's campaign to regulate lay marriage customs went hand in hand with its campaign to enforce clerical celibacy, and in both areas significant advances were made, although clerical marriage was certainly not stamped out. The principles for which the medieval church fought are largely accepted today, and their propagation in the Middle Ages did have some important effects. If marriages continued to be arranged for the most part by parents or feudal lords, there was now no getting round the fact that a marriage created purely by the mutual consent of the partners was valid. By implication, the church's doctrine of consent also improved the status of women in marriage: the woman's consent was just as important as the man's. The doctrine of indissolubility did not put an end to 'divorce', but it severely checked bigamy. Repeated exhortations to laymen to make public marriages also reduced concubinage, although the church's ambivalent attitude to clandestine marriages created unnecessary confusion on this front. The line between 'informal' marriage and concubinage was a fine one. Through

INTRODUCTION

its insistence that jurisdiction on marriage disputes was the exclusive responsibility of its own courts, the church also exercised at least nominal control over what it termed incest. This control seems to have been much more effective at the lower social levels than with the aristocracy and royalty; indeed, what evidence there is suggests that church views on marriage generally were more rigorously enforced among ordinary people than among the landholding classes. The nobles had the money and influence to bend the rules, but now at least there were rules to bend. The turning-point had undoubtedly occurred during the twelfth century, and it had occurred mainly because of the zeal, power and prestige of the reforming papacy, allied to the rapid dissemination of canon law and its enforcement through the ecclesiastical courts.

There were, of course, many questions relating to marriage on which church and lay views concurred, and one should not see the history of medieval marriage entirely in terms of a battle between the church hierarchy and the lay hierarchy. Both approved of the actual ceremony of marriage: clandestine marriages were condemned by the lay authorities just as strongly as they were by the church authorities. Both disapproved of abduction, and both saw reproduction as one of the principal functions of marriage. Not surprisingly it is the areas of disagreement rather than the areas of agreement about which we hear most. The effective indissolubility of marriage was the area in which the church gave most ground.

It is within this framework of marriage custom that the marriages of the kings of medieval England must be seen. It was accepted that kings and those who were likely to become kings made political marriages. The only exceptions to this rule in medieval England were William Rufus and Edward V, who never married, and Edward IV, whose marriage to Elizabeth Woodville was clearly a love-match (and politically inept). Many of them were betrothed or married while still children; most of them married foreign princesses; often the bride and bridegroom were of widely differing ages, spoke different languages, and had hardly met each other before the day of the wedding. This had obvious repercussions in the sexual and emotional fields. Denied the chance to marry the women they fell in love with, it is hardly surprising that kings felt little compunction about having affairs with them. We should be surprised at the number of kings in medieval times who do seem to have been faithful to their wives, rather than at the number who we know were not. For those who were of sufficient political importance, satisfaction of the normal emotional and physical desires often had to be extramarital.

36

CHAPTER 3

SEX, LOVE AND ILLEGITIMACY

ATTITUDES TO SEX AND LOVE

Attitudes towards sex and love have always varied enormously, and it is dangerous to single out a particular point of view as being typical of a particular time or place. On a comparative basis, however, there are some questions which it is worth at least trying to answer. For instance, adultery in upper-class circles in Victorian England was clearly regarded as scandalous. So what was the reaction to the fact that Henry I sired at least twenty illegitimate children in the twelfth century; to the relationship between Edward III and Alice Perrers in the fourteenth century; to Edward IV's flagrant womanising in the fifteenth century?

One reason why it is difficult to answer these questions with any certainty lies in the nature of the sources. The church did not have a monopoly on literacy in the Middle Ages, but the number of clerical authors was much greater than the number of lay ones. The church's attitude to love and sex is thus portrayed in far greater detail than lay attitudes. In theory, the church disapproved of sex. 'There is nothing which degrades the manly spirit more', wrote St Augustine, one of the most influential early church fathers, 'than the attractiveness of females and contact with their bodies.' This disapproval even extended to sexual intercourse in marriage: carnal lust was evil, and marriage, the remedy for carnal lust, was in one sense seen as an admission of failure, the failure of man to restrain his physical impulses and dedicate himself to a life of celibacy. This is why the church emphasised marriage as a union of two hearts, attaching such importance to mutual consent. The sexual act was for one purpose only: the propagation of the human race. It was not for pleasure. According to St Jerome, married couples who had sexual intercourse with each other purely for enjoyment were no better than adulterers:

> He who is too ardently amorous of his wife is also an adulterer. With regard to the wife of another, in truth, all love is disgraceful; and with regard to one's own wife, excessive love is. The wise man must love his wife with judgment, not with passion. Let him curb his transports of voluptuousness and not let himself be urged precipitately to indulge in coition. Nothing is more vile than to love a wife like a mistress.

INTRODUCTION

It was partly as a result of this attitude to the physical side of human relationships that the church did not develop a coherent doctrine on marriage before the late eleventh century. Some churchmen thought marriage so contemptible and carnal that the church should not involve itself in the matter at all, but simply leave it to laymen. Yet theory was considerably more stringent than practice. After all, large numbers of the clergy did not take their vows of celibacy too seriously. Once the church did establish its jurisdiction over marriage, it was up to the church courts to enforce ecclesiastical attitudes towards sexual behaviour on the errant laity, and in fact the later Middle Ages seem to have witnessed a gradual moderation of the punishments meted out for sexual misdemeanours. In the thirteenth century, the normal punishment for a proven adulterer or fornicator was to be whipped around the market place or churchyard; by the fifteenth century it was more usual for offenders to be made to wear penitential garb and carry a lighted candle in the church procession on Sunday. This is what the bishop of London made Elizabeth Shore do (at Richard III's request). The element of public humiliation had clearly become more important than physical castigation.

The church regularly issued decrees concerning sexual relations. Some canonists argued that there was a distinction between exacting the conjugal debt and rendering it. The latter was the duty of every spouse, while the former was sinful. In other words, no man or woman had the right to demand sexual intercourse from his or her spouse, but nor should the spouse refuse it if it was requested. Certain acts, such as bestiality and masturbation, were frequently forbidden, as were certain sexual positions, even between married couples: according to one regulation, oral sex was punishable by a three-year penance, rising to seven years if a nun or monk was involved. Aphrodisiacs were also prohibited: some women apparently believed that if they could persuade a friend to knead dough on their bare buttocks before giving the bread to their husbands, it would make the husband 'burn with greater love for them'. This and other forms of aphrodisiac were punishable by sentences of varying terms. More common were regulations on the frequency of sexual relations between married couples: Sundays, feast-days, the whole of Lent, and during pregnancies and menstrual periods were the most commonly forbidden times, and were often backed up with horrific stories of deformed children who had been conceived on Sundays, lepers who had been conceived during menstruation, and so forth. To what extent any of these regulations were enforced is impossible to say. What seems clear is that they stemmed from a basic belief, at least in official church doctrine, that sexual relations of all kinds were unclean, and should be avoided except when procreation was desired. 'Who does not know,' thundered Pope Innocent III (1198–1216) 'that conjugal intercourse is never committed without itching of the flesh, and heat, and foul concupiscence, whence the conceived seeds are befouled and corrupted.'

A certain degree of 'moral guardianship' was also written into lay jurisdiction. Early in the twelfth century the laws of Henry I declared that of two adulterers, the woman's fine must be paid to the bishop, while the man's must be paid to the king. Fines imposed by lay courts for sexual misbehaviour largely disappeared once the jurisdiction of the church courts had been established, but lords did retain the right to punish their serfs (unfree tenants) for such offences. A fine called *leyrwite* could be imposed by the lord's court on an unfree woman who fornicated, while for unfree women who gave birth out of wedlock a fine called *childwite* was exacted. *Leyrwite* was still sometimes exacted in fifteenth-century England, although serfdom was by now fast disappearing.

Lay attitudes to extramarital sex were, not surprisingly, more tolerant than ecclesiastical attitudes. There was one very important respect in which this was true. The church condemned adultery and fornication outright, regarding both man and woman as equally culpable. Laymen were more tolerant of licentiousness in men, but, at least as far as the propertied classes were concerned, were just as emphatic as churchmen on the need for chastity in women. The reason for this is not hard to find: adultery in a woman jeopardised the inheritance. A man with an unchaste wife could not be sure that the son who was going to inherit his property really was his son. Fornication by an unmarried heiress, if it became known, made her much less marriageable. When the French king Philip IV discovered in 1314 that two of his daughters-in-law had for several years been committing adultery with two knights, he imprisoned the two princesses and had the two knights publicly executed in barbarous fashion. It is quite impossible to believe that his reaction to the adultery of his son-in-law would have been so ferocious. Medieval men might boast of their sexual prowess, but wives and daughters were closely and jealously guarded, in upper-class circles at least.

This attitude led to a distinction between high-born and low-born women in the eyes of pleasure-seeking men: meddling with high-born women could lead to serious trouble, so men availed themselves of the services of low-born women. It seems to have been quite accepted that they should do so. Henry of Grosmont, duke of Lancaster, one of the most cultured nobles in fourteenth-century England, declared that although he loved the scent of fine ladies, he preferred to kiss the low-born, because they were more responsive. Prostitution was also common, and it was freely accepted that bachelors should frequent brothels if they wished to. Indeed, many towns and cities had official brothels, paying rent, subject to regular inspection and so forth. The red-light area of medieval London was Southwark, where the prostitutes were known as 'Winchester geese' because the house from which they operated was owned by the bishop of Winchester. The bishop was in good company: even the papacy owned a number of brothels in Rome.

Bawdy humour abounds in the plays, poems and other popular literature which survives from the Middle Ages, from the Mystery Plays to Chaucer's *Canterbury Tales*. There can be no doubt about the double entendre of the following riddle, in which the audience was meant to guess what was being described:

> I'm the world's wonder, for I make women happy. . . .
> I am set well up, stand in a bed,
> Have a roughish root. Rarely (though it happens)
> A churl's daughter more daring than the rest
> – and lovelier – lays hold of me,
> Rushes my red top, wrenches at my head,
> And lays me in the larder. She learns soon enough,
> The curly-haired creature who clamps me so,
> Of my meeting with her: moist is her eye!

The answer, of course, is an onion.

Most lay people, and most churchmen too, probably regarded it as quite normal that kings should take mistresses. Edward IV's contemporaries seem to have regarded his excesses with some amusement, although after his death political capital was certainly made out of them. Nevertheless it is interesting to note that slanders of a sexual nature seem to have been used increasingly as material for political propaganda in the fourteenth and fifteenth centuries. For instance, all sorts of stories about Edward III's infidelities circulated at the court of his French adversary; much was also made of John of Gaunt's libido, and of Edward IV's even before his death. One of the charges made against the duke of Suffolk when he was impeached in the parliament of 1450 was that he had committed adultery with a nun, and had fathered an illegitimate daughter by her. These were basically political smears, however, and it would probably be unwise to read too much significance into them.

English men never seem to have been regarded as great lovers. A Venetian who visited England at the end of the fifteenth century recorded his impressions as follows:

> Although their dispositions are somewhat licentious, I never have
> noticed anyone, either at court or amongst the lower orders, to be in
> love; whence one must necessarily conclude, either that the English are
> the most discreet lovers in the world, or that they are incapable of love.
> I say this of the men, for I understand it is quite the contrary with the

women, who are very violent in their passions. Howbeit, the English keep a very jealous guard over their wives. . . .

It is interesting that at almost exactly the same time, the German ambassador Nicolas von Poppelau wrote that he considered English women to be extremely beautiful but astoundingly impudent. The Venetian who thought the English incapable of love might have approved of the Scottish king James I. Captured by the English in 1406, he remained in honourable captivity in England for eighteen years, during which time he met and fell in love with Joan Beaufort, the granddaughter of John of Gaunt. In 1424 he eventually married Joan, and two months later returned with his new bride to Scotland. In his poem *The King's Quair*, James describes his feelings at the moment when he first set eyes on Joan:

> And therewith cast I down my eye that way
> Where, as I saw, walking below the tower,
> Quite secretly arrived there now to play,
> The fairest or the freshest budding flower
> That ever I saw, methought, before that hour,
> Which suddenly withdrew, and then did start
> The blood of all my body to my heart.
>
> And though a while I stood abashed then quite
> No wonder 'twas, because my senses all
> Were so o'erwhelmed with pleasure and delight
> Only through letting of my eyes to fall,
> That suddenly my heart became her thrall
> For ever, of free will; for of menace
> There was no token in her fair sweet face.

The love-match between James I and Joan Beaufort is a welcome reminder that, even at the highest level of politics, marriage could still sometimes be an affair of the heart; this was, however, a privilege enjoyed by few.

The taking of mistresses by kings led inevitably to the birth of royal bastards, for contraceptive techniques in the Middle Ages were far from advanced. Indeed, it seems likely that the ancient Greeks and Romans knew more about effective contraceptive techniques than did medieval men. The Catholic church's attitude to contraception needs no emphasis: the sole function of sexual intercourse was procreation. Contraception was unnatural and sinful. In the face of this church condemnation, there was little scope for the development of scientific methods of contraception, and what passed for contraceptive techniques were generally no more than folk superstitions, which now appear more amusing than efficacious. It is strange to find a man so learned as Albertus Magnus, the thirteenth-century

41

INTRODUCTION

Dominican scientist and theologian, stating that if a woman spat three times into the mouth of a frog, or if she ate bees before intercourse, she would not become pregnant; drinking the urine of a sheep or the blood of a hare was said to have the same effect. Even more fantastic was the idea, found in both the twelfth and thirteenth centuries, that the left testicle of the weasel, when wrapped in the skin of a mule upon which certain mystic words were written, and worn by a woman during intercourse, would prevent conception. One had to do it carefully, however:

> Remove the testicle as the moon goes down, and leave the weasel living; and give its testicle to be worn in the muleskin; it will serve as a sort of philtre, invincible and agreeable, against conception.

If widely practised, this method may well have created serious reproduction problems for the medieval weasel, but its value to humans is more dubious.

The one reasonably effective form of contraception which may have been practised quite widely in the Middle Ages was *coitus interruptus* (the fact that it was prohibited by the church is significant). But even if *coitus interruptus* was common, it is not nowadays regarded as one of the more reliable forms of contraception. In the Middle Ages, people had to accept that extramarital sex was likely to lead to illegitimate children. What then was the medieval attitude to illegitimacy?

BASTARDY IN MEDIEVAL LAW

One result of the church's attempts to regulate Christian marriage customs from about 1050 onwards was that a clearer demarcation line came to be drawn between legitimacy and illegitimacy. Before the late eleventh century, it must often have been very difficult to say whether a man was a bastard or not: monogamy was not well established, formal marriage was widely considered to be unnecessary and, since primogeniture was not yet the dominant form of inheritance pattern at any level of society, it must have seemed to many laymen that there was little point in trying to make a distinction between legitimate and illegitimate children. Thus in 1035 William the Bastard was widely acknowledged as his father's heir in Normandy, while in England in the same year the illegitimate Harold Harefoot gained the throne in preference to his legitimate brother Harthacnut. A hundred years later, it is clear that much had changed already: Robert of Gloucester may have been a popular choice to succeed his father as king in 1135, but there is no doubt that his bastardy counted crucially against him. By the end of the twelfth century, Geoffrey 'Plantagenet's' maternity made him a virtual non-starter. The change in attitude at this, the highest level of society, was a reflection of a much more deep-rooted change in attitudes to bastardy among both churchmen and common lawyers, a

42

change which wrought a profound and enduring deterioration in the legal rights accorded to illegitimate children.

Both ecclesiastical and common lawyers had good reasons to make a clearer distinction between legitimate and illegitimate children. For the common lawyers, the crucial point was naturally inheritance: the twelfth century was an age in which great efforts were made to apply more definite rules concerning inheritance. For the canonists, the argument in one sense led back to the problem of marriage customs: if illegitimate children were denied the rights accorded to their legitimate siblings, that was a great inducement to couples to make formal marriages in order to protect their children's future. From the mid-eleventh century, the church began to prohibit illegitimate children from entering the clergy. Dispensations could be obtained, however, and in fact these soon became fairly standard (in return for a payment, naturally). From the mid-twelfth century, this system was extended to the formal legitimation by the church of purely lay bastards – that is, lay men or women who had no desire to enter the church but who merely wanted to be officially legitimate. Joan, the daughter of King John, was the first lay royal bastard in England to be thus legitimated, in 1226. The very fact that by this time laymen considered such dispensations worthwhile shows the extent to which attitudes had changed.

Thus lawyers of all kinds were agreed on the need to penalise the illegitimate child in certain respects, and the main way in which this was done was by the enforcement in the common-law courts of the principle that bastards could not inherit from their parents as of right. By the end of the twelfth century, and probably for quite a few decades before that, this was an established common-law principle: the bastard was legally *filius nullius*, the son of nobody (which for practical purposes really meant the *heir* of nobody). But if it was the common-law courts which had to enforce this principle, it was up to the church courts to decide whether or not a man was legitimate. This was a natural extension of the church's claim to exercise jurisdiction over marriage disputes, and was clearly accepted in England during the second half of the twelfth century. The legal treatise which bears the name of Henry II's chief justice, Ranulf Glanville, and which was probably written around 1180, declared unequivocally that 'it does not belong to the king's court to enquire concerning bastardy'. In practice this meant that if a property dispute turned on the question of whether or not a man was a bastard, the process in the lay court was suspended and a writ was sent to the church court asking for a decision on the man's legitimacy. Having made its enquiries (usually through a local jury), the church court informed the lay court of its verdict, and the lay court could then determine the case. In the majority of cases, this co-operative procedure seems to have worked perfectly smoothly. In certain cases, however, difficulties arose: this was because canon and common lawyers were unable to agree on how legitimacy was to be defined.

It is in fact very difficult to define legitimacy. Ideas on who is legitimate and who is not will always depend on a number of other factors, such as the preoccupations and prejudices of those whose job it is to make laws, prevailing social and moral customs, precedents, and so forth. Substantive law on bastardy as applied by canon lawyers and common lawyers varied in a number of important respects, of which the most divisive was the question of so-called 'mantle-children'. These were children born out of wedlock (but not in adultery) whose parents subsequently married. The church considered such children to be automatically legitimated by their parents' subsequent marriage: at the wedding ceremony they were placed under the care-cloth (or mantle) which was spread over their parents, and became henceforward lawful children of the marriage. For about a century after the Norman Conquest it seems to have been customary to treat such children as legitimate for purposes of inheritance in the lay courts too, although their legitimacy never seems to have been officially supported by legal theory. By the 1180s, as *Glanville* (the legal treatise named after Henry II's chief justiciar, Ranulf Glanville) tells us, the common-law courts had come to the opinion that mantle-children should not be regarded as legitimate for purposes of inheritance:

> Although indeed the canons and the Roman laws consider such son as the lawful heir, yet according to the law and custom of this realm, he shall in no measure be supported as heir in his claim upon the inheritance; nor can he demand the inheritance by the law of the realm.

If, then, a case of inheritance in a lay court turned on the question of whether a child had been born before or after his parents' marriage (and with no registers of births or marriages such points were often difficult to prove in court), there was no point in sending a writ to the church court requesting a verdict on the child's legitimacy, as the answer would be 'legitimate' regardless of the date of birth, and the lay court would then be in the position of having to enforce a claim to inheritance which common law declared to be invalid. At a royal council held at Merton in 1236, this issue came to a head: the bishops, led by the fiery Robert Grosseteste, bishop of Lincoln, suggested that in future mantle-children should be heritable at common law. The barons refused: 'We do not wish to change the laws of England,' they are said to have declared unanimously. Not until the Legitimacy Act of 1920 was the law changed: thus long were the barons of Merton triumphant.

As a result of the stand taken by the barons at Merton, the procedure adopted by the lay courts in dealing with inheritance disputes which turned on the question of bastardy was altered: in future, common lawyers made a distinction between those cases which were sent to the church courts and those which were not. Only in cases where the substantive law on bastardy was identical would the church court be asked to give a verdict on a man's legitimacy. In fact this seems to have occurred on occasions before 1236 too (and no doubt this was what brought the issue to a head), but after 1236 it became the official practice of the lay courts. From the thirteenth century onwards, therefore, a younger son born after his parents' marriage would be granted the inheritance in preference to his elder brother who had been born before their parents' marriage, even though in the eyes of the church they were the equally legitimate children of their parents.

Nor was this the only point on which the canon and common laws on bastardy were at variance. Another was the thorny problem of children born to married women who were suspected of having committed adultery. From at least the twelfth century, English common law maintained that in all such cases there must be a strong presumption that the child was the son of his mother's husband. There were only two grounds on which the legitimacy of a child born in wedlock, and during the lifetime of his mother's husband, could be challenged: firstly, the proven impotence of the husband, and secondly, proven non-access by the husband to his wife. Until the eighteenth century, the rules governing non-access were stringent in the extreme, as exemplified by the thirteenth-century legal treatise which bears the name of Henry de Bracton:

> If the husband be absent from the realm or county for two years or
> upwards, it is to be strongly presumed that he could not have had
> access to his wife; and if he finds on his return that she is pregnant, or
> has a child who is then [presumably not more than] one year old,
> such child is a bastard.

This excessive reluctance on the part of English common lawyers to bastardise any child born to a married woman was not reflected in church law: the canonists were more concerned with actual paternity, and required much less stringent proof of non-access. What led the English common lawyers to impose upon husbands the duty of acknowledging as their own any children born to their wives was the desire to prevent the disinheritance of legitimate children; one of its by-products, as noted with approval by nineteenth-century historians, was to encourage husbands to keep a vigilant watch over the conduct of their wives. This law led to a well-known proverb in medieval England: 'Who that bulleth my cow, the calf is mine.' It was even quoted twice from the judicial bench in the fifteenth century, and Shakespeare adopted it in his *King John*. In France, where the lay courts followed more closely the canon law principle, it was easier for husbands to disinherit their children by claiming that their wives had committed adultery: the nemesis of such a principle came in 1420, when the Dauphin, the future Charles VII, was disowned and disinherited from the crown by his own father and mother. His father, Charles VI, was admittedly insane at the time; his mother, Isabella of Bavaria, who herself denied her son's royal paternity, was a known adulteress, referred to by her grandson Louis XI as 'a great whore'. Louis XI was also one of those who cast aspersions on the paternity of his contemporary Edward IV of England, but the rumour that Edward IV was a bastard never gained much credence in England, and it is significant that the argument was not used in the *Titulus Regis* (although it was hinted at). There were also rumours that Henry VI's wife, Margaret of Anjou, was an adulteress, but again these were no more than rumours.

The one English king who was the son of a known adulteress was Edward III, and it is significant that his paternity seems never to have been questioned. The rumours about Richard II's bastardy (on the grounds of Joan of Kent's adultery, as opposed to the validity of her marriages) seem to have been no more than political smears made at an opportune moment, and were never used officially as a reason to depose him. Thus once again the influence of common-law principles at the highest level is apparent: no case for the bastardy of Edward III, Richard II, Edward IV, or Henry VI's son Prince Edward would have stood a chance in an English common-law court. The case for Charles VII's bastardy might well have been upheld in a French court. Although the rules governing non-access have now been modified, the presumption of the legitimacy of a child born to a married woman is still very strong in English law.

The church's attitude to divorce also created serious problems with regard to legitimacy. After the twelfth century, as has been said, a marriage could not be dissolved; it could only be declared to have been invalid from the start. What then was the status of children born of that marriage? Logic, inexorably applied, could not avoid the conclusion that they were bastards, being born of an invalid marriage. In this instance, however, logic was at least partially tempered by humanitarian considerations. Both church and state recognised that such a policy would lead to the grossest injustices, and gradually a compromise was arrived at. By about 1330, it had come to be accepted by both canon and common lawyers that annulment of a marriage for precontract automatically bastardised any children of that marriage. In such cases it was difficult not to believe that at least one parent had knowingly acted in bad faith, and thus the sins of the parent were visited on the child. Annulment on grounds of consanguinity presented more problems. Canon law relied heavily on trying to establish the good faith of the parents: if at least one of the parents had been unaware of the consanguinity at the time of marriage, then in the eyes of the church the children were legitimate. Up until about the mid-fourteenth century, English common law worked on the same principle, but around this time the lay courts developed a harsher attitude to the children of consanguineous marriages: from this time onwards, the lay courts normally enforced the principle that any divorce between parents, including divorce for consanguinity, was legally retrospective, automatically bastardising the children and rendering them unable to inherit. The implications of this decision for the Tudor monarchy were immense. After the failure of his first two marriages, to Katharine of Aragon and Anne Boleyn, Henry persuaded parliament to accept the second Act of Succession (1536) declaring that his daughters Mary, the child of Katharine of Aragon, and Elizabeth, the child of Anne Boleyn, were illegitimate and could hold no place in the succession. By 1544, however, the king still had only one male heir, the sickly young Edward (born of his third wife, Jane Seymour), and the future of the Tudor dynasty was in jeopardy. Thus the third Act of Succession (1544) bestowed the crown on Mary and Elizabeth, in that order, regardless of the earlier bastardisations, if both Henry himself and the young Edward should die before producing any further heirs. Edward VI survived his father by only six years, and so it happened that two women, both of whom had been retrospectively bastardised by act of parliament, successively ascended the throne of England, and both occupied it until their deaths.

In these three cases then, mantle-children, suspected adultery by the mother, and divorce for consanguinity, the difference in substantive law applied by the canonists and the English common lawyers led the lay courts to abandon the practice of asking the church courts for a verdict on the defendant's legitimacy. There were one or two other cases in which the same principle was applied, but they were obscure and infrequent. The lay courts were in effect enforcing the common-law definition of bastardy, even though in theory all men accepted that only the church could give a verdict on a man's legitimacy. Those whom English common law regarded as bastards were not allowed their 'inheritances', regardless of what the church might think about their legitimacy; and although this angered some churchmen, most of them seem to have accepted that, where the passage of property was involved, it was up to the lay courts to enforce common-law principles. By the end of the thirteenth century, the same practice was followed in most Continental countries (although on the Continent the differences between canon law and secular law on bastardy were not so marked, so there were fewer opportunities for disagreement).

The distinction between those bastardy cases which were sent to the church courts and those which were not came to be defined in English law as 'general bastardy' and 'special bastardy'. 'Special bastardy' was the name given to those cases where substantive law differed; 'general bastardy' concerned more straightforward cases, where the two laws were in agreement, as for instance with the child of a couple who were alleged never to have married. There is no doubt that these complicating factors led to a certain amount of confusion, and through either chicanery or ignorance some cases did end up in the wrong court. From about the mid-fourteenth century, however, both procedural and substantive law in the lay courts seem to have become clearer, and henceforward the common law was administered with a greater degree of precision. English common law has often been denounced as being excessively harsh on illegitimate children. Yet the law was not all-powerful. English lawyers, whose unenviable task it was to draft and enforce laws which must be both logical and scrupulous, found that in theory there was no alternative but to penalise the bastard severely; in practice, however, people were a great deal more tolerant than the law would suggest.

SOCIAL ATTITUDES TO ILLEGITIMACY

English common law declared that a bastard could not inherit *as of right*. That did not mean that he could not inherit. The circumstances had to be favourable, however. This usually meant that the bastard's parents should not have any legitimate heirs, that his father should have recognised him as his own son and expressed a desire that he should be his heir, and that – at least among the higher social classes – the king or other feudal lord of the property concerned should acquiesce. The bastard therefore had to be lucky if he was going to become a landholder of importance primarily on account of his birth. In thirteenth- and fourteenth-century England at least, a form of quasi-adoption was recognised at law, whereby a father might legally acknowledge either his or his wife's bastard as his heir in the absence of legitimate issue. Justice Spigurnell declared in 1307 that

> Sir Henry de Berkely had but one wife, and never in her life did she conceive a child and yet he had six sons. After his death the eldest entered [the inheritance], and because he was holden and acknowledged as Sir Henry's son in his lifetime he retained the inheritance against the very heir [a collateral] by the judgment of the common council of the whole land.

The law was considerably more flexible than it appears at first sight. By the middle of the fourteenth century, it was sometimes no longer so much a question of law as of royal favour. By this time it was at least partly accepted, as it had not been in the thirteenth century, that land could be effectively bequeathed by will, which gave landholders the chance to distribute their properties in accordance with their own wishes rather than in accordance with the strict laws of feudal inheritance. Obviously this might create new opportunities for illegitimate children, but because such transactions were not yet fully defined at law, their success often depended upon royal acquiescence. Some were lucky, others were not. In 1346, a year before his death, John de Warenne, earl of Surrey, who was by now an old man and had no legitimate children, begged Edward III that

> in case he should depart this life without any such issue . . . all his castles, lands, manors and tenements in Surrey, Sussex and Wales should, after such his decease, remain to the king, to be bestowed upon some one of his own [bastard] sons . . . on condition that, in the person of such son and his heirs, the name, honor and arms of Warenne should be for ever maintained and kept.

Warenne's bastards were unlucky. The king wanted the lands to grant them to his friend the earl of Arundel (who had a claim to them by marriage), and he refused to sanction the deal.

More fortunate were the Beauforts, the most celebrated mantle-children in English history. At their official legitimation in the parliament of 1397, a year after John of Gaunt's marriage to Katherine Swynford, the actual mantle ceremony was apparently performed, all four children, by now adults, being placed under the care-cloth with their parents in parliament (although strictly speaking they were not what the church thought of as mantle-children, having been born in adultery). Richard II legitimated them in fulsome terms, pointing out that they were 'sprung from royal stock', and declaring them fully heritable at law. The Beauforts were exceptional, for they had royal blood in their veins. How often the great landholders of late medieval England used their new freedom of property disposition to benefit illegitimate children is difficult to say. It seems to have been more usual for a noble (certainly if he had legitimate heirs of his body) to bequeath gifts of cash or precious goods to his bastards rather than land: at his death in 1428 Thomas Montacute, earl of Salisbury, left 500 marks (£333) in his will for the upbringing and marriage of his illegitimate son (*pro filio nostro bastardo*).

The bastard's inability to inherit as of right was not confined to land alone: it extended, for instance, to offices held by the father which would normally be hereditary. If his father was a member of a trade guild, the bastard could not inherit his position, and since guild membership was the road to municipal office, bastards were normally excluded from this too. Nor could he enter the church without a dispensation, although in practice such dispensations were easily obtainable. These were major disabilities: incapacity to inherit has become virtually meaningless under the modern freedom of testamentary disposition, so that it is easy to underrate its former effect. Yet beyond this, there were no real attempts to penalise bastards for their defective birth. There were simply too many of them: recent research on the parish of Halesowen has shown that, for every two women who married, one woman gave birth to a child out of wedlock. The bastard could purchase property, unlike the foreigner. He was a free man, with the same rights in law and elsewhere as any other free man. The fact that he was *filius nullius* even led to a strange paradox in English law: from Anglo-Saxon times until about 1330, the bastard son of an unfree woman took his mother's status, but after about 1330 it was recognised that if he was the son of nobody he could not inherit his mother's (or father's) servility, and accordingly he was deemed to be a free man.

In some Continental countries this was not the case. In certain parts of thirteenth-century France it was claimed that a bastard, even if he was the son of free parents, was not himself free; he could not fight a duel with a free man, nor act as a witness in a criminal suit against a free man. In some parts of Germany, too, the bastard was said to be 'rightless' – unfree at law. To become a mason in Germany a man had to be legitimate. These disabilities in practice were only applicable to bastards born of humble parents, however, for it is quite clear that throughout Europe the bastard sons of noblemen, and particularly of kings, were recognised as being of the nobility themselves. In France, for instance, noble bastards were exempted from taxes along with other nobles. Some French and German historians have called the fifteenth century 'the age of bastards', because so many high-born bastards achieved political eminence: Jean de Dunois, for instance, 'bastard of Orleans', Joan of Arc's companion in war and the trusted counsellor of King Charles VII of France; or Anthony, the 'Great Bastard of Burgundy', son of Duke Philip of Burgundy, who was fêted like a king on his visit to London to take part in a tournament in 1467. The custom in some countries was more tolerant of bastards at the lower end of the social scale as well: in Scotland and Ireland, legal inheritance by bastards seems to have been possible through to the seventeenth century. In Wales, it was only after the English conquest of 1284 that inheritance was restricted to legitimate children. More often, however, the law concerned itself more with defining illegitimacy than with specifying the rights of illegitimate children: especially was this true of mantle-children, often recognised as fully legitimate by lay courts on the Continent.

If canon and common law were both against the bastard, there was nevertheless much sympathy for him on both sides of the fence. Church moralists of the Middle Ages declared that a man had a duty to bring up all of his children, legitimate or illegitimate. He had brought them into the world, and he should provide for them. The parish clergy could not afford to be too critical either, for up to the Reformation large numbers of them were themselves the sons of priests, and thus illegitimate. The fact that the church readily granted dispensations to allow illegitimate children to enter holy orders is a reflection of this humanitarian outlook. Among laymen, too, there was a general feeling that to leave any child unprovided for was a sign of failure. The illegitimate son must be given some sort of start in life, just as much as his legitimate siblings. Hence the attitude of the Vicomte de Castelbon in southern France, who, with admirable foresight, directed in his will that sums of money should be given to all his bastards already born or who might yet be born. It was naturally an attitude of mind which was much more likely to benefit the high-born bastard: no doubt the rigours of the law were enforced more sparingly when the father had wealth and influence and was concerned with the future of his illegitimate child. Yet it does seem true that at all social levels, there was no great stigma attached to bastardy in the Middle Ages. It is true that allegations of bastardy were commonly used for political slander, particularly in the later Middle Ages, but such allegations nearly always had a specific purpose: they were designed to show that a man or woman was not entitled to claim a particular office or property. That is very different from using the allegation of bastardy to cast a slur on a person's character or reputation. Medieval ears would probably have been deaf to slurs of this nature.

HERALDRY AND BASTARDY

In 1463 the Chief King of Arms to the duke of Burgundy wrote: 'A bastard may carry the arms of his father with a *baton sinister*.' The importance attached to the arms a man was permitted to bear in the later Middle Ages means that the treatment of bastards in the laws of heraldry is an important indicator of wider social attitudes to bastards at that time. Coats of arms were and still are heritable: the coat of arms borne by a man was a visible sign of the family from which he came. Yet in heraldic law, no two men were entitled to bear exactly the same coat of arms. Thus a system was developed whereby, during a man's lifetime, his sons had to have slight changes or additions made to their coats of arms, signifying that none of them was yet the head of the family. This system is known as 'heraldic cadency', and the changes or additions made to the coat of arms are known as 'marks of cadency', or 'marks of difference'. Heraldry had only really begun to develop in the twelfth century, and it was not until the fifteenth century that it became systematic. Yet heraldic cadency was clearly in operation before this: during the fourteenth century the obligation of cadet branches of a family to distinguish their arms from the primogenitary line was recognised almost universally. Along with marks of cadency developed marks of bastardy.

If coats of arms were heritable, and bastards could not inherit from anyone, could a bastard take his father's coat of arms (appropriately marked, of course)? In theory, the answer was no. In practice, however, it is abundantly clear that noble bastards did bear their parents' arms. If a nobleman acknowledged his illegitimate son and was prepared to allow

51

him to bear his arms, then as long as it was suitably marked no one was likely to object. The main point of marks of cadency was really to single out the primogenitary line from other lines. Illegitimate sons, like younger sons, were not their father's heirs (at least once primogeniture had become the norm): as long as the arms they bore demonstrated this fact, their right effectively to inherit arms was unlikely to be challenged. It has been suggested that marks of bastardy should not be considered as a part of the system of cadency, that they were 'marks of distinction' rather than 'marks of difference', specifically denoting illegitimacy, but this argument seems over-subtle: in practice – at least during the Middle Ages – there was little difference between marks of cadency and marks of bastardy. Not until the eighteenth century were more specific rules about marks of bastardy widely enforced. They were not developed in the Middle Ages as a punishment or a disgrace, but as an element of cadency, a means of heraldic 'differencing'. In many Continental countries bastards had the right to bear their father's arms, and it is clear that in England the same principle was in effect applied.

During the Middle Ages, marks of cadency and marks of bastardy were barely distinguishable from each other. These marks are called *brisures*, and could take many different forms. *Bends sinister* and *bends dexter* (lines imposed diagonally across the shield starting from the left or right side) were commonly used both for illegitimacy and for legitimate differencing. So were *bordures* (inset borders around the perimeter of the shield), of which there were variations, notably the *bordure wavy* (border drawn with a wavy line) and *bordure compony* (border divided into segments); *cantons* (miniature shields of the father's or mother's arms superimposed on the main shield) were also sometimes used. From about the fifteenth century, however, the range of options began to narrow. As the duke of Burgundy's Chief King of Arms noted, by the late fifteenth century the *bend* (also called a *baton* or, erroneously, a *bar*) *sinister* had established itself as the standard mark of illegitimacy, and as a consequence it was used less for legitimate cadency. In the eighteenth century, however, the *bordure wavy* began to be used as the standard mark of illegitimacy outside the royal family, and it is now used exclusively for that purpose. In Scottish heraldry, the *bordure compony* is the only mark of illegitimacy.

The royal arms have always been something of a law unto themselves, and the marks used for royal bastards have often been different from the marks used for other bastards. One device used for royal or quasi-royal bastards was the *bend* bearing the royal or parental arms imposed on a plain shield. Thus Sir Roger de Clarendon used the ostrich feathers and scrolls of his father, the Black Prince, set on a *bend* against a plain gold background (Plate 6a). Before his legitimation, John Beaufort used the royal arms of lions and fleurs-de-lis on a *bend* in similar fashion; after his legitimation, however, he abandoned this device and instead quartered the royal arms on the shield itself, within a *bordure compony* (Plate 6b,c). Ironically, this use of the *bordure compony* by the Beauforts led to the belief that it was a mark of illegitimacy, but in fact before this it had normally been used to denote legitimate cadency; only after this did it come to be used frequently to denote illegitimacy. By the end of the fifteenth century it was coming to be accepted that the *bend* (or *baton*, i.e., truncated *bend*) *sinister* was the usual mark to denote a royal bastard in both the French and English royal houses. Edward IV's bastard Arthur Plantagenet bore the royal arms quartered with the arms of March and Ulster, and traversed by a *bendlet sinister* (Plate 8), and later royal bastards followed him. Nowadays the *baton sinister* would not be allowed to any person other than a royal bastard.

CONCLUSIONS

The heraldic marks used to denote illegitimacy point in the same direction as much of the other evidence concerning high-born bastards in medieval society. In theory, the law penalised them severely; in practice, they were accepted into the aristocracy as the sons and daughters of their fathers, and usually given every opportunity to prosper in much the same way as other nobles. Moreover, the origins of an illegitimate family were soon forgotten. King John did not think it beneath him to marry Isabel of Gloucester, the granddaughter of Henry I's bastard Robert of Gloucester. James I of Scotland was content to marry Joan Beaufort only a quarter of a century after the family's legitimation. Writing in the seventeenth century, Sir George Buck, Master of the King's Revels, made his position on the matter quite clear:

> And let it not be thought any disparagement for a noble family to be descended from a natural issue, considering that there have been and are infinite number of noble and princely families which are derived and propagated from bastards or natural sons.

Aeneas, Romulus, Theseus, Themistocles, Hercules, William the Conqueror, the Stewart kings of Scotland, and the Beauforts are among the examples he gives, before concluding as follows:

> And this one example is above all, to wit, that Jesus Christ, the greatest and most noble king, was content to descend from Phares, a bastard.

English common law was by no means harsh on the bastard. It applied a more rigorous definition than did the law of many other countries on who should or should not be considered illegitimate, but this was at least partly compensated for by the rights which it accorded to those whom it called bastards. Frederick Maitland conjectured that the toleration of bastards in medieval English law might have been 'due to no deeper cause than the subjection of England to kings who proudly traced their descent from a mighty bastard'. The fact remains, however, that William the Conqueror was the last undoubted bastard to sit on the English throne in the Middle Ages. Royal bastards got a long way in medieval England, but they never quite got to the top (excluding technical bastardisations such as Edward V and, in the sixteenth century, Mary and Elizabeth I). In other countries, they sometimes did get to the top. When William II of Sicily died without issue in 1189, he was succeeded as king by his cousin Tancred, the illegitimate son of his father's elder brother. When the Holy Roman Emperor Conrad IV died in 1254, he was succeeded by his half-brother Manfred, illegitimate son of the great emperor Frederick II. The bastard Manfred was crowned king of Sicily in 1258, but was killed at the battle of Benevento in 1266 without having been able to persuade a hostile papacy to recognise him as emperor. Most successful of all the royal bastards in the Middle Ages was Henry of Trastamara, King of Castile. After strangling his legitimate half-brother, King Pedro 'the Cruel', with his own hands, Henry seized the throne in 1369 and kept it until his death ten years later, establishing a dynasty which was to rule Castile until the end of the Middle Ages. In 1383, fourteen years after Trastamara's triumph, the royal bastard João I of Portugal seized the throne which should have gone to his niece, and he remained king of Portugal for nearly fifty years. Other royal bastards also came close. In 1201 Pope Innocent III agreed formally to legitimate the two bastard sons of King Philip II of France, which made them second and third in line for the French throne; unfortunately for them, their legitimate brother Louis (VIII) lived long enough to succeed to the throne and to produce an heir to follow him. When Edward I was asked to adjudicate the succession to the Scottish throne in 1292, several descendants of royal bastards put forward their claims.

Royal bastards could never be ignored in medieval politics: there were too many of them around, and they had a head-start. Nor was there any real social stigma attached to bastardy in the Middle Ages. Although the rise of Puritanism and the promulgation of the Poor Laws in the sixteenth century led to much greater social disapproval of illegitimacy among ordinary people, kings and aristocrats continued to take mistresses with impunity and to rear their bastards in public. It is well known that four of our present-day English dukes are descended from the bastard children of Charles II. Only in the nineteenth century, with the 'Victorian revolution' of gentlefolk's morals, did illegitimacy really go out of fashion among the upper classes.

PART II

ROYAL BASTARDS
1066–1216

PART II

ROYAL BASTARDS
1066-1216

We shall never know the true number of bastards fathered by the medieval kings of England. The Appendix gives a list of forty-one whose identity can be established with reasonable certainty. In addition there are a number who have been described as royal bastards in the past, but whose royal paternity is in fact highly doubtful: rumours, fuelled by a desire to claim royal descent, however distantly, often sprang up decades or even centuries after a king's death. Sometimes kings were not very sure themselves: King John, for instance, referred to one of his probable bastards as 'Henry, who calls himself our son, but is really our nephew'. A few years later the king was clearer in his own mind, calling him 'Henry our son'. Some of Henry II's councillors apparently advised him not to acknowledge Geoffrey 'Plantagenet' as his bastard, because the woman Hikenai was 'base-born', and who could be sure that Geoffrey really was the king's progeny? Yet Henry readily acknowledged Geoffrey as his son, and Geoffrey went on to pursue a brilliant career in his father's service. In such circumstances it is quite impossible for a modern historian to be completely sure of any supposed royal bastard's true paternity. Moreover, there must be numerous royal bastards who have completely disappeared from the records: frequently we know of the existence of a royal bastard only because of a chance remark by a chronicler, or the chance survival of some royal writ or other official document. On the other hand it is clear that medieval kings had absolutely no compunction about acknowledging those children whom they were fairly sure they had fathered. So if the figure of forty-one is obviously a conservative one, it may not be entirely unrealistic: if it is right to assume that the medieval kings generally acknowledged and provided for their illegitimate children, then it is probably right to assume that some sort of record referring to at least a fair proportion of them would have survived.

The great advantage of royal bastards, as far as the king was concerned, was their loyalty. Being illegitimate, they were almost entirely dependent on the king for advancement. Legitimate sons, on the other hand, whose rights were enshrined in law, had much less reason to be loyal to the king who fathered them. English history is full of disputes between kings and their legitimate sons: Henry II and his children, Henry III and Edward I, Henry IV and Henry V, to name only the most obvious. By contrast, the record of loyalty to their fathers of the royal bastards is almost unblemished. Moreover, there was evidently a deep and strong affection between many of them and the kings who fathered them. After all, they were often the product of genuine love-matches, whereas legitimate sons often were not. Was it not bastards, as Shakespeare put it,

> Who in the lusty stealth of nature take
> More composition and fierce quality
> Than doth, within a dull, stale, tired bed,
> Go to th' creating a whole tribe of fops,
> Got 'tween asleep and wake?

There is abundant evidence that even the most hard-hearted of kings dearly loved at least some of their illegitimate children. When Henry I's legitimate son and heir, William Audelin, was drowned in the White Ship in 1120, the king was apparently equally distraught to hear of the death of his bastard son Richard, who had been drowned too. According to Orderic Vitalis, Henry had loved Richard as his own life. The devotion too between Henry II and Geoffrey 'Plantagenet' was legendary: when all the king's legitimate sons eventually rebelled against him, it was Geoffrey who remained at his father's deathbed and, when he died, made the arrangements for his funeral. 'You are my only true son,' Henry told him, and Geoffrey's subsequent violent feuding with both Richard and John was largely prompted by the belief that they had betrayed their father, and his father.

William the Conqueror was the first Norman king of England (1066–87), and he reigned by virtue of his conquest of the kingdom. In his Norman homeland, however, he ruled as his father's heir, in spite of the fact that he had been born out of wedlock. Yet his mother, Herleva, was no casual mistress of Duke Robert's; theirs was a long and stable relationship, it was simply that they never went through a formal wedding ceremony. The problem with Herleva was that she was low-born, the daughter of a tanner, and thus not a suitable wife for a Norman duke. Nevertheless, most of the Norman barons recognised the seven-year-old William as duke after his father's sudden death in 1035. On the other hand William's bastardy did not go entirely unnoticed. For some twenty years after Robert's death there were sporadic outbreaks of rebellion in Normandy, and some of William's opponents used the fact that he was illegitimate as an excuse to deny his right to rule. When he was besieging Alençon in 1051 the defenders are said to have waved animal skins from the walls of the castle to taunt him with the fact that he was descended from a family of tanners. This may be why he treated the people of Alençon with such savagery after storming the town. By 1060, however, William was securely established as duke in Normandy, and after Hastings the fact that he was a bastard was not an issue as far as his claim to the English throne was concerned, even though he was known to contemporaries as William the Bastard.

Despite his own illegitimacy (perhaps even because of it) William was widely praised by the chroniclers for his marital fidelity. His wife, Matilda, daughter of the count of Flanders, seems to have been a remarkable woman: when the casket containing her remains was opened in 1961, it was discovered that she was exceptionally small, hardly over four feet tall. She and her husband, the tall, russet-haired, powerful and domineering William, must have appeared a somewhat bizarre couple on ceremonial occasions, yet at her death in November 1083 he is said to have been grief-stricken. She bore him four sons and six daughters. The second son was William II (called Rufus because of his ruddy complexion), who succeeded his father as king of England, reigning from 1087 to 1100. Except for one Berstrand, who is mentioned in an unreliable eighteenth-century source as an illegitimate son of Rufus, there is no evidence for any royal bastards during the first thirty-five years of Anglo-Norman rule. With the accession of Rufus's younger brother Henry I, however, all this changed, and for over a hundred years not a reign went by without additions to the list of royal bastards.

CHAPTER 4

HENRY I'S BASTARDS

Henry I was one of the most effective kings ever to wear the English crown. He was of medium height, thick-set, with black hair which was already receding from his forehead at the age of thirty, deep, bright eyes, and a voice like thunder. Despite the voice, he was a man of few words; he preferred to listen and, once he had listened, to issue commands. When he issued commands, he expected to be obeyed; when aroused by disobedience or treachery, his temper was fearsome. He was a practical statesman of the highest ability, a man noted for his inflexible enforcement of the laws, his authoritarian handling of his barons, and his inveterate hoarding of money. He knew that to be successful a king must be rich, and he missed no opportunity to increase his wealth. Like his father and brother, he could be cruel to the point of savagery: he believed in ruling, at least in part, by fear. Yet he was respected as well as feared, for he maintained peace in England for most of his reign, and won a reputation as a man of learning and one who encouraged other men of learning to his court: his nickname was Beauclerc. In his private life he was methodical and, in every aspect except one, abstemious: he kept regular hours, was noted for his personal piety, never drank, and partook of a plain diet. He was, however, an incessant womaniser. He fathered, by various mistresses, at least twenty royal bastards, more than any other king in English history.

One of Henry's greatest achievements was to unite the two parts of his father's Anglo-Norman empire. William the Conqueror, at his death in 1087, had left Normandy to his eldest son, Robert Curthose, England to his second son, William Rufus, while to Henry, his third son, he left only a hoard of silver. Yet Henry was by far the ablest of the three. In 1100, after Rufus had been 'accidentally' struck by an arrow while hunting in the New Forest (there has always been a suspicion that Henry himself may have been implicated in his brother's death), Henry seized the English throne; six years later, he defeated his brother Robert at the battle of Tinchebrai and overran the duchy of Normandy. Robert Curthose was led away to prison, where he remained until his death in 1134. Thus for the last thirty years of his life, Henry I was ruler of both England and Normandy, the most powerful monarch in Western Europe.

The contemporary historian William of Malmesbury, while recognising the often brutal character of Henry's kingship, clearly admired his king: 'Inferior in wisdom to no king of modern time, he preferred contending by counsel rather than by the sword: if he could, he conquered without bloodshed. . . .Throughout his life he was wholly free from impure desires. . . .' In the light of his twenty known bastards, this last comment appears to come as something of a surprise, but it is worth noting how Malmesbury continues: ' . . . he was wholly free from impure desires for, as we have learned from those who were well informed, he partook of female blandishments not for the gratification of his lust, but for the sake of issue; nor did he condescend to casual intercourse, unless where it might produce that effect: in this respect [he was] the master of his inclinations, not the passive slave of desire.' Malmesbury provides us here with a fascinating view of the royal bastard in medieval society: not as the unfortunate by-product of a royal affair, the regrettable misfit likely to do little more than make demands on the royal purse, but as a child who could perform a useful role in the service of the king, who could provide very positive benefits for his or her father. Even the monk-historian William of Malmesbury could see the advantages in that. And when one looks at the way in which Henry I treated his bastards, it very rapidly becomes obvious that he could see the advantages too.

Although Charles II's brood of illegitimate children are more famous because of the dukedoms which were granted to four of them and because of the attention which has always been paid to his colourful mistresses, Henry's unofficial families also generated a vast network of relations in England, Ireland, Wales, Scotland, Brittany, Normandy and the French kingdom. Only two or three have disappeared in all but name, while of the others an assortment of information survives: details of their marriages, usually to men and women of political and material substance, of their major achievements and of the subsequent fortunes of their own families. Many of the sons were military leaders, initially in support of their father if they were old enough, later in the armies of Henry's legitimate daughter, Matilda, or his grandson Henry II. Several of the bastard daughters performed the less spectacular but equally significant function of marriage to the king's political allies: they were given to Englishmen, Normans, the duke of Brittany, and even the king of Scots, cementing relationships in much the same way as they would have if they had all been born on the right side of the blanket.

Robert of Caen, earl of Gloucester, who was born about 1090, is by far the best-known of Henry's bastards. For a quarter of a century he stood at the very centre of the English political stage. His career and personality will be discussed in detail at a later stage (pp. 74–93). His mother was probably a Norman woman from Caen, Robert's birthplace, and she was certainly not the only mistress whom Henry had enjoyed before he came to the throne in 1100. Ansfride, the widow of a knight, had given birth to at least two, and possibly three, of Henry's children by that date, while a mistress called Edith had produced a daughter who was married in 1103, and Sybil, daughter of Sir Robert Corbet, had also had a daughter, who was married in about 1107. William of Malmesbury says that on his accession to the throne – at which time he was thirty-two – Henry decided to stop using concubines and to 'settle down' with a wife. However, he clearly did nothing of the sort, at least not for long. Three other mistresses are known by name: Nest, daughter of the prince of South Wales, Edith, daughter of the lord of Greystoke (Cumberland), and Isabel, daughter of the count of Meulan and earl of Leicester. Of these Isabel was almost certainly the youngest, being born not before 1102 and possibly even later than 1107. The gentility of these ladies is striking, as well as the fact that at least half of them married afterwards and married well, in spite of liaisons with Henry which can have been no secret. A bride's virginity was normally all-important but it is perhaps not surprising that less disgrace ensued from a premarital affair if the bedfellow had been a royal one. One suspects, however, that in some cases at least, Henry may have arranged marriages for his former mistresses. Sybil married Herbert FitzHerbert, son and heir of Herbert the chamberlain and therefore a member of Henry's household. Likewise Edith married Robert d'Oilli, constable of Oxford castle. Isabel, however, married an earl, Gilbert de Clare, after Henry's death, a marriage which was clearly unaffected by her previous affair.

Nest was the only one of Henry's mistresses known to have been married at the time of their liaison. She was the wife of Gerald of Windsor, a man who worked as an agent of Henry I's in Wales. Pembroke castle and the surrounding area was in his custody. In about 1100, when Gerald married the Princess Nest, he was seeking to strengthen his position in the area and he also, no doubt, delighted in a new wife who was so beautiful that people called her the Helen of Wales. But if she was a beautiful wife she was also an unfaithful one. Apart from her seven legitimate children, who included several powerful barons, a bishop of St David's, and Angharad, mother of the historian Gerald of Wales, she also gave birth to one son by Stephen, constable of Cardiff (possibly the legitimate offspring of a second marriage), and another by Hait, sheriff of Pembroke. A tenth surviving child of this remarkable woman was Henry I's son, also called Henry, who was born some time after her marriage and probably before 1109. In that year Owain, son of Cadwgan ap Bleddyn, having heard of her great beauty, abducted Nest from the castle of Cenarth Bychan. He and fifteen companions broke in, setting fire to several buildings and, amidst the chaos, seized Nest and her children. It has been suggested, and one is hardly surprised, that she was a not unwilling party to the escapade but, whatever her attitude, it seems that the abduction of his mistress, if not simply his castellan's wife, was a direct challenge to Henry I. He arranged for the invasion of Ceredigion in revenge against Owain and his family.

Table 6 The bastards of Henry I

Name	Mother and date of birth	Spouse and date of marriage	Died	Additional information
Robert of Caen	Woman of Caen, *c.* 1090	Mabel, heiress of Gloucester, 1119	1147	Earl of Gloucester, 1121–2
Sybil	Sybil Corbet, 1090s	Alexander I, king of Scots, *c.* 1107	1122	
Rainald de Dunstanville	Sybil Corbet	Beatrice, 1140	1175	Earl of Cornwall, 1141
William	Sybil Corbet?, before 1105	Alice		? Still alive in 1187
Rohese	Sybil Corbet?	Henry de la Pomerai, before 1135		alive in 1175–6
Gundred	Sybil Corbet?			
Robert	Edith of Greystoke	Maud, Dame du Sap, after 1142	1172	Large estates in Devon
Richard	Ansfride, before 1100	Betrothed to Amice de Gael, 1120	1120	Drowned in White Ship
Juliane	Ansfride, *c.* 1090?	Eustace de Pacy, 1103		Later became a nun at Fontevrault
Maud	Edith (*not* of Greystoke)	Rotrou, count of Perche, 1103	1120	Drowned in White Ship
Maud		Conan III, duke of Brittany, before 1113		
Alice		Matthew de Montmorenci, constable of France		
Constance		Roscelin de Beaumont, vicomte of Maine, before 1135		Grandmother of Ermengard, queen of Scots
Maud				Abbess of Montvilliers
Isabel	Isabel of Meulan, 1120?	Unmarried		
Fulk	Ansfride?			Monk at Abingdon?
Gilbert	*c.* 1130?			
William de Tracy			1140?	Daughter Grace, matriarch of Tracys of Toddington
Henry	Nest, princess of South Wales, 1105?		1157	Sons took part in Strongbow's invasion of Ireland
Daughter		William Gouet III, lord of Montmirail		
?Daughter				Unsuccessful betrothal to Hugh FitzGervais, *c.* 1110
?Daughter		Fergus of Galloway		Mother of Uhtred
?Daughter				Unsuccessful betrothal to earl of Surrey, *c.* 1109
?Sybil of Falaise		Baldwin de Boullers		Called 'niece' of Henry I

Of Henry's other affairs nothing at all is known. With both Sybil and Ansfride he must have had more than a casual liaison, for between them they may have given birth to as many as eight of the twenty or so bastards, but the others may not have claimed his affections for long. It is possible that the other twelve known bastards were all born to different mothers, suggesting an astonishing number of extramarital affairs. When Henry had a so-called 'crisis of conscience' in 1130–1, he made dozens of gifts to ecclesiastical houses, especially to nunneries, and it is thought this may very well have been at least partly because of remorse for his years of licentiousness.

The five children thought to have been born to Sybil Corbet were Sybil, Rainald, Rohese, William and Gundred. It has usually been assumed that when a particular bastard of Henry's is said to be the brother or sister of another, the implication is that the two were full brothers or sisters. In view of the fact that for other bastard families this is clearly untrue, it would be unwise to place complete faith in such expressions of attachment. Yet Sybil Corbet's alleged children may indeed all have been hers. Sybil and Rainald certainly were.

The daughter Sybil was married to Alexander I, king of Scots, soon after his accession to the throne in 1107. There is no evidence that the match caused any astonishment amongst contemporaries. Royal blood was royal blood and in marriage, even to a king, one could overlook the illegitimacy of the intended bride. A political relationship and generous dowry were the important elements. Alexander loved his wife, and when she died, a young woman, in 1122 on the island of Loch Tay, he mourned her sadly and founded a church on the island in her memory. They had no children and the Scottish crown passed to Alexander's brother David two years later. Sybil's brother William (he is called both the queen's brother and brother of Earl Rainald) had followed her to Scotland as a member of her court. He may have been constable of Scotland, the first recorded appointment to that position, and he certainly witnessed charters of Alexander's in the early 1120s. Some time after Sybil's death William returned to England, where he married a woman called Alice and, forty years later, was holding four and a half knights' fees in Devon and Cornwall. It is likely that he becomes confused in the record, some time in the later years of Henry II's reign, perhaps with a William de Marisco, described as a brother of Earl Rainald, who was alive in 1187, and almost certainly with a William, 'brother of the chamberlain', who headed a naval expedition to South Wales in 1184. The confusion between these names is difficult to clear up, especially as a brother of Earl Rainald might also be called brother of the chamberlain: Sybil Corbet's eldest son by her husband would become chamberlain by hereditary right. To have witnessed a charter in 1120 the bastard William must have been at least fifteen, and men of seventy-nine or more, as he would have been in 1184, do not normally take command of naval expeditions. Although it is possible that he was still alive in 1187, he is most unlikely to have been active as a naval commander three years earlier.

About Sybil's other brother, Rainald, there is no doubt, for, unlike the shadowy William, he is well known as the earl of Cornwall, called also Rainald de Dunstanville, perhaps indicating the place of his birth. He helped to foment trouble against Stephen in Normandy, then headed a successful rising in the West Country in support of Matilda and was rewarded by her with his earldom in 1141. Rainald had married a wealthy heiress, Beatrice, daughter of William FitzRichard, 'a man of large estates in Cornwall'. It was not Henry I's policy to establish his bastards on large estates belonging to the crown; rather he used his powers of wardship and marriage to marry them off well. Most of Robert of Gloucester's great domain came to him through his wife and, although Rainald did not marry until five years after Henry's death, he was following a pattern which was well established. Thanks to the conditions of the Anarchy and his support for Matilda and then Henry II, a precedent was set that Rainald had direct control of the county and did not account for it to the exchequer. Much as Henry II must have disliked the situation he no doubt felt it unwise to strip a firm ally of considerable powers, and it was not until Rainald died in 1175, without a male heir, that the king again gained control of the revenues of the county, the earldom reverting to the crown.

Another of Earl Rainald's 'sisters', Rohese, married a powerful baron in the neighbouring county of Devon. Henry de la Pomerai had been a firm supporter of the king in the rebellion of 1123 and later became deputy constable in the royal household. He and Rohese were married while he was serving as a captain in the king's household forces. They prospered under Henry II with de la Pomerai performing various administrative duties in the royal service. In 1154, for example, he was to be found overseeing the purchase of £17's worth of seed for sowing the royal manors of Northamptonshire. He died in 1167, Rohese surviving him for some years, for she was still alive in 1175–6. Her sister Gundred would have vanished from the records had she not paid 24s. to the crown in 1130 for the land which she held in Wiltshire. She is called simply 'Gundred, sister of Rainald de Dunstanville', suggesting that she was a third daughter of Sybil Corbet by the king.

Apart from Sybil, queen of Scots, all of Sybil Corbet's supposed bastard family by Henry found residence if not a substantial power-base in the Southwest, along with Robert of Gloucester and another Robert, Robert FitzRoy. The latter Robert, son of Edith who married Robert d'Oilli, was clearly a considerable landholder, owing service for a hundred knights' fees in Devon in 1166. Perhaps this concentration was due at least partly to

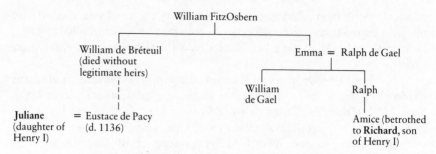

Table 7 Henry I's bastards and the Bréteuil inheritance

the fact that Sybil and Edith had themselves married West Country land-holders, and it may well have helped to bolster support for Matilda in the Southwest during the Anarchy. Although nothing is known of the upbringing of Henry's bastards (except Robert of Gloucester), it is not unlikely that they would have maintained contact with their mothers as well as with their father, and perhaps with their full brothers and sisters. Apart from the occasional reference to 'brother [or sister] of earl Rainald', there are other ways in which Sybil's family demonstrated its closeness: Rohese, for example, was granted Roseworthy manor in Cornwall by Rainald.

Another probable bastard family, that of Ansfride, seems to have remembered its relationship in adult life during events which threatened to destroy any friendship which they may have felt. Richard was definitely Ansfride's son by Henry, Juliane probably her daughter. They were both betrothed to French people whose houses claimed the inheritance in Normandy of William of Bréteuil (see Table 7).

The dispute surrounding the Bréteuil inheritance frequently involved Henry I. William de Bréteuil had no legitimate heirs, and in 1103 Juliane was married to Eustace de Pacy, William's bastard son, with promises from Henry that he would give consistent support against William's other kinsmen. The Norman inhabitants of the lordship of Bréteuil had voiced their approval of Eustace, in spite of his illegitimacy, because they preferred a native overlord to the Breton William de Gael and the Burgundian Reginald de Grancey, William de Bréteuil's nephew and more distant kinsman respectively.

For about sixteen years Eustace and his father-in-law remained on good terms. By 1119, however, Eustace was pressing Henry to let him have the castle of Ivry, which had belonged to his ancestors. Although promising to do so in the future, Henry was anxious to put off losing the castle and arranged in the meantime for Eustace to keep as hostage the son of the castellan, Ralph Harenc, in exchange for Eustace's two daughters. A treacherous piece of advice from a friend prompted Eustace to blind the castellan's son and send him back to his father. Henry was so shocked by this act that he allowed Ralph to put out the eyes of his own (i.e., Henry's) two granddaughters in revenge and to cut off the tips of their noses. Eustace and Juliane were naturally distressed, though one wonders that Eustace should have taken such a risk with his own daughters' well-being at stake. They made moves to fortify all their castles against Henry, and Juliane was sent to defend Bréteuil.

Henry soon arrived at Bréteuil with an army and was let into the town by the burgesses, who had no wish to provoke him. While he laid siege to his daughter in the castle she sent him a message, inviting him to negotiate. The chronicler Orderic Vitalis takes up the story. When the king entered the castle Juliane 'had a cross-bow ready drawn for the purpose [of murdering him] and shot a bolt at her father, but failed to injure him since God protected him. The king immediately had the castle drawbridge destroyed, so that no one could enter or leave. Juliane, seeing that she was completely surrounded and that no one was at hand to help her, surrendered the castle to the king, but could find no means of persuading him to allow her to leave freely. Indeed, by the king's command she was forced to leap down from the walls, with no bridge or support, and fell shamelessly, with bare buttocks, into the depths of the moat. This happened at the beginning of Lent, in the third week of February, when the castle moat was full to overflowing with the winter rains, and the frozen waters naturally struck numbing cold into the tender flesh of the woman when she fell. The unlucky Amazon got out of the predicament shamefully as best she could and, withdrawing to her husband who was then at Pacy, gave him a first hand account of her misadventure.' Thus was Bréteuil removed from Eustace's hands. Henry moreover restored all the lands of his ancestors to Ralph de Gael, younger brother of the Breton William de Gael, who had since died.

However, Louis, king of France, who frequently took the part of Henry's rebellious Norman subjects and wanted to see Eustace returned to power, advanced with a great army on Bréteuil, where Ralph heroically resisted him until an English force led by the royal bastard Richard turned his resistance into victory. A few months later Ralph, who feared that his Norman subjects would not long tolerate his rule and was worried about having such a far-flung patrimony (Gael, Montfort and other lands in Brittany as well as the Bréteuil lands), came to an agreement with Henry that his daughter Amice should be betrothed to Henry's son Richard, who had so ably assisted him against the French king's attack. Amice was to bring with her Bréteuil and the rest of the Norman estates. Richard, however, was drowned almost immediately afterwards in the wreck of the White Ship and thus never came into direct dispute with his own sister over the lands which they would both have claimed. Before his betrothal, moreover, Richard had interceded on Juliane's behalf when she and Eustace had walked barefoot into King Henry's tent at the siege of Evreux and fallen at his feet, begging forgiveness for their rebellious actions. Richard's intercession is the only evidence, indirect as it is, that he and Juliane were full brother and sister. His words were evidently effective, for Henry relented and, though unable to restore the lands which were now Ralph's, he gave Eustace an annuity of 300 silver marks. Eustace lived on at Pacy, a wealthy man, for seventeen years while Juliane some years after 1119 'abandoned the self-indulgent life she had led for the religious and, becoming a nun, served the Lord God in the new abbey of Fontevrault'.

Whereas Henry's relationship with his daughter Juliane had been strained, he seems always to have been devoted to his successful young son Richard, whose death at sea was almost as cruel a blow to him as the loss of his legitimate heir, William Audelin. According to Orderic he loved both William and Richard as his own life and Richard is elsewhere described as a magnanimous young man and a distinguished knight.

Not far from Pacy and Bréteuil in Normandy lay the lordship of Perche. In 1103, the year of Juliane's marriage, Henry married another of his bastard daughters, Maud, to Rotrou, count of Perche. It is no coincidence that Rotrou was a kinsman of the infamous Robert of Bellême and had long challenged Robert's claim to the patrimony of Domfort and Bellême. Robert of Bellême was disinherited by Henry in 1102 along with many others as a punishment for their resistance to his rule in both England and Normandy. In settling Bellême on Rotrou and giving him the hand of his daughter Henry was yet again imposing an arbitrary but, as he doubtless saw it, just arrangement. He saw to it that the leading claimant to land forfeited by a rebel was given the opportunity to realise a territorial ambition and thereby throw in his lot behind Henry's own policies. Indeed, Rotrou did just that and remained a firm friend of Henry's, being present at his death in 1135. Maud, his wife, daughter of another mistress, Edith, of whom nothing more is known, is best remembered for the part she played in the wreck of the White Ship (see below, p. 74).

Another Maud, daughter of an unknown mother, was betrothed some time before 1113 to Conan III, duke of Brittany (1112–48). The duke had become Henry's vassal, and in 1113 King Louis VI of France granted him the whole of Brittany along with some other disputed lands. Although Conan had accepted Henry's daughter as his wife, he was not anxious to perpetuate Brittany's dependence on the Anglo-Norman kings, so Henry's attempt to tame the duchy had little long-term effect. Yet he was not the only English king to try to acquire influence in Brittany by marrying his child into the Breton ducal house, for both William the Conqueror and Henry II did the same thing (see Table 8).

William's daughter was the first wife of Alan IV Fergant and they were

68

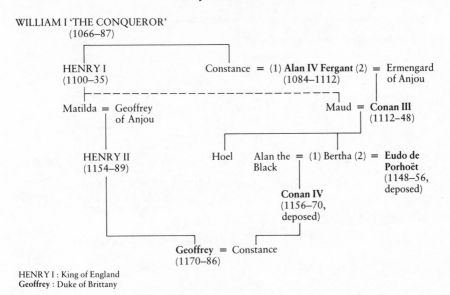

WILLIAM I 'THE CONQUEROR'
(1066–87)

HENRY I : King of England
Geoffrey : Duke of Brittany

Table 8 Marriage connections of the English royal house and the Breton dukes

married at a time of greater concord between the two families. Henry II, on the other hand, deposed the existing count, Conan IV, and married his seven-year-old son to Conan's four-year-old heiress, Constance, his second cousin once removed.

It was fortunate for Henry, with his vast dominions, that he was so well supplied with marriageable children. While the allegiance of Blois had been obtained some years before when Henry's sister married Count Stephen, Anjou, Maine and Touraine were under the rule of Count Geoffrey, to whom Henry gave his legitimate daughter Matilda in marriage in 1127. He used the marriages of his bastard daughters in exactly the same way and a glance at the map on page 70 shows how far he contrived to extend his influence in Normandy, Brittany and elsewhere through their marriage contracts. Doubtless this was what William of Malmesbury was talking about when he said that Henry 'partook of female blandishments . . . for the sake of issue'.

Maud, duchess of Brittany, Maud, countess of Perche, and Juliane of Pacy have already been mentioned, as has the fruitless betrothal of Richard to the heiress of Bréteuil and Montfort. There were at least five other French marriages arranged for Henry's bastards. An unnamed daughter married William Gouet III, lord of Montmirail, who was an important enough man to have his son and heir marry a daughter of the count of Chartres and Blois. The constable of France, Matthew de Montmorenci,

Brêteuil : lordship or duchy whose heir married or was betrothed to a bastard of Henry I
*Caen : Robert of Gloucester, hereditary castellan
†Montivilliers : Maud, abbess of Montivilliers

Scale

0   50
Miles

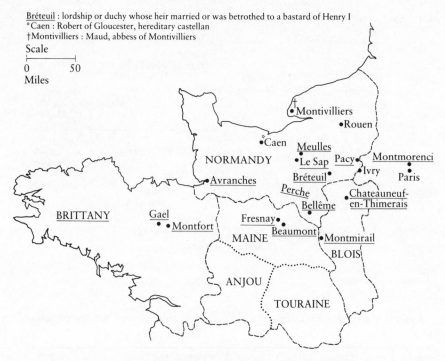

Territorial connections of Henry I's bastards in France

took Alice, another bastard daughter, for his wife. Matthew's father was Burchard de Montmorenci, who was a vassal of both the French and the English kings and fought with Louis against Henry I at the battle of Bremule in 1119. It is not known in what circumstances Burchard's son became betrothed to Alice, but it may have been that Henry was trying to woo Matthew from his French allegiance. Henry also tried to negotiate a betrothal between a daughter (unnamed) and Hugh fitzGervais, seigneur of Chateauneuf-en-Thimerais, who, like Rotrou of Perche, was a kinsman of Robert of Bellême, but the arrangement had to be dropped when the bishop of Chartres produced proof of their being related in the sixth degree. Yet another bastard daughter, Constance, was married to Roscelin de Beaumont, hereditary vicomte of Maine and, although it did not take place until 1142, a marriage was contracted between Robert, son of Henry and Edith of Greystoke, and Maud heiress of the lordships of Avranches, Meulles and le Sap.

Surprisingly little is known of the arrangements made by Henry for his daughters' dowries. The Devon manor of South Tawton for Constance is just about all that can be found. One assumes that he made use of the great forfeitures of land which took place in 1102 and 1106, when rebels and supporters of his brother, Robert Curthose, had their lands confiscated. This was more or less what happened in the case of Robert of Bellême's lands in 1103, when Maud was married to Rotrou, count of Perche. Juliane was also married in that year, and Sybil, queen of Scots, married Alexander I in or soon after 1107. Henry was certainly not a man who liked to grant large estates in perpetuity if he could help it, and the diplomatic benefits of having so many daughters must sometimes have been mitigated by the necessity of devising appropriate dowries.

The only two other women known to us by name who were definitely Henry's bastards did not marry. They were Maud, abbess of Montivilliers in Normandy, and Isabel, daughter of the Isabel of Meulan who later married Gilbert de Clare, first earl of Pembroke. Isabel was almost undoubtedly Henry's youngest bastard, just as her mother was his youngest mistress, and as far as is known she lived with her mother during and after the lifetime of her stepfather. For some reason this Isabel (or Elizabeth) has been confused with Sybil, queen of Scots, with the abbess Maud, and with another daughter who is said to have been the wife of Fergus, lord of Galloway. Fergus's elder son, Uhtred, was described by a contemporary English chronicler as a relation of Henry II's. From this evidence it may be reasonable to assume the existence of an eleventh bastard daughter. A twelfth daughter is also a possibility from the evidence of attempts to betroth William de Warenne, earl of Surrey, to an unnamed bastard of Henry's. The church again advised Henry against it because of consanguinity. Sybil of Falaise might have been yet another bastard. Married to Baldwin de Boullers, she is said to have been Henry's niece. There is no other known connection with the Falaise family, and the word 'niece' was sometimes used as a euphemism for an illegitimate daughter.

The four sons who have not yet been mentioned can be dealt with briefly. Fulk, who may have been a monk at Abingdon abbey, is likely to have been a third child of the widow Ansfride. About him and Gilbert, who was young and still unmarried in the 1140s, nothing else is known. William de Tracy died soon after his father, but by then he had a wife and a daughter, Grace. Henry FitzHenry, the son of Nest, married an unknown wife before his death in 1157 during Henry II's invasion of Anglesey.

The fortunes of some of the descendants of Henry I's bastards could fill a chapter or indeed a book in themselves. This is not the place to embark on the long and complex story of illegitimate royal lines, but the more notable figures among Henry's closest descendants should be mentioned.

Isabel, Robert of Gloucester's granddaughter who married King John is discussed later. She did not actually become queen but another of Henry's great-granddaughters did. In 1186 William the Lion, king of Scots, married Ermengard, daughter of Constance and Roscelin de Beaumont's eldest son.

The background to this curious match is interesting. Thirteen years earlier William the Lion had been captured by Henry II and was forced to accept harsh peace terms after his part in the rebellion against the English king. Relationships gradually improved between the two, so much so that in 1185 William had his great English estate, the honour of Huntingdon, fully restored to him. Soon afterwards he wrote to Henry asking for the hand of his granddaughter Maud, daughter of Henry the Lion, duke of Saxony. Since William was the girl's uncle, papal dispensation for the marriage had to be sought but it was not forthcoming. Some historians believe that Henry did not try hard enough to obtain it and that in giving a viscount's daughter to William instead of a duke's he was purposely imposing disparagement on the Scottish king. However, there is no evidence that William felt himself to be disparaged, and Henry gave the pair a magnificent wedding at Woodstock, followed by four days' feasting at his expense. Ermengard was the mother of Alexander II as well as of three daughters. She founded Balmerino abbey in 1225–9 and acted as mediator between her husband and the English king John at a treaty in 1212. She outlived her husband, who was already in his early forties at the time of their marriage, and she died in 1233.

Henry's bastard family penetrated every part of the Celtic fringe, for with Ermengard and her predecessor Sybil in Scotland, several uncles and cousins prominent in the Cornish peninsula, and Ermengard's great-aunt Maud a duchess of Brittany, there is also the Welsh family of Henry FitzRoy, son of Nest, to reckon with. After Henry's death during the invasion of Anglesey in 1157, his two sons, Meiler and Robert, took part in the Norman conquest of Ireland under Strongbow (Richard de Clare, earl of Pembroke). Meiler in particular became a great Anglo-Irish baron. He is described by his cousin, Gerald of Wales, as a swarthy, short-set man of great daring with long, muscular arms and legs. 'So intense was his thirst for fame that if perchance it had been denied him both to conquer and live, he would have chosen conquest even at the price of life.' If only, Gerald laments, he had shown generosity to the church and bestowed some of his newly acquired Irish land on her, instead of cruelly violating her liberties in common with all the other leaders of the Irish war.

The Cornish connection through Rainald earl of Cornwall diminished on his death without a legitimate male heir in 1175, when the earldom reverted to the crown. However, Rainald's own bastard, Henry FitzCount, was promoted to a position of extraordinary power for a brief period from 1215 when John granted him the county of Cornwall to farm until the realm should be at peace. Henry was already a man of some substance, acting as governor of Porchester castle from 1211 and being appointed sheriff of Cornwall, constable of Launceston castle and warden of the stannaries (tin mines) in 1215. The grant of the Cornish farm, renewed by

Henry III in 1217, did not confer the earldom on him, but it clearly recognised him as his father's son and, in time of civil strife, the best man to take on the administration of this remote county. After five years, however, Henry resigned the county to the king, took the cross, and died a crusader in 1222. The earldom of Cornwall passed to Richard, second son of King John and Isabel of Angoulême.

William de Tracy's daughter, Grace, whose marriage was far lower on the social scale than those of her high-class bastard aunts, nonetheless became the matriarch of a long-lasting house, that of Tracy of Toddington. Her second son, William, by her husband, John de Sudely of Sudely and Toddington, took his mother's name of Tracy, and his line did not become extinct until the death of Henry, eighth Viscount Tracy, in 1797.

It is difficult to know just how aware Henry II and his successors were of the men and women of illegitimate royal stock who were their cousins. Henry II certainly knew Ermengard, queen of Scots, to be his kinswoman, but gradually the more distant and less distinguished lineages must have fallen out of the family reckoning. It might be permissible to wonder how it was that Henry I managed to keep track of all his own illegitimate children, but there is no doubt that he did so. His mistresses and his bastards peopled his daily life and his every field of activity. When he died, quite suddenly, at a Norman hunting-lodge in December 1135, he was attended by five counts: his eldest bastard, Robert of Gloucester; Rotrou of Perche, the widower of a bastard daughter; William de Warenne, who was to have married another bastard daughter; Waleran of Meulan, and Robert of Leicester, both half-brothers of Warenne and full brothers of Henry's youngest mistress, Isabel. There could be no better illustration of the way in which his personal and working lives were so thoroughly interwoven, and of the ubiquity of his bastard family and its connections. As pawns (and even queens) in the game of diplomacy, or as commanders and counsellors whose loyalty to their father was usually unquestioned, Henry consistently employed his illegitimate children in the royal service in the same way as other, luckier kings employed their legitimate children. It was, of course, the cruellest irony of Henry's life that, although he fathered nine bastard sons and eleven bastard daughters, his only legitimate son predeceased him by fifteen years and, despite marrying again, Henry was unable to produce another legitimate heir to succeed him. The result was a succession crisis which plunged England into civil war for nearly twenty years, a civil war in which no one played a more decisive part than the oldest and most celebrated of those nine bastard sons, Robert earl of Gloucester.

CHAPTER 5

ROBERT OF GLOUCESTER

Just before twilight on 25 November 1120, Henry I set out from Barfleur in Normandy to cross the Channel to England. His son and heir, William Audelin, who was with Henry at Barfleur, decided to stay on and spend a merry evening there with several of his young companions before putting to sea. A great deal of wine was drunk, not only by William and his noble young friends, but also by the crew of the boat, the White Ship. It was a fine, clear evening. A gentle but steady wind augured well for the crossing. But when, towards midnight, the White Ship, the swiftest and most up-to-date vessel in the royal fleet, eventually put to sea, both passengers and crew were in an advanced state of intoxication. The ship never even reached the open sea. The drunken helmsman steered it straight on to a great rock at the mouth of the bay, lifting the prow clean out of the water. Soon the ship began to fill with water. After vain attempts to push it clear, a small dinghy was launched, and Prince William bundled into it. As he was rowed away, William heard in the darkness the cries of his illegitimate sister, the countess of Perche, imploring him not to desert her. He ordered the rowers to turn back. Once they did so, however, dozens of other men tried to clamber aboard, the dinghy overturned, and all aboard it were drowned. Only one man, a butcher from Rouen, survived the wreck, clinging all night to the masthead in the icy water, and living to tell the tale. For days they searched the beaches around Barfleur for bodies, but not more than a handful were ever recovered.

The disaster of the White Ship threatened to destroy everything that Henry I had laboured so purposefully to build up. He had intended that William should inherit all from him. Now his only surviving legitimate child was his daughter Matilda (also known as Maud). Born in 1102, Matilda had been married to the German emperor in 1114. Would the unruly barons of England and Normandy ever accept a woman to rule over them? It was Henry's intention that they should, but he was too realistic a man not to realise that her path to the throne would be strewn with pitfalls. If Matilda proved unacceptable, that left two possible candidates for the throne. One was Stephen, Henry's nephew, now twenty-four years old and count of Mortain, who had been brought up at Henry's court and whom the king both knew well and liked. The other was the king's favourite bastard, Robert of Gloucester.

At the time of the White Ship disaster, Robert was already aged about thirty. It has been said that his mother was Sybil Corbet, the probable mother of another five of the king's bastards, but this is almost certainly wrong. In fact he was probably born to an unnamed woman of Caen, in Normandy, in about 1090. Acknowledged by Henry from infancy, he was brought up in the royal household after his father became king, received a good education there under Henry's direct supervision, and by his early twenties had established himself as one of his father's chief military captains and most trusted councillors. From 1113 onwards he was a regular witness to royal charters, as 'Robert the king's son' (see Plate 2). In 1119 he played a major part in Henry's defeat of the French king Louis VI at Bremule. Henry is said to have placed great store by Robert's military ability, and to have taken him everywhere. In 1107 the king provided handsomely for his favourite bastard's future by marrying him to Mabel, heiress to the lordship of Glamorgan and the vast honour of Gloucester as well as many valuable lands on the Norman side of the Channel. Then in 1121–2 Robert's power and prestige were further augmented when Henry made him earl of Gloucester. With the death of William Audelin, Robert was now the most influential and respected of the king's male descendants. Henry looked to him as the guardian of his sister Matilda's interests, and must therefore accord to him the stature which would allow him to guard those interests effectively. The grant of this title to Robert was the only earldom which Henry created during his entire thirty-five-year reign.

In 1127, realising that his chances of fathering a new heir had all but disappeared, Henry summoned all the great men of England to a council at London and made them swear to recognise Matilda as his successor and to be faithful to her after his death. It was done, but reluctantly by many. One chronicler relates that Henry 'in that thunderous voice which none could resist, rather compelled than invited men to take the oath'. Twice more, in 1131 and 1133, the king forced his barons to renew their oaths to Matilda, but he knew as well as any man which way the wind blew. His son Robert, and his nephew Stephen, he treated with equal generosity, building each one up as a counter-check to the other, granting lands and honours to both, but never allowing the power of one to outstrip by far the power of the other. Yet already a fierce rivalry was building up between the two men. In 1127 there was a violent argument between them as to who should have precedence in swearing the oath to Matilda after the archbishop of Canterbury and the Scottish king. After much unpleasant wrangling, the legitimate nephew triumphed over the illegitimate son. But few men could fail to interpret it as a foretaste of the greater battle to come.

The crisis came at the beginning of December 1135. On 25 November, exactly fifteen years to the day after the White Ship disaster, Henry was staying at Lyons-la-Forêt, in Normandy. Against his doctor's orders, he ate a large dish of his favourite delicacy, lampreys, and then went hunting.

While out, he suddenly began to suffer terrible pains in his stomach, and had to be carried back to his bed. He was sixty-seven by now. Fever set in, and it soon became apparent that he was dying. The archbishop of Rouen was sent for. Robert of Gloucester arrived in time to say his farewells to his father. Shortly before he died, Henry was asked to whom he bequeathed his lands: he replied, yet again, to Matilda. On the night of 1 December, having received absolution from the archbishop for the third time in as many days Henry I died. For Robert, for Stephen, for Matilda, indeed for the whole people of England, the moment of truth had arrived.

Stephen was aged thirty-nine in 1135. A courteous, charming man, fond of children, kindly, with none of the insufferable arrogance so common among Normans of his class, he deserves to be more favourably remembered than he usually has been. He had great personal courage, a spirit that was never bowed in adversity, a strong distaste for the cruelties of war, but at the same time a deep-rooted desire to participate in all the traditional martial activities of his age and class. He loved to be chivalrous, courtly, generous to his followers: in the best traditions of the 'perfect gentle knight', he would humble himself to mix and eat with the poor. Over and again he revealed all the qualities of a good knight, but at the same time he showed clearly that it took more than a good knight to make a good king. He was not downright inept like some English kings, but he lacked judgment. He could never be a cunning man, nor even a clever one. His greatest fault was that he continually allowed himself to fall under the influence of others more strong-willed than himself, then, like the classically weak man who resents being dominated by others, would turn on those whose advice he had formerly sought. As a result of this he gained a reputation for untrustworthiness. At heart he seems to have been unsure of himself: not only of his ability, but also, one suspects, of the righteousness of his cause. He was weak-voiced, lacking in 'presence', not the sort of man who stood out in a crowd. At times, however, he could act with great energy and purpose: December 1135 was one of those times.

Stephen had been waiting for his uncle's death: waiting and planning. His plans had been well-laid, and he was not alone in his designs. The man under whose influence Stephen had fallen at this time was his younger brother, Henry of Blois, bishop of Winchester. Henry of Blois was typical of a certain type of bishop found throughout the Middle Ages: a brilliant administrator, unscrupulous politician, magnificently ostentatious in his lifestyle. His wealth was legendary, and his ambition knew no bounds, as was to be proved in the years that followed, for his loyalty to Stephen rested more on calculations of self-interest than it did on fraternal attachment. For the time being, however, the bishop was indispensable to Stephen's quest for the throne.

On hearing of the old king's death, the two brothers knew exactly what to do. Stephen, who was in Normandy at the time, made a dash across the Channel to London and managed to persuade the Londoners to 'elect' him as king, a privilege which they, somewhat dubiously, claimed. He then hurried down to Winchester, where the royal treasury was situated, and which was still the headquarters of the royal administration. Here, thanks to Henry of Blois's skilful groundwork, most of the old king's officials were prepared to recognise Stephen at once. One or two hesitated, however, including the archbishop of Canterbury. Henry and Stephen then played their trump card: a few hours before he died, they said, the old king had suddenly changed his mind about the succession, nominated Stephen, and released all his subjects from their oath to Matilda. Hugh Bigod, the royal steward, arrived in the nick of time and swore publicly before the archbishop that it was true. It was enough. Nothing now stood in the way of Stephen's coronation, which took place on 22 December, just three weeks after Henry's death. It was a remarkable achievement, the reward for years of careful planning and a few days of vigorous and decisive action.

Yet it was only a beginning. Stephen still hoped to establish a legitimate title to the throne, and he still had to gain the backing of the barons. He wrote to the pope, claiming that Matilda was illegitimate on the grounds that her mother had been professed as a nun before being plucked from the nunnery to marry Henry I; the pope, fearful of offending either party, refused to declare Matilda illegitimate. In practical terms, however, it was much more important for Stephen to win over the barons, and none more so than Robert of Gloucester. At the time of Henry I's death Robert was the greatest landholder in England. He had been devotedly loyal to his father, he had a reputation for piety and uprightness, and he had proved himself a superb military commander. Would his oath to accept Matilda as queen hold? The question which most worried Stephen in those early months of 1136 was, which way was Robert going to turn?

When Stephen dashed off to England to stake his claim to the throne, Robert, a dutiful son to the last, remained at Lyons-la-Forêt and supervised the arrangements for his father's funeral. Yet when Henry's body was taken across the Channel to be buried at Reading, Robert did not go with it. Was he biding his time, waiting for Stephen to make a mistake? There may have been some sense in such a wait-and-see policy, but Robert was behaving dangerously indecisively. He was himself approached by a party of barons, and urged to press his own claim to the throne: illegitimate he may have been, but the days were not yet gone when a royal bastard might aspire to the throne. The confusion and conflict of interests following Henry's death created precisely the sort of circumstances in which the royal bastard might thrust himself to the fore and surmount the disadvantage of his maternity, but Robert was either too uncertain of his chances or too loyal to his father's wishes to grasp the opportunity, and he declined the invitation. Yet even the most favourable interpretation of Robert's behaviour at this time still has to take into account the fact that he showed no greater desire initially to stand by his oath to Matilda than most of the other English or Norman barons. Indeed on 21 December 1135, the day before Stephen's coronation, he was one of a group of barons who met at Lisieux to consider the possibility of electing Stephen's elder brother, Theobald count of Blois, to the English throne. In the event Theobald, perhaps out of consideration for his two younger brothers, himself rejected the idea. Robert's motivation, however, is hard to divine. Was he out to stop Stephen at all costs, and hoping that Theobald's candidature might provide a temporary distraction? Or did he, as his panegyrist William of Malmesbury suggests, hope that the initial surge of support for Stephen would soon peter out when the English barons realised what sort of king they had landed themselves with, and that he, Robert, would then be in a far stronger position to press for the acceptance of Matilda? Whatever was in his mind, his plans backfired. For the next two years he dithered and dissimulated, and by the time he decided to throw his full weight behind Matilda, England had sunk into a state of anarchy from which there was no very obvious escape route.

Meanwhile Stephen was consolidating his early successes. As was his way, he bought off the Scottish king, and made promises and grants to the English barons in order to persuade them to do homage to him. The great majority of them were happy enough with this state of affairs, and by Easter 1136 almost every English landowner of note apart from Robert had recognised Stephen as king. In April, the royal court met at Oxford. Letters and personal messengers from the king had been sent in profusion to Robert inviting him to come and do homage to the new king, but he had ignored them all. Now, however, he crossed the Channel and came to Oxford. He would do homage to Stephen, he declared, but only conditionally: he would recognise Stephen as king, as long as Stephen promised to defend Robert's own interests and maintain his rank unimpaired. It was not the sort of homage which Henry I would have accepted from any man, and it is a sign of Stephen's weakness that he was prepared to accept such an equivocal oath of homage from a man who at heart was clearly his enemy. Yet accept it he did, and no doubt he was relieved to do so. Robert of Gloucester had become King Stephen's man.

For a year or two the uneasy alliance was maintained, but relations between the two men became increasingly strained. Stephen was soon beset by troubles on all sides, and he found himself constantly hurrying from one part of England to another in an attempt to quell the latest challenge to his rule. Meanwhile Matilda was successfully raising support for her cause in Normandy, and in the spring of 1137 Stephen was obliged to lead an expedition across the Channel. Robert went with him, but hardly had he disembarked in Normandy than he discovered that Stephen had laid an ambush for him. Forewarned, Robert managed to avoid the ambush and not surprisingly steered clear of the king's court for several days. A reconciliation was effected when Stephen confessed to complicity in the plot and made a formal apology to Robert, but by now it was becoming obvious to all that Robert was merely waiting for the right moment to unmask his hostility to the king and make an outright declaration of support for his sister's cause. When Stephen returned to England in the autumn of 1137, he had achieved nothing in Normandy, and opposition to his rule in England was continuing to mount. Moreover, he left behind him the man who above all might have turned the scales in his favour once more.

Robert remained in Normandy, spending the winter in company with his sister's supporters, the far from unwilling recipient of numerous entreaties, bribes and offers from them to make his final break with Stephen. At last, in May 1138, Robert understood that he could delay no longer. He sent messengers to Stephen, formally renouncing his homage, accusing Stephen of breaking his oath to Henry I in usurping the throne, and declaring that Matilda was the rightful heiress. Stephen retaliated immediately by confiscating all Robert's English estates. When the news broke that the earl of Gloucester had renounced his allegiance to the unhappy king there was a fresh wave of rebellions against Stephen's authority up and down the land.

It is difficult to understand why it had taken Robert so long to make the break which all of his contemporaries had evidently seen coming for a good while. William of Malmesbury tells us that Robert was searching his conscience throughout the winter of 1137–8, consulting numerous men of the church as to whether he could in good faith renounce his homage to Stephen, even though it had only been given conditionally, and even referring to a personal bull from the pope to Robert ordering him to stand by the oath he had sworn to Henry I back in 1127. More recently, and perhaps more realistically, some historians have pointed to the castles and titles promised to him by Matilda as the price she paid for his support. Yet what is strange is that, despite the fact that it was up to Robert to choose the moment at which he made his break, he seems to have been singularly ill-prepared for it. Had he followed up his renunciation with an immediate invasion of England on behalf of his sister, he and Matilda might well have carried all before them and settled the issue of the succession once and for all. The fresh wave of rebellions which he had sparked off in sympathy for Matilda's cause was threatening to destroy Stephen's government. By now, too, Stephen had fallen out with his brother, Henry of Blois. Tiring of his brother's pushiness, Stephen made only a half-hearted attempt to secure Henry's promotion to the archbishopric of Canterbury when it fell vacant in 1136. Henry had regarded this as no less than his due. Was he not, after all, the effective king-maker? Moreover, as it became increasingly obvious that Stephen had no intention of keeping the fine promises he had made to secure the church's support in 1135, Henry found it increasingly difficult to maintain his position as the man who had guaranteed Stephen's good behaviour. Stephen was vulnerable from every quarter. Yet Robert made no attempt to press home the advantage. He spent the summer in some desultory campaigning against Stephen's supporters in Normandy, then retired to Caen for the second successive winter. It is worthwhile at this point recalling the comment which one of the king's supporters made about Robert: 'As is his custom, he threatens much but does little, lionlike in his speech, but like a hare in his heart, great in his eloquence but insignificant through laziness.' To accuse Robert of personal cowardice was grossly unjust; he demonstrated his bravery on numerous occasions. But, despite his undoubted vigour as a military commander, he sometimes gives the impression of a man who needed to be goaded into action.

The year 1139 was a crucial year for Stephen. He had by now fallen under the influence of a pair of very uncelestial twins, Waleran and Robert Beaumont, earls of Worcester and Leicester respectively, who between them shared little love for Henry of Blois or for the church in general, and who by now had supplanted Henry and his ecclesiastical friends as the men who had the king's ear. In the early months of 1139 Stephen's fortunes were enjoying something of a revival. The Scottish threat had been neutralised by an English victory at the 'battle of the Standard' in the autumn of 1138. Robert and Matilda still showed no sign of crossing to England, and the spate of rebellions which had broken out in anticipation of their arrival the previous year had largely petered out. Stephen chose this moment to make a terrible mistake. Since the last years of Henry I's reign the highest posts in the English administration had been dominated by Roger, bishop of Salisbury, and his nephews, the bishops of Lincoln and Ely. Trusting in Henry de Blois's ability to keep Stephen under control, they had acquiesced in the usurpation of 1135 and had continued to run the administrative machine – rebellions permitting – along the lines laid down in the previous reign. Now, egged on by the Beaumonts, who hated to see such worldly and overbearing churchmen exercising such authority, Stephen determined to break the power of Bishop Roger and his family. He summoned them to a council at Oxford on 22 June 1139. Bishop Roger seems to have been reluctant to attend, considering that he would be 'as useful at court as a colt in battle', but attend they did. Stephen and the Beaumonts, however, had laid a trap for the bishops. On the night of their arrival a brawl was provoked between some of Bishop Roger's followers and some of the king's knights over the right to requisition certain lodgings in the town. Words were spoken, swords were drawn, and in a few minutes several men lay dead. The enraged king's knights made their way to the house where Bishop

Roger was staying and physically dragged him and the bishop of Lincoln before the king, demanding justice. The bishop of Ely, being younger and more agile, made good his escape to Devizes castle. Stephen demanded that the bishops hand over the keys to all their castles. This, the bishops considered, was less than just. Stephen threatened them all with the extreme penalty, and placed them in chains. Eventually the hapless bishops were forced to yield their castles to the king, but Stephen's rejoicing at his victory was soon cut short. His clumsy and brutal action had not only paralysed the central administration by removing at one stroke the men who had built it up, but had also alienated the support of the church. Henry of Blois was furious with his brother, and summoned Stephen before a legatine council to account for his actions. At the council, held at Winchester on 29 August, Stephen was forced into an abject apology, but was not prepared to make restitution. Relations between the two brothers had reached a new low. Before anything further could be done, however, Stephen was brought the news that he most dreaded hearing: on 30 September, Matilda and Robert of Gloucester had landed on the Sussex coast, at Arundel, with a force of 140 knights and 3,000 infantry.

Matilda was now aged thirty-seven. Born in 1102, the only legitimate daughter of Henry I, she was a striking and redoubtable woman. In 1110, when she was eight, her father had sent her to Germany as the future bride of the Holy Roman Emperor Henry V, and here she had proved a great success. She married the emperor in 1114, and remained with him almost continually until his death in 1125. Her experiences in Germany had a profound effect upon Matilda. Worshipped by her husband and, it seems, by his people, she grew up to be a very beautiful woman, inspiring a measure of devotion from the German people which she was never to inspire among her native English subjects. Brought up amidst the much more formal pomp and splendour of the imperial court, nurtured in the stiff, stilted ways of German etiquette, she learned what it was to cultivate the mystical aloofness of monarchy. It was a lesson that she later tried to adapt to English circumstances, with disastrous consequences. The death of her only legitimate brother in the White Ship altered her situation entirely. After the emperor's death in 1125, her father recalled her to England and began to groom her as his successor, but here her haughty and imperious manner cut little ice in the much less formal atmosphere of the English court. It was not simply because she was a woman that the English barons were reluctant to recognise her as Henry I's successor; they resented her arrogant affectations and her German mannerisms. Nor did her second marriage improve matters. In 1128 Henry I married Matilda to Geoffrey, count of Anjou, an astute and sophisticated politician, but a man who was seen as an enemy of the Anglo-Norman barons. It was a tactical mistake by Henry I, one of the few he made: his intention had been to secure his Norman border by a marriage alliance, but the effect of Matilda's new marriage was to make the barons even more determined not to accept her as their queen: the thought of Geoffrey of Anjou ruling over them was anathema to most of them. Yet despite her overbearing manner and unfortunate marriage, Matilda had many of the qualities required of a ruler. One contemporary said that she was 'a woman who had nothing of the woman in her', while another remarked on her 'masculine spirit'. She had a steely spirit devoid of sentimentality, a steady nerve in adversity, an iron will like her father's, and, like Robert, she was brave to the point of recklessness. She would have made a very passable dictator, revelling in the cult of personality, contemptuous of those who stood in her path. Her beauty inspired an almost blind loyalty in some of her followers; to many other men, unfortunately, she was very hard to stomach.

Matilda seems to have been caught flat-footed at her father's death in 1135. While Stephen made his celebrated dash for the throne, she remained with her husband. Naturally she was convinced of the righteousness of her cause – she had all those oaths to prove it – and naturally she was convinced of the necessity of taking some positive action to enforce her rights, but her husband Geoffrey showed no inclination to involve himself in English affairs, and if even her brother Robert was hesitating over his allegiance, then what chance might she have of making good her claim? Her helplessness deeply humiliated her. Moreover, it was not merely for herself that she was fighting, or rather failing to fight. In 1133 she had given birth to a son by Geoffrey, called Henry. In 1135, the two-year-old Henry was the only direct male descendant of legitimate birth from Henry I. Matilda was fiercely determined that one day her son should succeed to his grandfather's inheritance. As Stephen's mistakes multiplied, her hopes grew; when Robert renounced his allegiance to Stephen, they soared. Throughout the summer of 1138 and the following winter Robert and Geoffrey jointly picked off a number of Stephen's strongholds in Normandy. By the summer of 1139 much of the duchy was under Matilda's control. The time had come to bid for the throne which her father had bequeathed to her.

It seems to have taken Stephen some time to arrive at a decision as to how he should deal with this new threat from Henry I's daughter. His first reaction was to summon his trusted band of mercenaries and make a forced march to Arundel in the hope of nipping the invasion in the bud. He was too late. Robert, accompanied by a mere dozen or so knights, had already slipped off westwards to make his way to Bristol, the only one of his castles which had successfully held out against Stephen for the past fifteen months. On his way to Bristol, Robert met Henry of Blois. Whether this meeting was by accident or by design is not clear, but certainly Henry made no attempt to stop Robert. Instead, he gave Robert the solemn kiss of peace and friendship, and allowed him to continue on his way unharmed. Thus far had Stephen alienated the brother who less than four years earlier had fought tooth and nail to secure his coronation. Stephen himself did little better. Finding Robert gone, he determined to besiege Matilda in Arundel castle. So, leaving a besieging army around the castle, he himself set off to follow Robert. After a few days, however, he changed his mind, returned to Arundel, and raised the siege. Not only this, but he offered Matilda a safe-conduct to join Robert at Bristol, and even ordered Waleran Beaumont to escort her there. His chivalry may have been admirable, but the intention behind his action is far from easy to comprehend. Once again, Stephen had revealed his fatal inability either to devise or to execute a clear-cut and long-term plan of action.

The arrival of Robert and Matilda was the prelude to the two most bitter years of fighting in Stephen's reign. Those who had risen in rebellion against Stephen now found in Robert and Matilda the cause to justify their actions; those who had considered rebellion but not as yet dared to defy the king openly now took heart and united behind the figure of Henry I's daughter. Chronic instability bordering on anarchy was transformed into civil war. It was a miserable time for the people of England. Central government virtually ceased to exist; law and order gave way to the private and arbitrary dispensation of justice in the interests of the mightiest; barons imposed intolerable levels of taxation on their people, and enforced them at the point of a sword. 'When the wretched people had no more to give,' declared one contemporary, 'they robbed and burned all the villages, so that you could easily go a whole day's journey and never find anyone occupying a village, nor land tilled. Then corn was dear, and butter and cheese, because there was none in the country. Wretched people died of starvation. . . . They respected neither church nor churchyard, but took all that was inside and burned the church. . . . The bishops were constantly excommunicating them, but they thought nothing of it, because they were all utterly accursed. . . . It was openly said that Christ and his saints slept.' William of Malmesbury has left us with a gruesome description of how one of these robber-barons carried on, a notorious torturer called Robert FitzHubert who operated out of Devizes castle: 'He was the cruellest of all men within the recollection of our age, and likewise a blasphemer against God; for he used to boast gratuitously that he had been present when eighty monks were burnt together with their church and said he would do the same thing again and again in England. . . . He used to smear prisoners with honey and expose them naked in the open air in the full blaze of the sun, stirring up flies and similar insects to sting them.' Robert FitzHubert was eventually hanged for refusing to hand over Devizes castle to Matilda, but in the conditions which prevailed in England during these years there were many others who managed to establish similar private tyrannies within their localities.

It must be said, to his great credit, that Robert of Gloucester was never accused of the sort of indiscriminate plundering and murdering that was commonplace throughout England at this time. Even his enemies commented that he conducted his military operations, as far as was possible, with dignity and restraint, that he avoided unnecessary destruction, and that he treated his prisoners with far greater humanity than many of those against whom he fought. Using the powerful castle of Bristol as his headquarters, he managed to impose some sort of control over the Southwest of England, and established within that area a degree of peace and justice considerably greater than that which prevailed in many other parts of England. As commander-in-chief of his sister's armies, his problems were immense. Warfare at this time was hampered by very rudimentary systems of intelligence and communications. It consisted largely of the weary and time-consuming process of besieging castle after castle, a process which placed nearly all the advantages in the hands of the besieged – as long as their food and water held out – and which subjected the besieging army to protracted hardship, discomfort, and fear of counter-attack. Boredom and disease set in, supplies were often hard to come by, tempers were strained, and it was no easy task for a commander to prevent his troops from either deserting or indulging in random pillaging of the neighbourhood. Indeed, such pillaging was often an integral part of the besieging army's plan: devastation of the countryside surrounding a castle caused terrible hardship to the local population, but it also made it much more difficult for those defending the castle to obtain supplies. If a town or city resisted a besieging army for any length of time, it was common to allow the besieging soldiers, when eventually successful, to sack and plunder the town for a given length of time – usually a day or two – after it had been taken. The human misery inflicted by such a system of warfare was terrible. It speaks volumes for Robert that, while successfully upholding his sister's cause in England for many years, he managed to gain a reputation for moderation and clemency in warfare. At the same time, he did nothing to impair his reputation either for personal bravery or for incisive generalship.

For a year after Matilda and Robert's arrival in England, military stalemate prevailed. A series of dreary sieges and indecisive skirmishes left neither side with any overall advantage. In the autumn of 1140 negotiations for a treaty were held near Bath, but these came to nothing and soon the civil war was renewed. Not until the early months of 1141 did any decisive engagement take place. The earl of Chester, a notorious troublemaker who was married to Robert's daughter Matilda and was at this time siding with Robert and his sister, gained possession of Lincoln castle and began to plunder the town. The distressed citizens of Lincoln sent an urgent request for help to Stephen, who replied promptly by bringing up an army to besiege the earl's men in the castle. Leaving his soldiers to withstand the siege, the earl managed to escape towards the end of January 1141, hastily sought out his father-in-law, and returned with Robert to relieve the castle. So eager was Robert to force a battle with the king that, despite the icy weather and a racing current, he personally swam across the Trent, which was no mean feat for a man who had just passed his fiftieth birthday, and forced his troops to do likewise. Robert's army arrived before the walls of Lincoln on 2 February, to find that Stephen had already drawn up his forces in battle array. It was a short but vicious encounter, fought out in full view of the townsfolk lining the city walls above the battlefield. Stephen attempted a cavalry charge, which broke on the massed infantry of Robert's army. Robert's troops then counter-attacked, drawing the king's knights into hand-to-hand combats in which the advantage of their horses was neutralised. Then disaster struck for Stephen. His line of cavalry was broken at several places, and many of his foremost supporters immediately fled the field. The king himself, however, showed tremendous personal courage, remaining on the field even when he realised that his cause was lost: when his own sword broke he continued to deal great blows at his opponents with a Norwegian battle-axe handed to him by one of his young knights. Finally, surrounded on all sides by knights of Robert's army, he was struck on the head by a stone and fell to the ground. It was a magnificent display, and Robert recognised the fact. He too had been in the thick of the battle, and when he saw Stephen fall he at once rushed forward and ordered that no man was to harm the king further or to insult him. Stephen was led away to close but honourable confinement in Bristol castle, cursing his fate and the ignominy of his circumstances. Matilda's moment had come.

The man who now held the key to the situation was Henry of Blois, for if Matilda were to realise her dream and be recognised as queen of England, she would need the backing of the church. Henry was prepared to comply. He agreed to acknowledge Matilda as queen-designate, but only on condition that he should have full control over appointments to high office within the English church, as well as a major say in affairs of state. Thus in order to augment his own power, Henry was prepared to abandon utterly the brother whose coronation he had engineered. Matilda's plans began to go awry, however, when the citizens of London sent a deputation to her demanding Stephen's release. This was a severe blow, the clearest sign yet that the wealthy and powerful citizens of London had no intention of throwing their weight behind her. A few days later, a messenger arrived bearing a letter from Stephen's queen (also called Matilda). Not surprisingly, her request was identical to that of the Londoners: her husband's immediate release. The queen was a formidable lady: she too had sons to fight for, and she still controlled much of the area to the south of London. As Matilda was soon to discover, she was a lady to be reckoned with.

Unfortunately for herself, Matilda now revealed her own true colours.

Brushing aside these requests with disdain, she determined on a royal progress to London in preparation for her coronation. Once there, she behaved with extraordinary tactlessness: from the Londoners she demanded an enormous loan, and angrily refused to consider their requests for time to pay. From Henry of Blois, she demanded control over church appointments, pointedly ignoring his recommendations. At this point the queen sent an army to ravage the suburbs of the city and incite the citizens to rise up and expel her rival. They needed no second bidding. On 24 June 1141 the tocsin was sounded, and the enraged Londoners descended *en masse* on Westminster palace, where Matilda and Robert were just about to sit down to a banquet. Taken by surprise, outnumbered and in fear of their lives, they made a desperate dash through the night to Oxford, while the Londoners turned heel and opened their gates to the queen's forces.

The tide had turned against Matilda. Men began to slip away from her court, saying that it was wrong to keep an annointed king in prison. But worse was to come. Henry of Blois, his hopes dashed, now joined forces with the queen and set off to Winchester to put his defences in order. Matilda and Robert decided that the time had come to deal with the over-mighty bishop, so early in August they marched down to Winchester to arrest him. When they got there they found him gone, but they determined nevertheless to lay siege to the bishop's castle and palace, which he had left strongly fortified. Meanwhile, Henry sought out the queen and joined her in a forced march back to the city, where they in turn besieged Robert and Matilda. The situation, then, was of a double siege, with Matilda and Robert ensconced in the town, besieging Henry's troops who were blockaded within the episcopal castle, but being besieged themselves by a much larger army brought up by the queen and the bishop.

This double siege continued for several weeks, wreaking terrible destruction on the city, and severely testing the resources of Matilda's army, caught in the middle with major problems of supply. By early September, their situation was desperate, for the net had almost been closed around Robert and Matilda. The bishop's men in the castle were in a much better state: the castle had been fully provisioned before the start of the siege, and could have held out for several more weeks. There was nothing for it but for Robert and Matilda to try to get out while they still could. It was decided that Matilda should go on ahead with the main body of the army, while Robert with a few hand-picked followers should cover her escape and try to salvage what they could of the baggage-train. The break-out was planned for 14 September. Unfortunately the queen's army was ready and waiting for them. Matilda herself and a few close followers managed to break through the royalist ranks and fled to Devizes castle, but Robert soon realised that the baggage-train would have to be abandoned. He and his followers managed to engage the royalist army for long enough to allow

Matilda to make her escape, fighting with almost suicidal courage against tremendous odds. Robert himself even managed to get as far as Stockbridge, but here, as he attempted to ford the river Test to make good his own escape, he was caught by the vanguard of the queen's pursuing army and taken into captivity. The victorious royalists returned to Winchester, plundered the abandoned baggage-train, and mercilessly sacked the city. This was Henry of Blois's vengeance on his citizens who had deserted him.

Robert's selfless bravery earned him the highest commendations from friends and foes alike. It was entirely due to his actions that Matilda had managed to make her escape, and while many others of Matilda's party had fled from the field to avoid capture, he had stayed on with his handful of close personal followers to engage the queen's forces. 'What was greatly famed and brought him much honour,' recorded William of Malmesbury, 'was that no one saw the earl of Gloucester broken in spirit or even gloomy of countenance because of that mischance; such consciousness of his lofty rank did he breathe that he could not be humbled by the outrage of fortune.' The fact remained, however, that he and Matilda had lost their trump card. Now both sides, not just one side, had lost their commanders-in-chief. Robert was taken to Rochester castle, the prisoner of Stephen's queen; Stephen, meanwhile, remained in Bristol, in the charge of Robert's wife, Countess Mabel. Both women wanted to have their husbands back; both sides needed their leaders back; not surprisingly, thoughts quickly turned to the idea of an exchange of prisoners.

However, such a deal was easier in theory than in practice. The queen was shrewd enough to realise that a simple exchange of Robert for Stephen would decide nothing: the civil war would continue as before, and the adherents to Matilda's cause would be as numerous as ever. She began by trying to bribe Robert: if he would agree to an exchange, she said, then Stephen could remain titular king of England while Robert, as long as he agreed to abandon the claims of Matilda, could be virtual ruler of England under him. Whether the queen had sought Stephen's consent for such a deal is questionable, let alone whether she intended to honour it once the exchange had been accomplished. Robert was immovable: he refused to sanction any such deal without Matilda's consent, he declared, and the queen knew well what Matilda's reaction would be. Moreover, Robert had his own ideas about the exchange: an earl, he argued, was not equal in rank to a king; if Stephen were to be released, then not only Robert himself but all those who had been captured with him at Winchester too should be set free, to compensate for Stephen's exalted status. This was quite unacceptable to the queen. Several of Matilda's leading commanders had been captured at Winchester. When bribery failed to persuade Robert to change sides, the queen turned to threats. He had given his oath of allegiance to Stephen, she told him, and then broken it. For such an action his life was forfeit. If he were to be released and immediately resume the struggle on Matilda's behalf, then may God help him if ever he chanced to be captured again. Robert would not budge. His first oath had been to his sister: Stephen had taken the same oath. The difference between them was that Robert had later seen the error of his ways, while it appeared that Stephen had not. He was the oath-breaker, not Robert. Eventually both sides realised that to continue the negotiations was fruitless. The only sort of deal on which both sides were prepared to compromise was an unconditional exchange. The queen and her son Eustace rode to Bristol to inform Stephen of the agreement. On 1 November, Countess Mabel released Stephen. The queen and Eustace remained at Bristol as sureties for Robert's release. Two days later, Robert was released, and the queen and Eustace soon rejoined the king. It was nine months and a day since King Stephen had been captured. The seed of Matilda's triumph, sown by her brother on that dark winter's afternoon beneath the walls of Lincoln, had proved stillborn.

It was back to square one. To many, it must have seemed that nothing had changed. The whole dreary process of sieges and skirmishes, defection and deception, destruction and devastation, could start all over again as from the beginning, as from the moment a little over two years earlier when Matilda and Robert had landed at Arundel. In reality, however, much had changed. After the summer of 1141, when her own shortcomings had been so ruthlessly revealed by her treatment of those whose support she needed, when she had, with monumental bungling, succeeded in snatching defeat from the jaws of victory, it must have been clear to many of her supporters as well as to her opponents that it would necessitate a massive rebuilding of confidence in Henry I's daughter if her dream of becoming queen of England were ever to be realised. The very fact that, having captured and imprisoned her arch-rival, the man whose claim to be king of England she had consistently denied, she was then forced to release him in exchange for her brother, spoke volumes for the hopelessness of her cause should she ever lose the support of Robert. Equally, Stephen seemed to emerge from the events of 1141 with his reputation enhanced. His support had decidedly not collapsed with his own capture; his opponents had not even dared to depose him; Henry of Blois somewhat red-facedly tried to explain away the events of April and May 1141, and now swung the support of the church firmly behind his brother once more. The annointed king was king again, and few men believed that Matilda could ever deprive him of that title for as long as he lived. If Matilda at first refused to accept this, then during the long winter of 1141–2, which she and Robert spent at Oxford together, he succeeded in persuading her. Yet this did not mean that she should abandon the struggle; far from it. For Matilda had a son, the eight-year-old Henry of Anjou. It was not for herself that she and Robert now fought, but for Henry. Stephen had sons too, Eustace and William. After 1141, the battle for the succession to Henry I was virtually over; the battle for the succession to Stephen was just beginning.

It was with this in mind that Robert crossed the Channel in the early summer of 1142 to try to persuade Matilda's husband, Geoffrey of Anjou, to undertake an invasion of England. Geoffrey had never shown much interest in his wife's claim to the English throne, preferring to regard it as a useful way to distract Stephen while he methodically broke down the English strongholds in Normandy and added that valuable duchy to his own neighbouring dominions. Geoffrey's conquest of Normandy was now well advanced, and for a short time Robert joined him in the campaign. Early in October, however, news came from England that Matilda was in desperate straits, besieged by Stephen's army in Oxford castle. Robert persuaded Geoffrey to allow him to take the young Henry, now nine, back to England with him; the Angevin cause in England needed a new impetus, a new focal-point, especially if Matilda was about to be captured. Let the supporters of the cause see the fine young grandson of Henry I whose fate now lay in their hands. Geoffrey agreed, and Robert returned with his nephew, landing at Wareham on the Dorset coast with a force of some 300 knights. His army was not large enough to go to Matilda's relief at Oxford, but he hoped to draw Stephen away from the siege by diversionary tactics. As it turned out, Matilda was quite capable of looking after herself. December came, and with it a heavy fall of snow. The ground around Oxford was as white as a sheet. Stephen's men ringed the castle, preventing any supplies from reaching the garrison. But the siege had been dragging on for several weeks now, and the watch was becoming careless. Late one night, dressed all in white so that she would not be easily picked out against the snow, accompanied only by three knights, Matilda let herself down from the castle tower by a rope and walked across the moat, which was covered by a thick layer of ice. Then, without once being hindered or even accosted, she and her three companions walked straight through Stephen's lines, kept walking through the snow for six miles, and then rode to the friendly castle of Wallingford. Matilda was renowned for her lucky escapes: firstly at Arundel, where Stephen had let her go to join Robert, then at London when the citizens descended on her lodgings, then at Winchester, and now this, the most dramatic of all. Her flight through the night snows from Oxford is probably the most famous episode of the civil war. Stephen, needless to say, was not amused.

Matilda remained in England for another five years. The civil war continued, though not with the same intensity as in the years between 1139 and 1142, and Robert remained commander-in-chief of her armies throughout this period. With Matilda discredited in the eyes of many

English people, Geoffrey of Anjou refusing to be distracted from Continental ambitions, and their son Henry too young as yet to make an impact on the English scene, Robert more than ever came to be regarded as the mainstay of the Angevin cause in England. Although he never managed to gain a decisive advantage over Stephen, he did score some notable successes. In July 1143, by brilliant generalship, he surprised the king's army at Wilton, near Salisbury, and sent Stephen and Henry of Blois into headlong flight. Only the courageous rearguard action fought by Stephen's faithful steward, William Martel, saved both king and bishop from being taken prisoner on this occasion. In the following year Robert blockaded Malmesbury; when Stephen brought up an army to relieve the town, Robert turned his army to face the king, but Stephen, fearful of Robert's military reputation, declined battle and slipped away again.

Despite Robert's valiant efforts, support for the Angevin cause was ebbing away. Men were growing sick of civil war; they yearned for peace and a renewal of England's prosperity. In 1145, even one of Robert's sons turned against him. This was his fourth son, Philip, described by one contemporary as 'a man of strife, supreme in savagery, daring in what should not be dared, in fact a perfect master of every kind of wickedness'. It is not clear exactly why father and son quarrelled: perhaps a purely personal disagreement, perhaps a conflict of ideas over military strategy. Whatever it was, Philip soon repented of it, for he was struck down by a near-fatal illness and swiftly set off on crusade to the Holy Land. His rebellion against parental authority was symptomatic, however. The older generation was beginning to be upstaged. Matilda remained in England, ensconced for the most part in Robert's headquarters at Bristol, but her own cause was becoming increasingly irrelevant to the issues at stake, and she played little part in the war now. Henry of Blois was a mere shadow of the all-powerful prelate of ten years earlier; foiled in his bid for supreme power over the English church, no longer trusted even by his brother, he was to outlive nearly all his contemporaries, dying in 1171, but during the last twenty-five years of his life he devoted more and more time to the pursuit of his somewhat eccentric artistic tastes and less and less time to active politics. Stephen was still king, but by the late 1140s even he seems to have acquired a slightly passé air: he would remain king, there was little doubt about that, but his kingship was discredited and the real business of the day was the attempt to ensure a peaceful succession after his death.

Robert's own efforts were now nearing their end. Since the early months of 1143, he had virtually carried the Angevin cause in England single-handed. During these years his reputation as both statesman and soldier continued to grow. From Bristol he managed to control most of the West Country, and imposed here the sort of law and order which had been so disastrously lacking since Henry I's death. His military superiority over

Stephen had been decisively proven on several occasions, and while Robert remained in control in the West Country, Stephen seems to have taken the attitude that it was best to leave well alone rather than court disaster by mounting a major campaign. So Stephen stayed mainly in the East, and England remained a divided country. Robert knew well that Matilda would never become queen, but it was no longer for her that he was fighting; it was for her son, his nephew. In fact his last encounter with the young Henry was not entirely cordial. In the early months of 1147 Henry, now aged thirteen, a brash, resolute youth of great determination and very little patience, decided to have a go at conquering England. He arrived with a motley band of renegade knights and wild mercenaries, no money with which to pay them, and little idea of what to do once he had crossed the Channel. Robert had disapproved of the escapade from the start, and when after a few weeks Henry arrived on his doorstep at Bristol begging for money to pay his troops, he was given a less than enthusiastic welcome from his uncle. Far from handing over cash, Robert promptly escorted his nephew from Bristol back to Wareham, put him on a ship, and told the captain to make sure the young lad got back to Normandy. But Henry never forgot his uncle. A few years later he was back, and this time it was a very different story. When Henry did eventually become king of England, he was as aware as any man that it had been Robert, 'earl of Gloucester, of glorious memory', who more than any man had made it possible for him. It was Robert's chief legacy to English history.

One of Robert's last acts was to found a Cistercian abbey at Margam in Glamorgan, in the summer of 1147. Throughout his life he had been a benefactor of the church: he and Countess Mabel had already taken under their special protection, in 1130, the Cistercian abbey of Neath, made numerous gifts to Gloucester abbey and other religious houses, and founded a Benedictine priory dedicated to St James outside the walls of Bristol. It was in this priory that Robert had asked to be buried. His death came quite suddenly. In the autumn of 1147 he began to prepare a new expedition against Stephen, who had taken advantage of the young Henry's failure to encroach further to the West. Then, towards the end of October, when preparations for the campaign were virtually complete, news came that Robert had contracted a fever. He had led a tremendously active life, and was still robust enough to lead an army on horseback, but he had now reached the age of fifty-seven, old by medieval standards. The fever was a virulent one, and could not be checked. The end came quickly. He died on 31 October 1147, at Bristol castle, with his wife Mabel by his bedside, and was laid to rest beneath a tomb of green jasper stone in the priory which he had founded.

Robert's character is elusive. The qualities for which he was praised by contemporaries were thoroughly conventional ones, and in many ways he comes across as a thoroughly conventional sort of man. It may be that the quality of greatness which some men saw in him stemmed not so much from any especially distinguishing characteristics or talents as from an ability to do the basic things in life well. The English political stage during King Stephen's reign was dominated by figures of proven mediocrity. Against such a background, Robert stood for traditional virtues and traditional values. From the time when he first began to hold military commands under his father, he stands out as a consistently successful military leader; during the civil war of Stephen's reign, he was the best general in England. As a statesman he was more limited, lacking both the decisiveness to exploit an opening and the clear-sightedness to formulate successful policies. He was, however, regarded as an upholder of justice and honour, a man of integrity and trustworthiness, and these were uncommon virtues in Stephen's England. He was an upright and pious man, a patron and respecter of the church and of scholars, 'a man of great cleverness and learning', according to the contemporary chronicler Walter Map, and even something of a scholar in his own right: it is said that he translated at least one book from Latin into French. He used to 'regulate his day so wisely that he did not neglect his knightly duties for letters, nor letters for knightly duties', according to another contemporary. Such an interest in learning, nurtured no doubt by his father, Henry I, was rare among even the greatest laymen at this time.

The real question-mark which hangs over Robert's career concerns his changes of allegiance between 1135 and 1138. Yet in some ways it is difficult to see what else he could have done. He delayed longer than any of the other great English magnates in offering his allegiance to Stephen, which certainly shows that he was reluctant to break his oath to his sister, and by the time he came to Stephen's court at Oxford at Easter 1136 his range of options had narrowed: either he accepted Stephen's *fait accompli*, albeit conditionally, or he broke decisively with the new king and declared for his sister Matilda: the latter course would, at that time, have left him almost completely isolated from the rest of the English barons, and would have led to the immediate loss of his enormous English estates. Robert knew his sister, and had never been entirely happy about the prospect of her succession: hence his readiness to go along with the attempt to persuade Theobald to accept the crown in December 1135. If not even her husband was prepared to help her to gain the throne, and if the English baronage had thrown their support behind Stephen almost to a man, what chance had Robert of standing in his way? To declare for Matilda at this stage would have been a rather futile and potentially suicidal gesture. Far better to bide his time and let Stephen make the mistakes. He clearly was not the staunchly incorruptible man of honour portrayed by William of Malmesbury; he was a pragmatist, but a pragmatist with a strong streak of loyalty in him. His refusal to abandon Matilda after 1138, even when bribed and threatened by his captors in the autumn of 1141, even when the tide began to flow strongly against the Angevin cause in the last two or three years of his life, stands in stark contrast to the wheeling and dealing of so many of his contemporaries. The collapse of the Angevin cause (albeit temporarily) after Robert's death is the plainest indication of how much it had owed to him.

In assessing Robert's achievement, and even more his personality, there is one problem in particular which is almost insurmountable, that is, the violent partiality of most of the contemporary chroniclers. Robert himself patronised two of the most celebrated chroniclers of the twelfth century, William of Malmesbury and Geoffrey of Monmouth; indeed, William of Malmesbury dedicated both his *Gesta Regum* and his *Historia Novella* to Robert, and in both works, not surprisingly, he tends to be praised in fulsome terms, while the apparent ambiguities in his behaviour between 1135 and 1138 are glibly explained away. Geoffrey of Monmouth described his patron as a man 'whom philosophy nurtured in the liberal arts, and whom an innate competence made superior to other warriors in the arts of war', whereas those men who supported Stephen, such as Baldwin FitzGilbert, could describe him as 'lionlike in his speech, but like a hare in his heart, great in eloquence, but insignificant through laziness'. The majority of historians – though with one or two notable exceptions – have tended to praise Robert's qualities and to acknowledge the difficulty of his position in the years after 1135, rather than to condemn him for duplicity. After all, even one of his contemporary opponents admitted that he 'restored peace and tranquillity throughout his dominions, and greatly improved their condition'. Without necessarily accepting the panegyrics of Malmesbury and Monmouth, it does indeed seem that Robert's military ability, his aptitude for learning, and above all his integrity, were a cut above most of his contemporaries.

Four months after Robert's death, Matilda left England, her hopes shattered, her support disintegrating, her faction now effectively leaderless. Yet in the long term the cause for which Robert had striven was to be vindicated. In 1153, after young Henry of Anjou had defeated Stephen in a series of campaigns, the king agreed to disinherit his own sons and recognise Henry as his successor. When Stephen died in the next year, Matilda was still alive to see her twenty-one-year-old son accede to the throne almost entirely unchallenged. It was sad that Robert himself did not live to see his nephew crowned: Henry II was soon to demonstrate that he had been a king worth fighting for.

CHAPTER 6

GERVAIS OF BLOIS

There is no evidence that King Stephen was an adulterer, nor did he have a reputation for womanising. His wife, Matilda, was the daughter of the count of Boulogne, and the niece of Henry I's first wife, Matilda (see Table 1). The match had been arranged by Henry I in 1125, and it seems to have been both happy and fruitful: Matilda was clearly a pillar of strength to her husband throughout the troubles of his reign, and she bore him two sons and a daughter, apart from other children who did not survive infancy. Perhaps fortunately, she died in 1152, and was thus not obliged to witness Stephen's disinheritance of their sons from the throne in favour of Henry of Anjou in the settlement of 1153.

In his youth, however, Stephen had had an affair with a Norman woman called Dameta – practically nothing else is known about her – and she had given birth to a son, Gervais, who became abbot of Westminster. He is always known as Gervais of Blois, possibly because he was born there, possibly because he was descended from the counts of Blois (Stephen's elder brother Theobald was count of Blois). Dameta seems to have had two other sons, Almaric and Ralph, who were called brothers of the abbot when they witnessed two of Gervais's charters. There is no certainty that they too were Stephen's bastards by Dameta, but it is a possibility. He may also have had an illegitimate daughter, whose name is unknown, for Hervey, viscount of Léon in Brittany, is said to have married a bastard daughter of Stephen's some time before 1139. If she existed, she was clearly born long before Stephen became king. It is unlikely, however, that he had any other illegitimate children. A bastard William is mentioned in both seventeenth- and nineteenth-century genealogies, but there does not appear to be any contemporary reference to him; it may be that later historians confused him with Stephen's younger legitimate son, who was called William.

Gervais's appointment to the abbacy of Westminster by his father in 1136 is the first thing that is known of him. Throughout the Middle Ages Westminster was one of the two or three wealthiest religious houses in England and the abbot occupied a position of considerable standing. There seems to have been little problem in securing the necessary dispensation, though he was a bastard and probably very young, and in 1138 he was ordained by the papal legate. Unlike Geoffrey 'Plantagenet', future archbishop of York and another royal bastard, Gervais was quickly accepted by the Westminster monks in spite of his irregular appointment. It has been said that since the previous abbot, Herbert, had reduced the abbey's finances to a parlous state the monks were probably prepared to accept any reasonable candidate, while a royal one might be able to use his position to help put things right. An indication of the extent to which Herbert had allowed the Westminster estates to be dispersed is given by the fact that in 1129–30 the monks were prepared to pay 1,000 marks to purchase the authority to reappropriate them.

Gervais was not the best man to deal with the administration of a large abbey which had seen better times. In 1138 his father was barely forty years old and Gervais may well have been less than twenty. His preparation for office was not untypical of that for royal appointees to positions of high ecclesiastical honours: he may only just have taken orders and can hardly have known much about the management of large estates. However, it is doubtful that he allowed the condition of the monastery to sink to a disastrous level, as historians have believed for hundreds of years. The main charge against him has always been that he dissipated the monastic estates by granting land to his friends without the consent of the monks, for a very low rent and in perpetuity. He was undoubtedly guilty of granting the manor of Chelsea to his mother and her heirs for an annual return of £4, but a recent study of all the available records suggests that Gervais was not a particularly bad administrator under the circumstances. His unfavourable reputation has largely depended on the fifteenth-century historian Flete, who in his *History of Westminster Abbey* seems to have blamed Gervais unfairly for many of the problems which subsequently faced the abbey.

A papal bull addressed to Gervais in 1139 instructed him to maintain proper discipline, to keep laymen and knights outside the monastic precinct, to reassemble the abbey's lands and rents, some of which had become the perquisites of individual monks, to recover the churches and tithes which had been dispersed without the consent of the monks, and not to redistribute any assets without such consent. Although the bull has usually been seen as a personal rebuke to Gervais, it is important to realise that it was written in the second year of his abbacy and was almost certainly aimed at clearing up the wrongs perpetrated by Gervais's predecessor. It is unfortunate that little else is known of his own abbacy, because the cloud cast upon it by the retrospective accusations of Flete, the misinterpretation of the papal bull and the fact that he was deposed early in the reign of Henry II, is difficult to dispel. He successfully recovered manors and other benefices for Westminster and resisted the monks of Malvern priory in their attempt to become independent of Westminster. In 1148 his uncle, that worldly bishop Henry of Blois, put his name forward with two others as candidates for the vacant see of Lincoln.

Family interest was the key to Gervais's rise and fall as abbot. Having been his father's appointee as abbot, he has never lost the taint of corruption for, amongst other things, granting a monastic estate to his mother, and when his family support evaporated on the death of his father in 1154 it was only three years later that he was removed from office to be replaced by Laurence, a firm Angevin supporter. It is not true, as was once alleged, that the pope had tried to depose him in 1146, and when it came his actual deposition was almost certainly on account of his identification with Stephen's lost cause.

Gervais lived only three more years after being deposed, and was buried in the south cloister of Westminster. His epitaph reads:

> De regum genere pater hic Gervasius, ecce,
> Monstrat defunctus, mors rapit omne genus.

> (Here lies father Gervais, born of kingly stock,
> In his decease we learn that death spares no man.)

In spite of all that Gervais must have done at Westminster during his twenty-year abbacy, good or bad, it was his royal paternity which the composer of these lines chose to commemorate. This is all the more inappropriate in that Gervais was not born a royal bastard. At his birth, which probably occurred *circa* 1115–20, few people can have imagined that his father would one day be king of England. It was only by virtue of the White Ship and all that resulted from it that Gervais came to enter that special category of royal bastards.

CHAPTER 7

HENRY II'S BASTARDS

By 1154, the year in which the twenty-one-year-old Henry of Anjou became King Henry II of England, he was already the ruler of a vast complex of territories in France, generally known as the Angevin Empire. From his father, Geoffrey of Anjou, Henry had inherited Anjou, Maine and Touraine; England and Normandy (which he saw as his rightful inheritance anyway) had been settled on him by agreement with Stephen in 1153, and came to him on Stephen's death in 1154; Aquitaine came to him by right of his wife, Eleanor, in 1152, and the east coast of Ireland was conquered in his name in the 1170s. He also managed to establish effective control over Scotland and Brittany, and it was said that he could have ridden from the Cheviots to the Pyrenees without ever leaving his own dominions. Energy he needed, and energy he had. He was a king who had little time for the pomp and circumstance of monarchy. Because of the enormous extent of his dominions he was frequently involved in military action, but, although he pursued his aims with vigour, it is said that he despised violence and hated war. He preferred to be riding and hunting or engaging in conversation with intellectuals; indeed, he was widely read and 'remarkably polished in letters'. Active, restless, often impatient, he could tolerate privation and danger, but not personal affronts to his authority. His temper was legendary. In 1166 John of Salisbury, the foremost English scholar of his day, described one of the king's eruptions in a letter to Thomas Becket:

> I heard that when the king was at Caen and was vigorously debating the matter of the king of Scotland, he broke out in abusive language against Richard du Hommet for seeming to speak somewhat in the king of Scotland's favour, calling him a manifest traitor. And the king, flying into his usual temper, flung his cap from his head, pulled off his belt, threw off his cloak and clothes, grabbed the silken coverlet off the couch, and sitting as it might be on a dung heap started chewing pieces of straw.

Eleanor of Aquitaine also had a reputation for a lively temper. Divorced from Louis VII of France in March 1152, she was married barely eight weeks later to Henry. Eleanor was eleven years older than Henry. She was thirty and had been Louis's wife for fifteen years but, although they had two daughters, there were no sons of the marriage and Louis needed a wife who would give him an heir. He and Eleanor were third cousins once removed, and their consanguinity was the pretext on which the marriage was declared null. Strangely enough Henry and Eleanor were related to almost the same degree, but there was no need to manufacture a divorce in their case, for over the next fifteen years Eleanor bore Henry no less than four sons who survived to manhood.

From what is known of Eleanor before her marriage to Henry, she was a beautiful, headstrong woman, perhaps indiscreet in her flirtations with men other than Louis, and certainly infuriated by his increasing piety. Yet during her thirty years and more of married life with Henry her activities are barely touched upon by chroniclers, and one can do little more than speculate about the nature of their relationship, up until, that is, her attempt to join their sons' rebellion against him in 1173. She was imprisoned by Henry, probably for the rest of his reign, although he seems to have allowed her to appear publicly on occasion after 1183. By 1173 their marriage must have broken down, but it is possible that it had only deteriorated during the last few years.

Opinion is divided about whether Henry II had mistresses after he married Eleanor and before the major family rows of 1170 onwards, and whether adultery had something to do with their estrangement. William of Newburgh believed that Henry's adultery began only after Eleanor was past child-bearing age. He must have known about the bastards Geoffrey 'Plantagenet' and William Longsword, and presumably he thought that Geoffrey was born before Henry and Eleanor married in 1152. However, William Longsword, who was much younger, might have been born before 1170 and there were rumours of other infidelities.

Eudo de Porhöet, ex-count of Brittany, claimed in 1168 that the English king, while holding his daughter as a hostage for peace, had made her pregnant 'treacherously, adulterously and incestuously. For the king and Eudo's wife [Bertha] were the offspring of two sisters' (Matilda and Maud, one the legitimate, the other an illegitimate daughter of Henry I). Some years earlier, it is said, Henry had lusted after the sister of Roger de Clare, earl of Hertford, she being the 'most beautiful woman in the realm'. More serious, perhaps, but still no more than a rumour, was the whispered claim that Alice, the daughter of the French king, who was being kept in Henry's guardianship until she was old enough to marry his son Prince Richard, had been seduced by the king and even, according to one version, given birth to a daughter who did not survive. Richard and Alice never married, although the unfortunate princess was kept at the English court for over twenty-five years. Henry's possible affair with her was, some would argue both then and now, a good enough excuse for Richard to set Alice aside, for he would have been entering into an incestuous relationship with a woman who had been seduced by his father. Political considerations were probably, however, more important in the failure to marry, and the whole question of Henry's treatment of the French princess remains unresolved.

98

Hugh of Avalon, bishop of Lincoln from 1186, was thought by some to be the bastard son of Henry II, so generously did the king treat the young Carthusian monk. If, as is extremely doubtful, the unsubstantiated allegation has any truth to it, Hugh would have been born to a mistress of Henry's younger days, before his arrival in England in 1154. Morgan, provost of Beverley (1201) and bishop-elect of Durham (1213) was, however, almost certainly the son of King Henry, his mother being the wife of Ralph Bloet. Indeed, his bastardy prevented the confirmation of his election as bishop by the pope. One can therefore be fairly sure that he was another royal bastard, even though it is strange that he should be so little known while his half-brothers, Geoffrey and William, were generously supported and acknowledged by the king. The circumstances of Morgan's birth must have been different. To be provost of Beverley in 1201 he need have been no more than about twenty; he was probably born late in Henry's reign, with the result that his father died before he could establish Morgan's career. It seems likely that he was brought up in the Bloet household, for later in life he was given an opportunity to assert that he was Ralph's own son. That was in 1213, the year he sought papal confirmation for his election to the see of Durham. It was not altogether an auspicious year in which to be pursuing an appointment which had King John's blessing, for, until Pope Innocent received John's abject submission in June, the interdict which had blighted the spiritual and political life of England for some years was not lifted and Innocent was hardly likely to be generous with dispensations for bastardy in the English king's favour. However, the exact date of Morgan's visit to the Roman curia is unknown. Apparently Pope Innocent felt sorry for Morgan, for he had come all the way to Rome in good faith hoping for the papal blessing, and now found himself unexpectedly disappointed. The pope therefore called him aside, and told him that if he was prepared to swear that he was really the son of Ralph and his wife Nest, rather than of the king and Nest, then he would very readily confirm him as bishop of Durham, but that if he continued to insist that he was the son of King Henry, then his illegitimate birth obliged Innocent to refuse confirmation. This put poor Morgan in a quandary: whether to deny his royal blood, or to forgo his hopes of a bishopric. He retired to consult with a friend. The friend's advice was unequivocal: on no account must a man deny his royal blood, a far more worthy endowment than a bishopric. So Morgan returned to the pope, told him that it was unthinkable that he should deny his father the king, and went away a disappointed man. No doubt he thought the world an unfair place: forty years earlier, when his half-brother Geoffrey was elected bishop of Lincoln, another pope had granted a dispensation for bastardy. But at least Morgan could console himself that his royal paternity was now official.

Another possible mistress of Henry's later years, called Bellebelle, is mentioned in the Pipe Roll for 1184, when the king ordered that various cloaks, hoods and other clothing should be bought for her. But while Bellebelle and Morgan's mother may have been the king's bedfellows during the last dozen or so years of Henry's reign, the evidence for his adultery during the previous twenty years is not substantial, except of course for his well-known affair with Rosamund Clifford between about 1173 and 1176.

Henry's two most celebrated bastards were Geoffrey 'Plantagenet' and William Longsword. William Longsword was probably born just before or just after the king's affair with Rosamund. There is no evidence to substantiate the long-held belief that William was her son, though from the point of view of his age he could have been; his mother was possibly that Hikenai or Ykenai who produced Geoffrey, for in Henry III's reign William claimed the estates of a Roger of Akeny. However, there must have been a great difference in Geoffrey's and William's ages, the former an archdeacon before 1170, the latter not mentioned in the record until 1188, when he received land from Henry II. The likelihood of their having the same mother is not therefore very great.

The name Longsword originally belonged to William, duke of Normandy, who died in the middle of the tenth century. The surname is thought to have been used by William Clito, son of Robert Curthose, and it later passed from Henry II's bastard to his descendants. Before long William was to add another title to his name, for in 1196 Richard I promised his half-brother the daughter and heiress of the earl of Salisbury. Two years later they were married, although Ela can have been little more than ten at the most. The third earl, as William became (see Plate 3b), was an ally of both King Richard and King John, and it was during John's reign that he first came to public notice. By the time of his death he had been sheriff of eight counties, lieutenant of Gascony, constable of Dover castle and warden of the Cinque Ports, constable, too, of Winchester, Portchester and Southampton castles and warden of the Welsh Marches. Most, if not all, of these posts would have been delegated for a sum of money. In addition he had sometimes been sent on diplomatic missions, for example in 1212 when he went to Flanders on the king's business, and he had often received commands in the king's army and navy. In 1214 he was made marshal of the king's army in Flanders when it joined forces with the German emperor Otto IV against the French king, Philip Augustus, in the disastrous Bouvines campaign. At the battle of Bouvines Longsword was taken prisoner, to be released a short while later in exchange for the son of the count of Dreux.

There are records of a great number of gifts made by King John to the bastard brother whom he evidently liked and promoted so highly. The king's household accounts also reveal that he and William frequently gambled together. Williams's lands in England and Normandy included the castle and honour of Eye (Suffolk) and the castle of Pontorson. The king also gave him wardships and marriages, money, timber, wine, venison, his own ship, the *Constance*, and quantities of fish. Small wonder that the earl of Salisbury should have been associated with John through thick and thin, witnessing his charters and participating in some of the darker deeds perpetrated by that unpopular monarch. Unlike many royal servants, William did not desert John during the period of his excommunication, and one contemporary even remarked that William would do anything John asked of him. In 1212 he arrested the clerk of the exchequer, Geoffrey of Norwich, at Dunstable after Geoffrey had withdrawn his services following the promulgation of Pope Innocent III's bull excommunicating John. The unfortunate clerk was made by John to wear a heavy leaden cope so that he died of misery and want, and Longsword's apparent complicity in this misdeed did not enhance his reputation.

Longsword remained faithful to John throughout the baronial revolt and the enactment of Magna Carta, except for the final months of John's life, when he went over to the rebel side. In the civil war following Magna Carta, some of the rebel English barons offered Prince Louis of France the crown of England if he would help them get rid of John. He accepted, and Longsword was one of those who helped him attack the south coast of England. As a royal servant during the minority of Henry III, however, he was as faithful as he had usually been to John and equally indebted to the young king for gifts of land and money and for important public office.

Longsword was also genuinely religious and extremely generous to the church. His will is occupied almost entirely by gifts to religious houses and charities. After clearing his debts, he issued instructions for profits of a wardship to go to his own Carthusian foundation at Heythrop, along with a gold chalice encrusted with emeralds and rubies, a gold pyx, vials of silver, beautiful silk and satin vestments and a thousand ewes, three hundred muttons, forty-eight oxen and twenty heifers. Nineteen other houses were to receive bequests in descending order down to ten oxen for the house of St Radegund, a Premonstratensian abbey outside Dover.

In 1220 he and his wife, who was destined for an even greater role in the church, becoming abbess of her own foundation, Lacock abbey in Wiltshire, laid foundation stones for the new cathedral of Salisbury. It was in the cathedral that William himself was buried in 1226. His tomb and effigy are still to be seen there (plate 3a), although in 1790 they were moved from their original site in the chapel of the Virgin to the easternmost bay of the south arcade of the nave. Longsword's attachment to the Virgin Mary was profound. Since the day of his knighthood it is said that he kept a candle burning before her altar. He also attributed the saving of his life to her when, during a terrifying storm at sea, he and the sailors saw the vision of a lovely maiden at the masthead, whom he alone knew at once to be the Virgin Mary. Naturally enough the storm soon abated and they completed their journey in safety.

Unlike his bastard brother Geoffrey, whose light shone most brightly during their father's reign and who lived a troubled life under Richard and John, Longsword, who was probably too young to go far while Henry II reigned, married well under Richard and served both his brother John and his nephew Henry III to the best of his ability, except for the brief period of indecision in 1216–17. It is interesting that Richard does not seem to have felt threatened by his existence in the way that he clearly was by Geoffrey's. No doubt Longsword's youth and lack of a strong attachment to their father were partly responsible for this.

Longsword's eldest son was also called William Longsword, but for some reason he never received his father's earldom. He himself claimed that it was because of some legal obstacle, rather than because Henry III disliked him. Instead he received a grant of 60 marks (£40) *per annum* from the exchequer until such time as his claim should be decided. It is interesting to note that the younger William's son married Matilda, great-grand-daughter of Walter Clifford and great-niece of Fair Rosamund. This marriage as much as anything else suggests that Rosamund could not have been the elder William's mother, for it would have been between second cousins once removed, and there is no record of a dispensation having been sought. The coincidence is intriguing, however, and by that marriage the Clifford estates merged with those of Longsword, for Matilda was her father's heir.

CHAPTER 8

GEOFFREY 'PLANTAGENET'

The story of Geoffrey 'Plantagenet', eldest and most remarkable of Henry II's bastards, is the story of a man who was born with all the talent and ambition to take him to the highest offices in his father's kingdom, yet whose extraordinary ability to make enemies, and inability to tolerate or compromise with those who opposed him, dogged him throughout his life and ultimately brought him to ruin and exile. No one was quicker to recognise Geoffrey's qualities than his father, and for good reason, for the strengths as well as the flaws of the father's and the son's characters were strikingly similar. Both were fiercely determined, immensely energetic, and single-minded to the point of arrogance; both had fearsome tempers; both found themselves confronted by others as obstinate as themselves, and neither cared much for the path of moderation. Between them, however, there was no hint of dissension. While Henry lived, he did everything in his power to further Geoffrey's career: his dying wish was that his favourite bastard should be elevated to the archbishopric of York. In return, Geoffrey was his father's most steadfast and devoted councillor, serving Henry with great success both as war-captain and as chancellor of England. In the final, bitter days of Henry's reign, when the dying king was at last brought low by his own turbulent brood of legitimate sons, Geoffrey refused to accompany his father to the scene of his humiliation, because he said it would break his heart to witness the spectacle. Two of these rebellious sons, Richard the Lionheart and John, in turn succeeded Henry to the throne, and his father's death proved to be the turning-point in Geoffrey's life. Overnight, the staunch upholder of the rights of the crown against all its enemies became himself one of the foremost of those enemies, and the remaining twenty-three years of his life were spent in continuous and acrimonious feuding with his royal half-brothers.

Despite the fact that there is no contemporary warrant for the name, Geoffrey is commonly known nowadays as Geoffrey Plantagenet. He was probably born in 1151, the son of a woman called Ykenai or Hikenai whose identity is mysterious. One chronicler said that she was a woman of low birth and character, but she may in fact have been the daughter of a knight. Shortly after Henry's accession to the English throne in December 1154, Geoffrey's mother brought her little boy to court and presented him to his father. Later, it was to be whispered that he was not the king's son at all, and that the young king had been tricked into acknowledging him as his son by Geoffrey's mother. This can only have been malicious gossip. There was clearly no doubt in Henry's mind that the three-year-old Geoffrey was of his own blood: he acknowledged him at once, took him into the royal household, and never regretted it. What Queen Eleanor thought of the arrangement is not recorded, but she never showed any affection for Geoffrey, and in later years she probably regarded him as a threat to her own children – and with some reason.

Henry and Eleanor had plenty of children of their own. Their first child, William, born in 1153, died three years later, but between 1155 and 1167 a further four sons and three daughters followed, all of whom survived childhood. Henry's sons by Eleanor were the young Henry, born in 1155, Richard, born in 1157, another Geoffrey, called Geoffrey of Brittany because he later became duke of Brittany, born in 1158, and John, born in 1167. Along with them in the royal household, and on a footing of virtual equality with them, the little royal bastard Geoffrey lived and grew up. In time, every one of Henry's legitimate sons – and not only his sons but his wife as well – was to rebel against him. Not without reason have they been called 'the devil's brood'. In contrast, the base-born Geoffrey remained faithful to his father through all the troubles which embittered Henry's later years. No doubt it was expedient for him to do so: legitimate sons, whose inheritances were established in law, could afford to rebel, whereas illegitimate sons had no rights in law, and were therefore entirely dependent on royal favour. In this case, though, there was more to it than expediency: there was great affection between Henry II and his first-born bastard – greater affection than he showed for any of his legitimate children, except perhaps the youngest, John.

From an early age, the king decided that Geoffrey should follow a career in the church, and when he was still 'a mere boy' – the exact date is not certain – he was put into deacon's orders and made archdeacon of the diocese of Lincoln. This was a wise and tactful move on Henry's part. Geoffrey was, after all, his eldest son, and it was not unthinkable that a royal bastard might be regarded as a serious candidate for the throne. It is abundantly clear that Henry's second legitimate son, Richard, did indeed regard his illegitimate brother as a threat, and this probably goes much of the way towards explaining the animosity between these two half-brothers. A career in the church was not only an easy way to provide for Geoffrey, it also deprived him of any possible claim to the throne – as long, that is, as he was ordained a priest. Yet throughout his father's reign, Geoffrey steadfastly held back from ordination: to become a bishop, or even an archbishop, a man did not technically need to be ordained a priest. He needed only to be in minor orders, such as the deacon's orders which

Geoffrey had assumed when he became archdeacon of Lincoln, and minor orders were not irrevocable. Thus Geoffrey's refusal to undergo ordination as a priest does lend some support to the contemporary rumours that his real ambition was ultimately to become king of England. Nevertheless, he accepted high office in the church: in April 1173, Henry persuaded the canons of Lincoln cathedral to choose Geoffrey as their bishop. It was just at this time, however, that the king's family problems were coming to a head, and Geoffrey was soon to find himself serving his father in a very different, and most unspiritual, capacity.

For about twenty years, Henry's marriage to Eleanor had been not only fruitful but apparently happy. By 1173, however, it was clear that their personal relationship had broken down. It may be that Henry had already begun to live with Fair Rosamund, and that as far as Eleanor was concerned this was the final straw; or it may be that the volatile and wilful Eleanor, now aged fifty-one, finally decided to break free of Henry's grip. She was a woman who liked to have her own way: yet in her second husband she had found an even more domineering and obstinate character than her own, and for twenty years now she had been reduced to playing a role of almost total subservience. The overpowering personality of Henry II was producing a similar reaction in his legitimate sons. John was only six in 1173, but the three elder sons, young Henry, Richard, and the legitimate Geoffrey, were eighteen, sixteen and fourteen respectively: hungry for real power, eager to make their mark in the world, they found their authority and independence stifled at every turn by the heavy hand of their father. Granted but a little power, they ached to be free of his domination. Egged on by their mother, and confident of the support of barons both in England and on the Continent who resented Henry's harsh government as much as they did, they planned a rebellion. In the spring of 1173 they slipped away from Henry's court at Chinon, near Tours, and raced to join Henry's arch-enemy, the French king, at Paris. Eleanor, disguised as a man, tried to follow them, but was discovered and brought ignominiously back to face her husband. The damage, however, had been done. For King Louis, it was the chance he had been waiting for, the chance to manipulate the dissensions within the English royal family in order to strike a decisive blow at his over-mighty neighbour. In England, a number of leading landowners, including four of the earls, declared openly for the rebels. Throughout his vast empire, the flag of revolt was raised against Henry. He was facing the greatest crisis of his reign.

At the time of the outbreak of rebellion, Geoffrey was probably aged twenty-one or twenty-two. His experience of warfare was minimal, since he had been brought up in the expectation of a church career, but his election as bishop of Lincoln a few weeks earlier had greatly increased his stature within the kingdom, and as it turned out he was to play a crucial role in suppressing the revolt. Geoffrey had no doubts as to where his loyalty lay. All around him men were wavering in their allegiance to his father, waiting to see how events turned out before committing themselves to either side. The heartland of the rebel cause in England was the Midlands, where several of the leading landowners had declared for the king's sons and against the king, but the potential support for the revolt was widespread throughout England. What made the situation even more dire for Henry was that William the Lion, king of Scotland, also declared for the rebels, and launched an invasion of northern England. Initially, those who were loyal to the king could do little but hold their own. Fighting both in England and on the Continent continued throughout the summer of 1173 and over the following winter, but the longer the revolt continued, the more it became obvious that the king was gradually gaining the upper hand. Shortly after Easter 1174, the English rebels joined with the king of Scotland in one last attempt to secure victory. William the Lion invaded and laid siege to Carlisle and other northern strongholds, while the Midland rebels raided Northampton and captured the important castle of Nottingham. The king's fate hung in the balance.

Geoffrey had already been busy collecting contributions throughout his diocese for his father's cause, but now he decided that more positive action was necessary. He returned the money which he had collected, and instead exhorted the men of Lincolnshire to follow him personally to the North to crush the rebels. He began by besieging one of the leading northern rebels, Roger of Mowbray, in his castle of Kinardferry in the Isle of Axholme, in the fens by the lower Trent. Having successfully starved Mowbray's forces out and captured Roger himself, he razed the castle to the ground, marched north, and captured another of Mowbray's castles, at Kirby Malzeard. A third castle, at Thirsk, was neutralised by the erection of a fort at neighbouring Topcliffe. Geoffrey's next task brought him into conflict for the first time with a man who was later to be one of his most persistent enemies, Hugh de Puiset, the grandiloquent bishop of Durham. Puiset had not actively joined the rebels, but he had, at the least, connived at their schemes. Geoffrey now sought him out, compelled him to give pledges for his future loyalty to the king, ordered him to stop his dangerous meddling, and moved on to confront the king of Scotland, who was besieging Bowes castle. At the approach of Geoffrey's army, King William promptly abandoned the siege and retreated to Alnwick in Northumberland. A few days later, on 13 July, William the Lion and a small party of Scottish knights were surprised outside Alnwick by some of Geoffrey's followers, led by the sheriff of Yorkshire, and the Scottish king was himself captured. It was the crowning achievement of the campaign against the rebels. With the capture of the Scottish king, the revolt in England collapsed, and Geoffrey returned in triumph to meet his father, who was busy mopping up pockets of rebel resistance, at Huntingdon. On seeing Geoffrey again, the victorious Henry cried out, 'Base-born indeed have my other children shown themselves; this alone is my true son!'

By his quick and decisive campaign in the early summer of 1174, Geoffrey had proved much more than his loyalty. He had shown himself to be forceful and resourceful, personally brave, a man of action, and a man of great military skill, prepared to throw himself against opponents in situations where the odds were clearly against him. His father's confidence in him had been repaid with interest, and from now on both his relationship with the king and his own career blossomed. As for Henry's relations with his own family, it was evident to all that they could never be the same again. Although a peace was patched up after the collapse of the rebellion, and Henry in fact treated his rebellious sons with considerably more generosity than they deserved, an atmosphere of lingering mistrust continued to permeate the political history of the remaining fifteen years of Henry's reign. Queen Eleanor, however, played no further part in that history. From the time of her arrest in the spring of 1173 until Henry's death on 6 July 1189, she remained his prisoner, closely although honourably confined at Winchester, a sad, discarded, lonely woman passing through her middle age in what must have seemed to her to be circumstances of extreme boredom and humiliation. It was left to her favourite son, Richard, to release her and restore her to the dignity which her station demanded when he became king.

From this time onwards, Geoffrey became one of his father's closest and most trusted councillors. Once King Henry had assured himself that the rebellion in England was entirely stamped out, he returned to his duchy of Normandy in October 1174, taking Geoffrey with him. For the next two years Geoffrey was regularly either with his father or undertaking missions for him in England or on the Continent. Meanwhile, Henry was trying to persuade the pope to confirm Geoffrey's election as bishop of Lincoln. Although the canons of the cathedral had elected him (at Henry's behest), there were still obstacles to be overcome before he could be consecrated: one obstacle was his youth, for he was still only in his early twenties, while another was his illegitimate birth. Bastards were not normally allowed to take holy orders of any kind, so a special dispensation had to be obtained from the pope. After two years, this dispensation was eventually forthcoming, but still Henry would not allow Geoffrey actually to receive his confirmation, deciding instead to send him to study at the cathedral school at Tours, where he received an education which was to stand him in good stead later in life. When he returned to England, he was once more actively employed in his father's service, and seems to have found no time at all to attend to the spiritual affairs of his diocese. 'He was more skilful to fleece the Lord's sheep than to feed them,' remarked one contemporary, and it may well have been true. As a man much more intimately connected with the royal administration than with the well-being of the English church, he gained a reputation for being an efficient and uncompromising tax-gatherer, a man who enjoyed all the revenues associated with his office but made no attempt to fulfil its responsibilities, a churchman of exceptional worldliness in an age when worldly churchmen were far from uncommon. On the other hand, he also applied some of his administrative efficiency to the running of his diocese, for he was active in recovering the cathedral's estates, and in encouraging scholars to come to the cathedral school, making it one of the chief centres of English learning at this time. Moreover, he was personally a generous benefactor to his cathedral, purchasing for it, among other things, two large and very fine bells, out of his own money.

Nevertheless, it was clearly a situation that could not go on for ever. Geoffrey had been elected bishop of Lincoln, that election had been confirmed by the pope and blessed by the king, yet by 1181, eight years after that election, he still had not been consecrated, let alone ordained as a priest. In that year, Pope Alexander III decided that the matter must be settled one way or the other: he wrote to Henry ordering that Geoffrey be compelled either to receive consecration immediately, or to resign and allow another man to be consecrated as bishop. Geoffrey, still hoping to have his cake and eat it, wrote to the pope asking for a further respite for three years, but the king had other ideas. Geoffrey had proved himself too efficient an administrator, and Henry now planned to raise him to the post of chancellor of England, the highest position in the royal administration after the justiciar. A deal was made between father and son: Geoffrey agreed to resign his bishopric of Lincoln, in return for which he would not only become royal chancellor, but would also be compensated for his lost revenues with a whole host of offices and lands in both England and France. These included the archdeaconry of Rouen, the treasurership of York cathedral, and two castles in Anjou. It was not only a very generous offer from Geoffrey's point of view, it was also a further vote of confidence on Henry's part. Geoffrey's new titles and acquisitions were reported to bring him in an annual revenue of over £650, spread roughly evenly on either side of the Channel. He formally resigned the bishopric of Lincoln at Marlborough on Epiphany Day, 6 January 1182, and the ceremony of resignation which took place throws an interesting sidelight on Geoffrey's character. It seems that he was a rather indistinct speaker, and when he came to recite his speech of resignation the archbishop of Canterbury twice had to stop him and ask him what he was saying. On the second occasion the historian Walter Map, who was present at the ceremony and afterwards recorded the story in his chronicle, replied on Geoffrey's behalf, 'French of Marlborough.' By which he meant apparently that there was a local tradition that anyone who drank of a certain well in the town spoke bad French for the rest of his life.

Geoffrey remained chancellor of England for the next seven and a half years, until the end of Henry II's reign. It was not a very happy twilight to what had in many ways been a reign of great achievements. In 1183 the king passed his fiftieth birthday, and now at last the immense energy which had once caused the French king to remark that Henry seemed rather to fly than to walk or ride was beginning to decline, the memories of the glittering successes of the early years of his reign beginning to fade. His will remained unflinching, his capacity for work remarkable, but increasingly he appears as an isolated and aging figure, fighting a ceaseless battle to restrain the ever-growing ambition of his violent and impatient sons, and gradually, very gradually, beginning to retreat in the face of such relentless selfishness. In 1183 the eldest of his legitimate children, the young Henry, died of dysentery in the middle of yet another rebellion against his father; despite all that his son had been guilty of, the king was said to be overcome with grief at the news. In 1186 his third-born legitimate son, Geoffrey, followed his elder brother to the grave: 'a hypocrite in everything, a deceiver and a dissembler' was how one contemporary described this least-known of the 'devil's brood'. He had died after suffering a wound at a tournament in Paris, whither he had taken himself in order to conspire with the new king of France, Philip Augustus, against Henry. That left only Richard and John: Richard, the legendary Lionheart whose fame as a courageous warrior and brilliant general has endured through the centuries, but who was in reality a cold, harsh and faithless man, as slippery as an eel, possessed of a heart of stone rather than that of a lion. Richard was now approaching thirty, whereas his youngest brother, John, was not yet twenty: in the course of time, John was to give ample proof that he was no less endowed with the unpleasant qualities of the Angevin dynasty than any of his brothers. Up until this time, however, he had been faithful to his father, and he remained, as he seems to have been almost since his birth, the undoubted favourite of Henry's four legitimate sons.

In the last few years of his life, Henry decided that the only way to keep Richard in check was to play him off against John, to refuse to confirm him in his succession to the English throne or to the king's French dominions, so that the threat of his being disinherited in favour of his younger brother, John, would always be hanging over him. It was a plan which backfired. In 1187, news reached Western Europe of the fall of Jerusalem to Saladin. A new crusade was proclaimed, and Richard was eager to join it, but not until he felt reasonably sure that his inheritance would not be snatched from his grasp while his back was turned. Philip Augustus of France, a much more far-sighted and astute statesman than his predecessor Louis, began to work on Richard, raising doubts in his mind over his father's intentions, offering fair promises for the future in return for treachery against his father now. At a conference in November 1188, Henry refused point-blank to confirm Richard in his succession, whereupon there was a violent quarrel between father and son, the meeting broke up in disorder, and the two men stormed off in opposite directions: Richard to rejoin King Philip of France, Henry to set his castles in a state of readiness for the approaching conflict. Whether Henry really did intend to disinherit Richard in favour of John it is impossible to be sure: he may well have wanted to, and he made no effort to conceal his desire from Richard. But the old king's health was now failing fast: through the early months of 1189 proposed conferences between father and son continually had to be postponed because Henry was too sick to attend them. It must have been evident to Richard that he had only to exercise a little patience, and all would soon be his. But this was not his way: he was determined not only to wrest his inheritance from his father but also to humiliate him as much as he could in the process. In the early summer of 1189, he began waging open war, backed by King Philip, against the dying Henry.

Throughout this final crisis of the reign, the faithful Geoffrey remained with his father, acting as Henry's chief-of-staff in the last campaigns. After the collapse of the conference in November 1188 he was dispatched by Henry to secure the king's French castles against Richard and Philip. In June 1189, his father sent him to alert the garrisons of Normandy to the outbreak of war. Having done this, Geoffrey then hurriedly raised a fresh force and raced back to cover Henry's retreat into Anjou. For retreat was now all that was left to the king. Men could see which way the wind blew, and few had the stomach to fight for a dying king against the man who would shortly be his successor. He knew that he had no option but to sue for peace, and in the first week of July a new conference was arranged at Ballan, near Tours. Geoffrey begged permission to be allowed not to accompany his father: he would be overcome, he said, at having to witness this final humiliation. Henry rode the few miles from his headquarters at Chinon to Ballan, his body feeble and convulsed with pain, and there met Richard and Philip. Even Philip was moved to pity, and offered his cloak so that Henry could rest on the ground. Henry refused the offer. He had not come to negotiate. He had nothing left to negotiate with. He had come to listen, to agree to the terms imposed upon him, and to go home again. The terms were read: he was to submit himself to the French king for all his Continental territories, he was to acknowledge Richard as his heir, and he was to pardon all those who had gone over to Richard's side during the past few months. Henry duly listened, agreed, and departed. Yet even now, before he left, he found time for one last gibe at his perfidious son. Seizing Richard by the shoulder, he hissed, 'God spare me until I may be revenged upon you!' Then, being too sick to ride, he was borne back to Chinon on a litter.

Back at Chinon, Henry asked for a list of those who had deserted him for Richard in the past few weeks. Geoffrey tried to keep the list from him, but the king insisted that it should be read out. The first name on the list was John's. It was the final, the most bitter, act of treachery. In the end, even his dearest son John had turned against him. He ordered them to stop reading. Now, at last, the will to go on living had gone from him. The pain and the bitterness took hold of him, and he began to rave deliriously about the faithlessness of his sons. Geoffrey remained with him throughout his last hours, patiently trying to calm his father's ravings. Occasionally Henry returned to sanity: he blessed Geoffrey, the one son who had remained faithful to him through all; he expressed his desire that Geoffrey should be elevated to the archbishopric of York. Then he lapsed into a coma. On the morning of Thursday 6 July 1189, he died. He was fifty-six.

For Geoffrey, the world had turned upside down. His sense of personal loss was overwhelming. His devoted service to the king who had fathered him had been the lynchpin of his life, the solid rock upon which an immensely successful career had been built, while his personal relationship with Henry had been a constant source of strength and stability. He had devoted all his great energies to the maintenance of the English crown against its enemies, and now it was the greatest of those enemies who was himself to assume the crown. From now on, Geoffrey was alone in the world. Up until now, his own personality had been largely submerged by that of his father; he had acted as an extension of his father's will, the dutiful son and servant responsible for enforcing the decisions which Henry made. In moments of crisis he had invariably shown qualities of determination and decisiveness, but ultimately there had always been a much greater power at his back. Now, with only himself to fall back on, he was forced to reveal very different qualities, forced himself to take a leading part in the affairs of the kingdom, and more often as an opponent of royal authority than as its supporter. It soon became clear that Geoffrey Plantagenet was not a man who could be ignored, that he had inherited the obduracy and quarrelsomeness of his father in as full a measure as had Henry's legitimate sons.

Richard and Geoffrey were not only political enemies, they were also personal enemies. Close in age, they had long been rivals. The reputation for military skill which Geoffrey had won in 1174 irked Richard, who longed for nothing more than to be renowned for his prowess in arms. Richard had always suspected Geoffrey of having designs on the English throne. Geoffrey, for his part, could never forgive Richard for his perfidy to their father. When the two men met, for the first time for several months, on the evening of Henry's death at Chinon, where Richard had come to pay his last respects to his father, each could be forgiven for feeling somewhat apprehensive about the intentions of the other. Richard stayed only long enough to gaze briefly at his dead father's face, say a short prayer, and then, leaving Geoffrey to make arrangements for Henry's funeral, went off to attend to his new responsibilities. Four days later they met again, when the dead king was buried in the nearby abbey church of Fontevrault. Richard asked Geoffrey to resign the chancellorship of England, which he did. The new king was, however, prepared to honour his father's dying wish: he nominated his half-brother for the archbishopric of York, and on 10 August a majority of the cathedral canons duly elected Geoffrey. Geoffrey was soon to find that the validity of his election was disputed, and the trouble which this caused him placed a powerful weapon in Richard's hands. For the moment, however, Richard needed to make friends, not enemies, and was in conciliatory mood. He desired nothing more than to be off on crusade, but before doing so he had to ensure that his kingdom would be well governed in his absence, and that nothing which might jeopardise his inheritance should occur while he was away.

Geoffrey's election as archbishop of York immediately brought him into conflict with two men who were to prove his bitterest foes during the next few troublesome years. The first was Hugh de Puiset, bishop of Durham, the most powerful churchman in the northern province of the English church after the archbishop of York. Puiset had been bishop of Durham since 1152. He was now approaching seventy, an enormous hulk of a man with a voice like the roar of a lion, eloquent and worldly, ostentatiously extravagant in his lifestyle, addicted to hunting, a consummate intriguer and a very astute politician. He and Geoffrey had clashed before, in 1174, when Geoffrey had forced him to give pledges for his loyalty during the great rebellion. Puiset, a proud and selfish man, resented being crossed. He had not been present at Geoffrey's election to the archbishopric on 10 August 1189. Nor had Hubert Walter, the dean of York, the second principal enemy whom Geoffrey made at this time. Hubert was unashamedly ambitious, and extremely able. Like Geoffrey, he had served faithfully in the royal administration under Henry II. He was to do so again under Richard; indeed, in a few years he was to reach a position of pre-eminence in the kingdom, second only to the king when he was in England, and virtual ruler of it when Richard was abroad. In 1186, the canons of York had put forward Hubert's name to the king as their next archbishop, but Henry had refused to sanction their choice. Now, with the election of Geoffrey, he felt cheated. A minority of the York canons had dissented strongly from Geoffrey's election. Without powerful leadership, they would no doubt soon have been overridden, but Puiset and Hubert Walter now determined to put themselves at the head of the dissenting party and to try to secure the annulment of the election. It was the opening round of a battle between Geoffrey and his opponents at York which was to last right through Richard's reign, and well into John's.

From the start, Richard was able to use Geoffrey's problems with his own canons as a lever on his half-brother. Despite the protests of Puiset and Hubert, he agreed on 16 September to confirm Geoffrey's election to the archbishopric, but only on condition that Geoffrey would receive ordination as a priest, and thus allay Richard's lingering fears that his father's bastard might still prove an acceptable candidate for the throne. Having received ordination, Geoffrey was promptly dispatched to the North to escort the king of Scotland to Canterbury, where he had agreed to swear fealty to Richard before the latter's departure on crusade. On his way north, however, Geoffrey found time to visit his cathedral at York, and immediately became embroiled in a dispute with the dissident canons there because of his refusal to appoint various men of their party to offices within the cathedral. The canons protested to Richard, who ordered that Geoffrey's estates should be seized. Thus by the time Geoffrey returned to Canterbury with the Scottish king, he found that Richard had once more turned against him. Queen Eleanor, recently released from her sixteen-year imprisonment, was back at court and whispering rumours about her husband's bastard. Puiset and Hubert were both with the king, urging Geoffrey's immediate demotion. He was surrounded by enemies, enemies who chattered that he was the son of a whore, and thus unfit to be an archbishop. All sorts of stories reached Richard's ears: it was said that Geoffrey had been observed to place a golden bowl-cover on his head and remark that it was a head eminently suited to the wearing of a crown; that he had trampled on a portrait of Richard, declaring that the new king had done nothing to deserve his crown. It was a situation which Richard could hardly fail to exploit. He had no desire to deprive Geoffrey of his archbishopric. What he did want was money, to finance his crusade. In return for a promise of £2,000 in cash by Easter, Richard agreed to restore Geoffrey's estates to him. It was no better than blackmail. It was scarcely two months since the king had confirmed his election, and now he was being asked to pay an enormous sum for the privilege of not having that confirmation revoked. Yet Geoffrey had no option but to agree. He returned to York to attempt to raise the money. Meanwhile, on 11 December 1189, Richard crossed from Dover on the first leg of his journey to the Holy Land. He was not to set foot in England again for over four years.

Geoffrey arrived back in York at the beginning of January 1190, and within a few days found himself in a sharper contest than ever. On 5 January, the eve of the Epiphany, he proposed to attend Vespers in the cathedral church in state. Those canons who supported him escorted him into the choir in solemn procession, but when they arrived there they found that the candles were already lit and the service had started without them.

Whether they had been late in arriving, or whether the dissident canons had decided to begin the service early to spite the archbishop they hated, there could be no doubt that a deliberate insult had been intended. Geoffrey's quick temper was aroused instantly. He ordered the singers to be silent in no uncertain terms, and began to sing the service himself. As soon as he did so the treasurer, one of the leaders of the dissidents, ordered the candles to be extinguished. The candles were the sole responsibility of the treasurer, and no amount of threats from Geoffrey could persuade any of the canons to relight them. He had to finish the service in the dark. As soon as it was over, he suspended the church from divine service and declared that it would remain suspended until an apology was forthcoming.

On the following day, matters went from bad to worse. Geoffrey, to his credit, offered to be reconciled to the dissident canons if they would apologise for their actions. The church was full of clergy and citizens who had come to witness the struggle. The two sides met in the choir, but the treasurer and his followers refused to apologise, and tried to provoke the citizens into a riot against their new archbishop. Unfortunately this backfired somewhat, for a riot did indeed follow, but the citizens took the part of Geoffrey rather than of the canons who opposed him, and it was left to Geoffrey to stop them falling on the treasurer and killing him. The discomfited dissidents took flight. Had Geoffrey, having gained a notable moral victory, been content to let matters rest there, he might have been able to secure his position with the canons once and for all. Unwisely, he tried to press home his victory by excommunicating the treasurer and another canon, and closing the church to all services. The consequences of the whole affair were disastrous for Geoffrey. The citizens of York, now fully aware of the tenuous nature of Geoffrey's hold on the archbishopric, refused to grant him a loan. Hugh de Puiset took the opportunity of stirring up further trouble for his rival by forbidding any of Geoffrey's tenants to make any payments to him. He had to return to the king at Easter without the money which he had been ordered to bring with him. He found Richard in France, told him his story, and Richard promptly confiscated his estates once more.

Yet again, circumstances had combined to place Geoffrey at his half-brother's mercy. Yet again, Richard knew well enough what he wanted from Geoffrey. He was prepared to rescind half the total debt of £2,000, as long as Geoffrey found £500 to give him at once and promised to pay a further £500 into the exchequer as soon as he could raise it. What Richard really wanted now was a promise from Geoffrey that he would not return to England for three years, that is, for as long as Richard expected to be absent on crusade. Richard had already extracted such a promise from his brother John. The king knew that it would be difficult enough for his appointed ministers to govern England in his absence without having his royal brother and half-brother on hand to serve as rallying-points for any potential opponents. In return, Richard promised to intercede with the pope to persuade him to agree to Geoffrey's consecration as archbishop of York, which, hopefully, would put an end to the dispute concerning the validity of his election. Geoffrey agreed; he had to agree. He returned to his academic home, Tours, where he remained for fifteen months. Richard went south to Marseilles, took boat to Sicily, and then on to the Holy Land. Hardly had he left France, however, than all his worst fears about the government of England during his absence began to be confirmed.

When he left England in December 1189, Richard appointed two justiciars to govern the kingdom jointly while he was away. One was Hugh de Puiset, Geoffrey's arch-enemy in the northern church, the other was William Longchamp. It would be hard to imagine a worse-matched pair. Puiset, the massive, magnificent bishop of Durham, descended from a great house of ancient nobility, soon found that he shared very little in common with his co-justiciar. Longchamp was a new man, and proud of it: he came from relatively humble origins, and had worked his way to prominence as a clerk under Geoffrey in the royal chancery in King Henry's later years. He was short, ugly and deformed – more like an ape than a man, said one contemporary. He walked with a limp, though if anything it seemed to make him walk faster than other men: he moved around 'like a flash of lightning'. He had tireless energy, arrogant self-confidence, and a decided lack of tact. He was a Frenchman, and made little effort to hide his contempt for the English. He would tolerate no opposition. He was unflinchingly, even ruthlessly, faithful to Richard, but next to the king's cause he placed the advancement of his own family. He had both the best and the worst qualities of the self-made man.

It took less than two months for Longchamp and Puiset to fall out. For much of the first half of 1190, the two men struggled to gain the upper hand, but by the middle of the year it was clear that Longchamp had won, and for the next year he was supreme. The eclipsed Hugh de Puiset began to search for ways of turning the tables on Longchamp, and he did not have to wait too long to find one. Early in 1191, John returned to England. He claimed that Richard had released him from his promise not to return for three years. Few men believed him, but it was of little consequence: it would be difficult for Longchamp to take action of too drastic a nature against Richard's brother, the probable heir to the English throne. Nevertheless, John's return placed Longchamp in an exceedingly awkward situation, for Longchamp's high-handed methods had alienated large sections of the baronage, and these men now turned to John to provide the focal point for opposition to the justiciar. John, realising that here was an opportunity to stir up the sort of dissension which might lead to his own seizure of the throne in his brother's absence – for nothing was in reality nearer to his heart – lost no time in espousing the cause of the disaffected. Hearing distant and delayed reports of the troubles in England, Richard sent Walter de Coutances, archbishop of Rouen, to mediate between the two factions, but Coutances soon found himself siding with John after a fruitless attempt at arbitration. The country was sliding inexorably into civil war. At this point, in September 1191, Geoffrey decided that he too must return to England.

Geoffrey had finally received his formal consecration as archbishop of York. It had been performed, at the request of Richard, and with the blessing of the pope, by the archbishop of Tours on 18 August 1191. He set out for England immediately and, despite Longchamp's attempts to prevent him crossing the Channel, arrived at Dover on 14 September. Like John, he claimed that Richard had released him from his oath, but Longchamp's men were ready for him. He received orders to proceed immediately to Dover castle, which he ignored. Hastily disguising himself, he made his way to a horse which was ready and waiting for him on the beach, and set off at full speed for the priory of St Martin in Dover. One of Longchamp's men recognised him and set off in pursuit, managing to seize Geoffrey's horse by the bridle, but Geoffrey, still agile at the age of forty, struck out with his right leg, dug his spur into his adversary's horse, and managed to get away. He reached the priory just as the canons were starting Mass. Within a few minutes the canons found their church surrounded by armed men.

The siege continued for four days. The knights sent by Longchamp demanded that Geoffrey take the oath of allegiance to the king and to the justiciar. Geoffrey, with his customary tact, replied that he had already sworn to be faithful to the king, but as for Longchamp, he had no intention of taking an oath of allegiance to a traitor. On the second day, a Sunday, the soldiers took possession of the church, but still they stopped short of physically dragging an archbishop from his sanctuary. Eventually, on the following Wednesday, their patience exhausted, they seized Geoffrey by the arms and legs and dragged him from the church, his head banging down the steps of the altar where he had been assisting at Mass. He was taken to Dover castle.

News of the outrage spread rapidly. It was only twenty years since Archbishop Thomas Becket had been murdered by four knights in Canterbury cathedral, an act which had profoundly shocked the whole of Christendom, and the parallel was obvious to all. The saintly Bishop Hugh of Lincoln excommunicated the offenders. Geoffrey became a national hero, though only briefly. For Longchamp, the affair was a disaster. Trying to undo what he had done, he swiftly sent messengers ordering Geoffrey's release, but it was the death-blow to his already crumbling authority in the

1 An impotence trial. From a late thirteenth-century North French edition of Gratian's *Decretum*, with commentary by Bartholomeus Brixiensis (Walters Art Gallery, W.133, fol. 277)

2 Charter of Henry I, 7 January 1121, notifying that he has granted the see of Hereford to Bishop Richard. The witness list includes (three lines from the end, in abbreviated form) the name of Robert (of Gloucester), the king's son: *Roberto filio regis*. The charter was issued shortly before Robert's elevation to the earldom of Gloucester; here his name heads the list of laymen below the rank of earl. The seal shows a representation of Henry I seated on his throne. (British Library Harleian Charter III B.46)

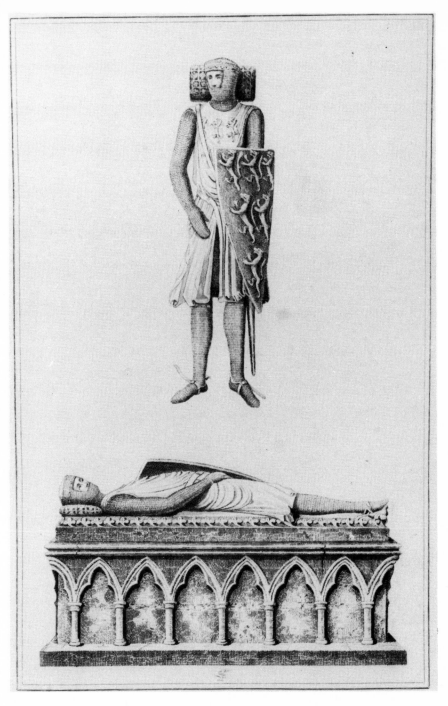

3(a)   Tomb and effigy of William Longsword (d.1226), earl of Salisbury, son of Henry II, in Salisbury cathedral

3(b) Seal of William Longsword

4 Below left Effigy of King John, Worcester cathedral. One chronicler wrote of John that he 'deflowered the wives and daughters of his nobles: not a woman was spared if he was seized by the desire to defile her in the heat of his lust.' He was the father of at least seven bastards

5 Below right Joan Skerne, daughter of Edward III and his mistress Alice Perrers. Rubbing of memorial brass in the church of All Saints, Kingston-upon-Thames. Joan married the lawyer Robert Skerne, and they lived at Down Hall in Kingston. This memorial brass was commissioned after Robert's death in 1437

4

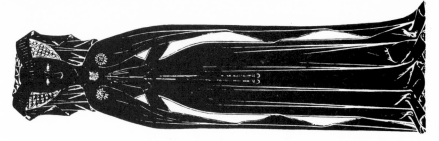

5

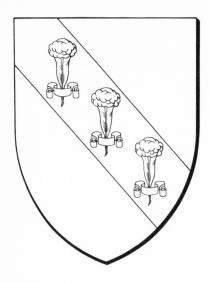

6(a) *Top left* Arms of Roger de Clarendon, son of Edward the Black Prince and his mistress Edith de Willesford. Roger adopted the ostrich plume and scroll of his father's favourite badge, set on a *bend* against a plain gold background. The paternal arms on a *bend* against a plain background were commonly, though not exclusively, used to denote illegitimacy in the fourteenth century

6(b) *Top right* Arms of John Beaufort, son of John of Gaunt and his mistress (later his wife) Katherine Swynford, before his legitimation in 1397. John adopted his father's royal arms as a *bend* of England (*bend gules charged with three lions passant guardant or*) with a label of France, set against a plain background

6(c) *Left* Arms of John Beaufort after legitimation. John has now quartered his father's royal arms on the shield itself, within a *bordure compony*; his adoption of this device led, ironically, to the belief that the *bordure compony* was a mark of illegitimacy, whereas in fact it had normally been used before this to denote legitimate cadency

7   Oil-painting of Edward IV (1461–83), by an unknown artist, but probably based
on a portrait drawn from life. The chronicler Dominic Mancini said of Edward that he
'pursued with no discrimination the married and the unmarried, the noble and the
lowly; however, he took none by force. He overcame all by money and promises, and
having conquered them, he dismissed them.' Edward fathered at least three bastards.
(Royal Collection, Windsor Castle)

8 Arms of Arthur Plantagenet, Viscount Lisle (d.1542), son of Edward IV and his mistress Elizabeth Lucy. Arthur bore the royal arms quartered with the arms of March and Ulster (of which his father was earl), traversed by a *bendlet sinister* to denote illegitimacy. The *bendlet* (or *baton*, a truncated *bendlet*) *sinister* was by now becoming the usual mark to denote a royal bastard. (Society of Antiquaries MS.442, Garter Roll 16 Henry VIII)

kingdom. Geoffrey was released on 26 September after eight days in captivity, made his way to London where he received a martyr's acclaim, and by 3 October had joined John, Hugh de Puiset and the other malcontents at Oxford. Longchamp had achieved the apparently impossible: uniting Geoffrey and Puiset in a common aim. After a fruitless attempt to parley at Reading on 5 October, he made a dash for the Tower of London and blockaded himself within it, hurling spiritual anathemas at all those who dared to oppose him. Longchamp might still have saved himself: the citizens of London were divided, trusting no more in John and Geoffrey than they did in the justiciar himself. But John, as usual, promised all for the future, and the citizens admitted him with his followers. A great assembly was held at St Paul's: Geoffrey recounted the story of his arrest at Dover and succeeded in arousing the Londoners in fury against Longchamp. It was decided that he must be deposed from the justiciarship and replaced by the archbishop of Rouen. John became regent, and was recognised as Richard's heir. A delegation led by John, Geoffrey and Puiset went to the Tower to inform Longchamp of the decision. At first he swooned, but once he had been revived with a liberal sprinkling of cold water he set about trying to bribe John and argue with the bishops. It was to no avail: the disdainful little Frenchman who had made no secret of his contempt for the English had now united Englishmen from all classes and of all political persuasions in a common desire to be rid of him. He was forced to accede to the demands of his opponents, and was then allowed to go. He set off at once for the Continent. To complete his misery, no sooner had his boat landed on the coast of Flanders than he was seized, robbed and held to ransom by a band of Flemish mercenaries.

Once the Longchamp affair had subsided and order had been restored to the southern counties, Geoffrey returned to York determined to enforce his authority over the unruly canons who had made a mockery of his last visit. Needless to say, he arrived now with far greater authority than on previous occasions: the pope had confirmed his election, he had been formally consecrated as archbishop, his treatment at the hands of Longchamp had elevated him to the status of a champion of popular liberties, and there was even a chance that, having once made common cause with Hugh de Puiset over the Longchamp affair, he might now be able to reach some form of agreement with his high and mighty northern neighbour. It took no more than a few weeks for all these hopes to be dashed. As a demonstration of his new-found authority, Geoffrey decided that he should be solemnly enthroned as archbishop in his cathedral. The enthronement, a magnificent affair, was held on 2 November 1191, but Puiset failed to turn up. Geoffrey summoned him to account for his absence. Puiset ignored the summons, so Geoffrey excommunicated him. The dissident York canons, realising that they could still count on the support of Puiset in their struggle to be rid of Geoffrey, refused to co-operate with the officials whom Geoffrey had appointed, so he excommunicated them too. When the prioress of Clementhorpe refused to agree to Geoffrey's plans for reorganising her nunnery, she was excommunicated as well.

Quite why Geoffrey behaved as he did at this stage is difficult to understand, but during the next few years he seems to have been consistently at pains to reveal the worst and most uncompromising side of his character. It is true that many of the men with whom he had to deal were no less arrogant and obstinate than himself, but for a further decade the northern province of the English church, of which Geoffrey was nominal head, continued in utter turmoil, amidst a welter of accusations and counter-accusations, excommunications and counter-excommunications, and it is impossible to avoid laying much of the blame for this on the behaviour of its archbishop. Geoffrey seems to have had a genius for tactlessness. When Queen Eleanor summoned him and Puiset to come before her and settle their differences by mediation, he insisted on appearing in solemn procession, with his archiepiscopal cross carried erect before him, at the Temple in London: he knew full well that the archbishop of York might only have his cross borne before him within his own northern province, but the vacant archbishopric of Canterbury had not yet been filled at this time, and it was a situation which Geoffrey was trying to exploit to his best advantage. He merely succeeded in enraging several of the bishops of the southern province – i.e. those subject to the authority of Canterbury rather than York – as well. Refusing to be reconciled with Puiset until the latter made a solemn promise of obedience, he returned to York and within a few months had once again excommunicated several of his canons for contumacy. The canons' reply to this was to close the minster, forbid the ringing of bells, strip the altars, lock up the archbishop's stall in the choir, and block up the door by which Geoffrey entered the church from his archiepiscopal palace. They then walked out, leaving him to his personal servants.

By now men who had originally been Geoffrey's supporters, men who had served him loyally for many years and had in return been rewarded by him for their service, were beginning to turn against him. Simon of Apulia had been Geoffrey's personal agent in Rome in 1190. He had been the leader of Geoffrey's retinue on the occasion of his celebrated return to England in September 1191. Now, in 1193, the position of dean of the cathedral became vacant. Geoffrey first promised it to Simon, then, having secured Simon's election by the canons, he informed Simon that he had changed his mind and decided instead to give the post to his brother, Peter (Peter was probably not a royal bastard, but a half-brother of Geoffrey's on his mother's side). Simon refused to give up the post, an angry scene followed, and both parties appealed to the king. When Richard, now back from the Holy Land, summoned Geoffrey to his presence, Geoffrey failed to appear, and Richard confirmed Simon's appointment. From this time onwards the new dean became one of the archbishop's implacable foes, and he took with him into the party of opposition several other men who had formerly been Geoffrey's supporters. By this time, however, new trouble was brewing for Geoffrey, for in May 1193 his old opponent at York, the former dean, Hubert Walter, was created archbishop of Canterbury.

Looking at Geoffrey's career in retrospect, one gets the impression that it was in about 1193 or 1194 that he reached the point of no return. No more than five years had elapsed since his father's death and his own nomination to the archbishopric of York, yet in those few short years he had managed to alienate almost everyone with whom he had come into contact. The great majority of the canons at York, even those whom he had appointed himself, were now ranged against him. Virtually every one of the English bishops had become his personal enemy. Increasingly he has the appearance of a man set apart from others, bearing a grudge against the world and all who lived in it, a lonely and desperate figure driven deeper into holes of his own making, for whom the path of reconciliation could only lead to total surrender. Between him and Hubert Walter there seems to have been a peculiarly intense hatred. His first action following Hubert's election to the archbishopric of Canterbury was to appear before him at a council in London with his cross borne erect before him; and on leaving the council to make his way to the Continent to find King Richard, he sought out little-known tracks and byways so that he could bypass Canterbury and continue to have his cross borne before him through Hubert's home territory without encountering opposition. When Richard pleaded with him not to insist on having his cross borne before him at the king's coronation in April 1194, Geoffrey responded by boycotting the coronation altogether. (Richard had been crowned at his accession in 1189, but now decided to mark his return and resumption of full power with a second, symbolic, ceremony.)

Hubert, for his part, was determined to undermine Geoffrey's authority in the North. He remembered, as did Geoffrey, the time when he had been dean of York and had been forced to accept Geoffrey as his superior. Then he had felt balked, but now the tables had been turned. Hubert was a practical statesman of the highest ability, and when Richard conferred upon him the title of chief justiciar as well as archbishop of Canterbury in December 1193, he made the wisest decision of his reign. Hubert's power was now immense, for he was head of the English church, and head of state in the king's absence. Hubert sent a commission to investigate Geoffrey's conduct of affairs in his arch-diocese. Geoffrey refused to appear before it, and once again his estates were seized. The findings of the commission were damning: the only spiritual function which the archbishop of York discharged, so they claimed, was that of excommunication. For the rest, he spent most of his time hunting and hawking. The canons whom he had excommunicated were reinstated. He was ordered in future to issue no sentences against any of his canons without the consent of the whole body of canons. His authority had been rendered worthless; he realised that his position in England was untenable, and at the end of 1194 he left to find Richard on the Continent. He was not to set foot in England again for over five years.

Meanwhile, Pope Celestine III had decided that the course of events at York could no longer be tolerated, and summoned Geoffrey to Rome to explain his behaviour. When Geoffrey refused to obey the summons, the pope suspended him. Once again Geoffrey turned to Richard to ask him to intercede for him with Celestine but, having begun by begging a favour from the king, he then went on to rebuke Richard for the immoral life that he led, and warned him that he ought to mend his ways. Richard could take no more. He flew into a violent rage, ordered Geoffrey from his presence, and once again confiscated his estates, which he had previously agreed to restore.

So matters continued, unresolved and with no apparent hope of resolution. While he remained in France, Geoffrey exercised no authority in his arch-diocese. In 1198 the new pope, Innocent III, tried to effect a reconciliation between the archbishop and his canons, but when the canons were informed that they were once more to have Geoffrey in their midst, only one of them, a man called Hugh Murdac, declared himself ready to receive him back, whereupon the unfortunate man was promptly excommunicated by Simon of Apulia, who was still dean. Before the pope could take any further action, King Richard was dead, killed by a sniper's bolt while besieging the castle of Chalus-Chabrol, on 7 April 1199.

With the death of Richard, Geoffrey might have been forgiven for thinking that the worst of his troubles were now over. Richard's profound animosity towards his illegitimate half-brother, and the intense personal rivalry which had embittered relations between the two men, meant that he had always been willing to exploit Geoffrey's misfortunes to the best of his ability. Geoffrey's relationship with John was quite different. For nigh on sixteen years, until John's final treachery to his father in the summer of 1189, they had been the only two of Henry II's sons who had genuinely enjoyed his confidence and affection, the only two who regularly travelled round with Henry on his great journeys from one end of his vast dominions to the other. In 1191, they had acted together to rid the country of Long-champ. Although the events of 1189 must have soured their relationship somewhat, and although Geoffrey had remained loyal to the king when John's impatience to wear the crown had led him to start a rebellion in the autumn of 1192, there had been no personal clashes between the two men as there had been between Geoffrey and Richard. There was over fifteen years' difference in their ages, too, which greatly reduced the likelihood of personal rivalry. At the time of his accession John was only thirty-two, whereas Geoffrey was approaching fifty.

John had most of the worst qualities of his father, and some of the best ones. In his youth he seems to have been regarded as an idle waster. In later years, although he retained his fondness for sensual pleasures, he also developed a capacity for hard work. Ultimately, he was every bit as energetic a king as his father had been. He had a sharp and inquisitive mind, an ability to grasp detail, and an inclination to meddle in everything. Like all the Angevins, he was intolerant of opposition, and ruthless in suppressing it. His personal cruelty was demonstrated on many occasions. Cunning, devious and untrustworthy himself, he was eternally suspicious of others. He never gained the reputation for personal bravery which both his father and his brother had enjoyed. He regarded the acquisition of wealth as of primary importance to the monarchy, and seldom displayed the generosity which had enabled both Henry and Richard to win men over. It is true that he lived in an age of rapid inflation, but his unpleasantly blatant greed was one of the most important factors contributing to the many disasters of his reign. By the time he died in 1216, he had lost Normandy to the French, quarrelled so violently with the pope that the whole of England had been laid under interdict for six years, and been forced by his exasperated barons to concede the most famous charter of liberties in English history – Magna Carta. Even so, his reign ended in civil war. Despite the problems which he faced, in an age when monarchy was so personal, much of the blame for the political turmoil of his reign must rest with John himself. He had, as a recent biographer has remarked, 'the mental abilities of a great king, but the inclinations of a petty tyrant'.

Initially though, John had even more need to be conciliatory than had Richard ten years earlier, for his claim to the throne was disputed by his nephew Arthur, and powerful men must be convinced that he was a king worth fighting for. Soon after Richard's death, John and Geoffrey met at Rouen and swore to be brothers and friends to each other. For several months the new king remained in France, consolidating his hold on his Continental dominions, and Geoffrey remained with him. In February 1200 they returned to England together. It was the first time that Geoffrey had set foot on English soil for over five years, but now, with the promise of royal support to back him up, he must have been hopeful of being able finally to subdue his opponents at York. And so, initially, it turned out. One of John's first acts on his return was to summon the recalcitrant dean, Simon of Apulia, to effect a reconciliation with Geoffrey at Westminster. Simon duly appeared, and was persuaded to acknowledge Geoffrey as his archbishop. In return, Geoffrey recognised Simon as dean, and agreed that all past differences should be sorted out by consultation with the canons. Under the watchful eye of the king, the two men swallowed their pride, agreed to forget the past, and solemnly gave each other the kiss of peace. Geoffrey then returned to York.

It was, unfortunately, the briefest of reconciliations. Within a few weeks of Geoffrey's return, the archdeaconry of Cleveland, one of the richest pickings in the arch-diocese of York, fell vacant. Geoffrey nominated one of his followers for appointment, but the canons, led by Simon of Apulia, refused to sanction his choice; instead, they elected Hugh Murdac – that same Hugh Murdac who was the only canon to support Geoffrey's reinstatement in 1198, and whom the dean had then excommunicated for voicing that support. Hugh had since been reconciled to his fellow canons, but Geoffrey was furious at the canons' opposition and now retaliated by excommunicating him. Thus the wretched Murdac, having once been excommunicated for supporting his archbishop against the canons, was now excommunicated for a second time for supporting the canons against the archbishop. So once more the administration of Geoffrey's arch-diocese was in turmoil: the reconciliation had proved as shallow as many men must have suspected that it would be. Both sides, as usual, appealed to the king.

Geoffrey now committed an act of singular stupidity. His standing with the king was high. So far, John had shown himself willing to throw his support behind his brother in a way that Richard had never done. But when John now summoned Geoffrey to accompany him back to France, Geoffrey ignored the summons. At the same time, he refused to allow John's officials to collect a tax on the lands of the archbishopric. At a stroke, he had forfeited the royal support which had been the main cause of his restoration to his archbishopric only a few months earlier. John, not surprisingly feeling betrayed, ordered that all Geoffrey's estates should be seized. Geoffrey responded by excommunicating the sheriff of Yorkshire and all those others who, he claimed, had poisoned John's mind against him. He also found time to excommunicate the townspeople of Beverley, a number of whom had broken into one of the archiepiscopal parks. After a few welcome months of harmony, Geoffrey once more found himself in the same absurd position as he had been in throughout most of Richard's reign, faced by both a hostile king and a hostile cathedral administration, each feeding off the other in their attempts to outmanoeuvre him. He had little but his own folly to blame.

For the next few years, his life followed much the same depressing pattern as it had in the 1190s. He was usually able to buy John's support back with promises of money, but no sooner had he done so than he once again lost that support by some act of gross tactlessness or simple pig-headedness.

The York canons, emboldened by the knowledge that the king found their archbishop as exasperating as they did, continually snapped at his heels and thwarted his attempts to reduce them to obedience. In 1201 the king appealed to the pope against his archbishop. In return for the promise of £1,000, John agreed not to press his suit at Rome, but by March 1204 matters within the cathedral had reached such a desperate state that the king had personally to take the canons under his protection against Geoffrey. Early in 1205 the new bishop of Durham, Philip de Poitiers, the entire body of canons at York, and the heads of fourteen religious houses in Geoffrey's arch-diocese jointly appealed to the pope, in the king's presence, against sentences of excommunication and suspension imposed by Geoffrey. At this stage there can have been few men of influence in the northern province of the church who had not been excommunicated by the archbishop at some time in their careers; it had become almost a qualification for high office within the arch-diocese. Once again Geoffrey managed to patch up his relationship with the king with an offer of money when the two half-brothers met at Worcester in January 1207. By this time, however, matters were hurrying to a conclusion. It must have become obvious to all that peace would not be restored to the cathedral until Geoffrey had been got rid of. For nearly two decades, the administration of the northern province of the English church had been subordinated to the bitter and divisive personal wranglings of its chief officials. Geoffrey was still only fifty-five, and showed no signs of either mellowing or dying. So it was that a final trial of strength had to be fought out, one in which Geoffrey again appears to have seen himself as the fervent champion of ecclesiastical liberties, but which once again ended in his own ruin. And this time, there was to be no going back.

In February 1207, only a few weeks after his latest reconciliation with Geoffrey, John tried to impose a tax on the entire clergy of the country. His need for money was desperate: three years earlier, King Philip of France had overrun Normandy, and since then John had been engaged in a continuous series of costly and futile campaigns to try to recapture the duchy. The bishops, led by Geoffrey, refused to countenance the tax. John, in desperation, demanded a proportion of one-thirteenth of all the goods and chattels belonging to lay people in England. Then, ignoring the opposition of the bishops, he ordered the archdeacons from each diocese to levy the same proportion from every member of the English clergy. The royal writ to the archdeacons was issued from York, almost as if John was deliberately trying to goad his principal opponent among the bishops into an act of open defiance. At this point the other bishops, seeing that resistance was pointless, climbed down and allowed the tax. Geoffrey, in his inimitable manner, rose straight to the bait. He immediately forbade the collection of the tax in his arch-diocese, under pain of excommunication.

Too late, he realised that he stood alone. The incensed King John, determined to have his money, began muttering personal threats against his half-brother. No one dared resist his demands. Geoffrey, in fear of his life, fled overseas into French-occupied Normandy. His last act before leaving England, appropriately enough, was to hurl sentences of excommunication against all those who either collected or paid the tax, together with all spoilers of the church in general.

Geoffrey never set foot in England again. Naturally, the king seized his estates. Within a few months John had become embroiled in a much greater quarrel with the church, over the question of the appointment of a new archbishop of Canterbury, a quarrel which was to result in Pope Innocent III's excommunication of the king and the laying of the whole of England under interdict. So although Geoffrey managed to secure the pope's support for his cause, in practical terms that support was worthless. He lived on for another five years, an unfriended, embittered, lonely figure, growing old in exile, powerless to help his own cause, a pathetic shadow of the once mighty archbishop of York. He died on 18 December 1212, at the monastery of Notre-Dame-du-Parc, a house of the Grandmontine order near Rouen, and was buried in the monastic church there. It was, appropriately, a monastery which had been especially favoured by Henry II: he had brought the men of Grandmont there from Aquitaine, to take care of a leper-house which he had established on the site of his old hunting-lodge outside Rouen. If Geoffrey had lived but a few more months, he would have had the satisfaction of witnessing John's eventual submission to the papacy, the raising of the English interdict, and very probably his own restoration to his archbishopric of York. Perhaps it was fortunate that he did not.

'Reflections on his story are needless,' concluded one of Geoffrey's biographers, and in a way they are. Yet one is left with a lingering sense of uneasiness about Geoffrey, a feeling that although many of his actions are explicable in terms of his irascible, uncompromising and abrasive personality, there still remains much that, for sheer pig-headedness, borders on the inexplicable. He was a man of the fiercest qualities: unshakeable in his loyalty to his father, unflinching in his determination to impose his will upon his canons at York, unwavering to the end in his determination to resist royal demands for taxation. The change which was forced upon him after 1189 was almost as sudden as the change which overcame that other great twelfth-century English churchman, Thomas Becket, when Henry II foolishly forced Becket to become archbishop of Canterbury. Becket was a man who excelled in role-playing: as the king's chief lay minister, he saw it as his duty to further the interests of the crown with every weapon at his disposal; when he became archbishop of Canterbury, he devoted all his energies to resisting those demands. Whatever his part, he acted it to the full, and in the end he paid for it with his life. There are many similarities between Geoffrey's career and that of Thomas Becket. Geoffrey too fulfilled his roles with almost blind disregard for the consequences. Like Becket, he never really wanted high office in the church: he was happiest during the years that he served as his father's secular chancellor, and when he became archbishop of York he tried to govern his cathedral with all the high-handed authority of a lay lord, making little allowance for the more complex decision-making machinery of the church. Although worldly, he was personally pure: they could call him whoreson, but never whore-monger. He was not a cunning man: his strength lay not in artful trickery, but in the passionate intensity of his convictions. He was quite unable to exploit situations to his advantage, as politicians like Hubert Walter and Hugh de Puiset did. Finding himself unable to beat them at their own game, and being a man whose patience was very rapidly exhausted, he repeatedly resorted to drastic action on occasions when a little diplomacy would have been repaid a hundredfold. Under Geoffrey, the northern province of the English church passed through one of its darkest hours. Yet for over thirty years he was a towering figure in English history, and although it was his own arrant self-righteousness which steered him inexorably on the path to self-destruction, in the end it is difficult to deny him a certain misguided greatness.

CHAPTER 9

THE BASTARDS OF RICHARD I AND KING JOHN

The reigns of Richard I (1189–99) and John (1199–1216) were both dominated by the difficulty of holding together Henry II's empire. Richard is deservedly famous as a soldier, above all as a crusader, yet his long sojourn in the Holy Land, his year's captivity in Germany, and his wars against his rebellious subjects in France conspired to keep him away from England for all but six months of his reign. Indeed, English contemporaries often complained of the way he treated their country: he seemed to regard it as nothing but a bottomless coffer to finance campaign after campaign, to say nothing of his famous ransom of £100,000.

Despite eight years of marriage to Berengaria of Navarre, Richard failed to provide an heir. It has sometimes been suggested that he was homosexual, but this is extremely unlikely. The allegation is based solely on two thoroughly ambiguous remarks by the chronicler Roger of Howden, and there are many other stories told of Richard, or remarks made about him, which point clearly to the fact that he was heterosexual (see for instance, p. 14). He is also known to have fathered at least one bastard. This was Philip de Cognac, born to an unknown mistress some years before Richard became king. Philip is a shadowy figure of whom very little is known for certain, and who is better known to most as the bastard Philip de Faulconbridge in Shakespeare's *King John*. Richard gave him the castle and honour of Cognac (Charente), hence his name. Amelie, daughter of the lord of Cognac, may also have been given to him in marriage.

The only noteworthy exploit attributed to Philip was the murder of the vicomte of Limoges, whom he held responsible for the death of his father. In the spring of 1199, Richard went to besiege the castle of Chalus-Chabrol in the Limousin, where the vicomte, Adhemar, was resisting his lordship. A crossbow bolt fired by a lone sniper on the walls of the castle struck the king in the shoulder, gangrene set in, and he died on 7 April. Although Richard is said personally to have pardoned the sniper before he died, Philip apparently considered that Adhemar was to blame, and subsequently sought him out and murdered him. Whether there is any truth in the story – recorded in only one chronicle – it is difficult to say. Philip is next heard of in England in 1201, when he sold his lordship to King John and promptly disappeared from the records.

Richard's death had come unexpectedly, and because he had left no legitimate children the succession to his enormous dominions was disputed. Was the rightful heir John, the fourth and now the only surviving legitimate son of Henry II, or was it Arthur, only child of Geoffrey, Henry II's third son (see Table 2)? By primogenitary custom Arthur was Richard's heir, but primogeniture was not universally accepted in either England or France, and Arthur was but a boy of twelve. What really mattered was to secure the support of a sufficient number of powerful men on either side of the Channel, and this John managed to do. Within a few weeks he had been crowned king of England, and despite all the disasters of his reign, he managed to keep his hold on the crown until his death in 1216. It is worth noting that despite the succession dispute, which might have created the sort of situation which a royal bastard could turn to his advantage, it is clear that no one even considered the idea that Philip de Cognac might be a candidate for the throne.

John had a reputation for lasciviousness. 'He deflowered the wives and daughters of his nobles: not a woman was spared if he was seized by the desire to defile her in the heat of his lust' – so wrote the Cistercian chronicler of Meaux. A French chronicler claimed that John lusted after beautiful women greatly, and thereby caused shame to the great men of his realm, by whom he was hated. Neither of these writers was unbiased, but John certainly had many mistresses and at least seven bastards.

John was married twice, his first wife being Isabel of Gloucester, grand-daughter of Henry I's bastard Robert of Gloucester. He seems to have paid little attention to her. She bore him no children in their ten-year marriage, and he divorced her on grounds of consanguinity (they were second cousins) in 1199, shortly after becoming king. His second wife was Isabel of Angoulême, who was married to him in 1200. Seven years later she did what her namesake had been unable to do, and gave birth to the future Henry III. Whatever the quality of their marriage may have been, there is little doubt that, while few if any of his seven or eight bastards were born after 1200, John continued to take mistresses to the end of his life.

The careers of his bastards were, with one exception, insignificant in comparison to those of Henry I's and Henry II's bastards, and his mistresses are known by little more than name, if that. The damoiselle Susanna, a 'friend of the king's' was given a tunic and super-tunic in 1213; £30 was paid to a royal mistress in 1209; a chaplet of roses was sent from the justiciar's garden to another mistress in 1212. Somewhat more ambiguous references occur: 'Alpesia, the queen's damoiselle' was ordered to be brought under escort to the king on 14 July 1214; in 1205 a tun of wine was sent on John's instruction to Henry Biset to be given to his wife, and so on. Sometimes the women were of unknown or low birth but, if the Meaux chronicler was correct, John had no qualms about seducing aristocratic ladies. Eustace de Vesci's wife might have been one who experienced his advances, for it is said that de Vesci was hated by the king 'because he had placed a common woman instead of his wife in the royal bed'. Robert FitzWalter claimed that his daughter Matilda, wife of Geoffrey de Mandeville, had been seduced by John. Both de Vesci and FitzWalter, it must be said, were particular enemies of John's, being leaders of the baronial rebellions which convulsed the later years of the reign. Their claims, made partly in justification for their rebellion against John, can hardly be considered reliable. The French chronicler quoted earlier was almost certainly depending to some extent on their testimony for his information about John's treatment of his nobles' womenfolk.

One of John's bastards, however, was undoubtedly the son of the sister of William, earl of Warenne. There is also an extraordinary document which has always teased the imagination of historians in stating that 'the wife of Hugh de Neville gives the lord king two hundred chickens that she may lie one night with her lord, Hugh de Neville'. Whether she was being used by John as a mistress against her will, or being detained as a hostage, or whether something entirely different should be deduced, will continue to be a matter for speculation. Equally suggestive and just as puzzling is the way in which John assisted the heirs of Hawise, countess of Aumâle, after her death. Instead of demanding a vast sum of money for the relief of her barony by her son William de Fortibus, John took nothing. Moreover, he forgave the fine of 5,000 marks which Hawise had only just begun to pay for her inheritance on the death of her husband, and he also gave William's new bride a marriage-portion worth 40 marks a year. Might Hawise have been a favourite mistress? Returning to the realms of certainty, however, two other mistresses are known by name, being the mothers of two of John's bastards. Hawise (but not the countess of Aumâle) gave birth to Oliver, the king's son. She had some claim to land in Kent and it is possible that she was a Tracy. Finally, bringing the number of possible royal mistresses to at least a dozen, 'Queen' Clementia is said to have been the mother of Joan, John's only known illegitimate daughter.

Although nothing whatever is known about Clementia, the same is not true about her daughter, for Joan married Llewelyn ap Iorwerth, prince of North Wales, in 1206 or 1207 and she became an influential figure in diplomatic affairs between England and Wales. During an attack by John on North Wales in 1211, Llewelyn was so hard pressed that 'by the advice of his liegemen, [he] sent his wife, who was the daughter of the king, to make peace between him and the king in any manner that she might be able'. Llewelyn was granted a safe-conduct and John accepted his submission for Joan's sake. The English king was dissuaded from another expedition into Wales when Joan warned him of treachery amongst his barons in 1212, and three years later her intervention secured the release of some Welsh hostages. She maintained a friendly relationship with Henry III, meeting him formally on occasion in the Marches, and in 1229 she and her son David did homage to the king at Westminster, presumably on behalf of Llewelyn. Three years earlier Pope Honorius had declared her legitimate, but without prejudice to Henry III or the realm of England. It has been suggested that this implies that she was the child of the divorced Isabel of Gloucester, but there is no evidence that Isabel had any children and in 1226 Joan would have been seeking legitimation as the wife of an important prince, rather than because she had incurred bastardisation through the divorce of her parents. In any case the church did not insist on bastardisation by divorce until later.

Joan's own children were David and Ellen. David succeeded his father as prince of North Wales in 1240, and Ellen married first John Scot, earl of Chester and heir to the Scottish throne before he died in 1237, then Robert de Quinci. Joan's two stepdaughters were called Gladys and Margaret. Gladys's stepson was William de Braose, who had at one time been taken as a prisoner to one of Llewelyn's castles. One version of the story suggests that he managed to endear himself to the prince and his family and, after he had been ransomed, Llewelyn discovered that he had been having an affair with Joan. Whether or not this is true Llewelyn did later (1230) find him in Joan's bedchamber, having perhaps tricked him to go there so that he would fall into a trap. De Braose was hanged and, according to an old ballad which portrays Joan as William's lover, she was led, while still unaware of what had happened, to view the hanging:

> 'Lovely princess', said Llewelyn,
> 'What will you give to see your Willim?'
> 'Wales and England and Llewelyn,
> I'd freely give to see my Willim.'

Historians have been cautious in accepting Joan's role in the episode as anything other than her husband's accomplice, and the pair must have been on good terms by the time of her death in 1236 or 1237, for Llewelyn built a Franciscan house in her memory and over her grave at Llanvaes in Anglesey. The coffin was removed during the Reformation and used afterwards as a horse trough, but it and the covering slab, said to portray the princess, were rescued in the early nineteenth century and taken to Baron Hill, Beaumaris.

Joan's illegitimate brothers figure only marginally in contemporary affairs. Oliver helped in the repulse of the French forces during the last year of John's reign and again under Henry III, when he took part in the defence of Dover. The castle of Tonge, the manor of Erdington and (temporarily) the estate of Hamedon were granted him in the early years of Henry III's minority. In 1218 he joined the Fifth Crusade and died the following year at Damietta in unknown circumstances. His body seems to have been brought back to England, because the antiquarian William Camden (1551–1623) recorded its burial place in Westminster Abbey. Geoffrey, the king's son, held the honour of Perche and was at the head of a band of mercenaries who were to embark at Dartmouth on an expedition to Poitou in 1205. He died the same year. Another son, Richard de Dover or de Chilham, son of the earl of Warenne's sister, was a captain in John's army during the baronial revolt. During Henry III's minority he remained faithful to the royal house and was active in a campaign against Prince Louis in 1217. In 1214 he had been given an heiress in marriage, Rohese, daughter of the lord of Dover and baron of Chilham.

John, Henry, Osbert Giffard and perhaps a Eudo (or Ivo) and another Richard are the names of the remaining bastard sons. Osbert Giffard is easily confused with a contemporary of the same name and goes almost unrecorded; John was perhaps a clerk at Lincoln, where he was being supported by the custodians of the see in 1201; a Richard, the king's son, who might possibly have been a different man from the lord of Dover, was constable of Wallingford castle in 1216, and in 1240 a 'Eudo FitzRoy', said to be the illegitimate son of King John (who had been dead for twenty-four years by now), was mentioned. He may have been the same person as the royal bastard Ivo recorded at about the same time. Henry FitzRoy received lands in Cornwall and married a minor heiress. King John referred to him, somewhat euphemistically, as Henry 'who calls himself our son, but is really our nephew'; however, there is no evidence that he was instead a bastard of Richard's or Geoffrey's and later in John's reign he is referred to as 'Henry our son'.

Whether John was really the unprincipled ravisher of all beautiful women is debatable. His reputation for lechery, as for so much else, depends partly on unreliable and unfriendly sources, but nonetheless he did have a considerable number of known bastards, more than any medieval king apart from Henry I, and at least a few of his somewhat shadowy mistresses are documented. The twelfth century was undoubtedly the golden age for royal bastards in England, yet the relatively insignificant careers of John's bastards stand in sharp contrast to the careers of many of Henry I's and Henry II's bastards. By the early years of the thirteenth century, there are clear signs that things were changing: William Longsword was the last royal bastard to rise to the peerage in England for over three hundred years; Morgan's inability to persuade Pope Innocent III to overlook the consequences of his birth in 1213 is as telling as Joan's decision to apply for official legitimation by Pope Honorius III in 1226. Materially, she stood to gain nothing from it, for it was specifically stated that she should be excluded from the inheritance of any of her father's lands. It was simply a reflection of a long-term and deep-rooted change in attitudes towards bastardy, a change which affected royal bastards just as much as it did humbler ones.

PART III

ROYAL BASTARDS
IN LATE
MEDIEVAL
ENGLAND

Royal bastards played a much less conspicuous role in late medieval English history than they had done under the Norman and Angevin kings, and the reasons for this were twofold. Firstly, the late medieval English kings on average produced far fewer illegitimate children than their predecessors: of the eleven kings who ruled England between 1216 and 1485, only four brought clearly identifiable illegitimate offspring into the world (Edward II, Edward III, Edward IV, and Richard III). The total number of bastards produced by these four (excluding doubtful attributions) was just nine, less than half the number which Henry I had managed on his own. Secondly, the offices, privileges and status accorded to royal bastards declined. No longer did they attain high office in church or state. Not until the sixteenth century did a royal bastard once again rise to the peerage; the heirs to the tradition established by Robert of Gloucester and Geoffrey 'Plantagenet' were not the royal bastards of late medieval England, but the illegitimate children of Henry VIII and Charles II. However, there was more to this than just a change in attitudes towards bastardy. Personality invariably played a large part in determining the treatment accorded to royal bastards. Deprived of the automatic status accorded to the legitimate offspring of a king, they could only hope to achieve real political prominence or high office on the merits of their individual ability. After all, Henry I granted an earldom to only one of his nine illegitimate sons, and everything we know of Robert of Gloucester suggests that he was fully worthy of the honour. The evidence we have concerning most of the royal bastards of late medieval England does not suggest that they were particularly suitable candidates for high office. Nevertheless, some of them certainly left their mark on English history.

It is extremely unlikely that Henry III (1216–72) had mistresses; certainly no bastards of his are recorded. It is possible, though unlikely, that Edward I (1272–1307) had an illegitimate son. There is a tradition that Sir John Botetourt, one of the knights of Edward I's household, was really the king's bastard, and it is true that Botetourt's origins are mysterious: he styled himself Lord of Mendlesham (Suffolk), and other members of the Botetourt family held property in East Anglia, but there is no clear information as to who his parents were. It is also true that he was especially favoured by Edward. From at least 1285 he was a knight of the royal household, and pursued a long and active military career until shortly before his death in 1324. He also became a regular member of the royal council, was admiral

135

of the North Sea fleet, and in 1305 received a personal summons to parliament, making him one of the 'lords' rather than the 'commons'.

However, the evidence for his royal paternity is far from conclusive. The solitary reference upon which the tradition is based is a genealogical table in the chronicle of Hailes abbey (in the British Library), where his name is in fact written in over an erasure, which makes its authenticity highly questionable. Also, Botetourt's coat of arms (*Or*, a saltire engrailed *sable*) carries no hint of royal blood. It is true that there were rumours of youthful indiscretions on the part of Edward before he became king. In 1265, for instance, when imprisoned by Simon de Montfort's followers at Dover castle, he is said to have fallen in love with an unnamed lady whom his mother sent to him to help him escape; this rather vague legend may be no more than a corruption of a similar story told about Richard the Lionheart when he was imprisoned by the German emperor. Soon after this, however, the more reliable chronicler of Bury St Edmunds reported rumours that Edward was taking an unseemly interest in the earl of Gloucester's wife. What we know of Botetourt's career suggests that he was probably born about this time, but unless further evidence is forthcoming it would be best to discount him as a royal bastard.

Edward II (1307–27) did have an illegitimate son, but we know practically nothing about him apart from the fact that he was called Adam, was probably born around 1310, and accompanied his father on the Scottish campaign of 1322. Edward III (1327–77) had three illegitimate children by Alice Perrers, all born during the last fifteen years of his reign. There is also a later and thoroughly unreliable tradition that he was the father of Nicholas Litlyngton, abbot of Westminster from 1362 to 1386. In fact Litlyngton called himself 'son of Hugh and Joan', and although his parentage is not certain, it is very likely that he was a member of the Despenser family. It may be that he was the illegitimate son of Edward II's great favourite Hugh Despenser the younger. Litlyngton was professed as a monk by 1333, at which time Edward III was twenty-one, which makes it virtually impossible that Edward could have been his father. In 1352, when he was prior of Westminster, Litlyngton ordered that alms should be dispensed to the poor each year on the anniversary of Edward II's deposition: if Hugh Despenser was his father, this may have been an oblique way of honouring his memory, for Hugh had been grotesquely executed during the revolution which deposed Edward II.

Edward III's three children by Alice Perrers were given the less than striking names of John, Joan and Jane. Joan and Jane were of little consequence: they were still small children when their father died, and although he had tried to provide for at least one of them, they suffered from the aura of public disapproval which surrounded their mother at the start of the new reign, and rapidly sank into obscurity. Neither of them made distinguished marriages: Jane married a man called Richard Northland, about whom very little is known, while Joan married a Kingston-upon-Thames lawyer called Robert Skerne. Although she submitted a petition to the parliament of 1394 claiming that her step-cousin John de Windsor owed her £4,000, there is no indication that either she or her sister succeeded in recovering more than a fraction of their mother's vast properties. In 1406 she even allowed her claim to the manor of Gaines-in-Upminster, where her mother had spent her last years, to be bought out in return for a life rent of £26. Nevertheless, it is clear that the Skernes were very comfortably off. They lived at Down Hall in Kingston, and after Robert Skerne's death in April 1437 a splendid monumental brass depicting the figures of himself and his wife was commissioned, and eventually placed over the marble casket which contains their bodies. It may still be seen in the church of All Saints at Kingston, where the figure of Joan (Plate 5), in covered horn head-dress, tight-fitting gown, and loose cloak with a cord across the breast, is ample testimony to the standard of living enjoyed by her and Robert.

CHAPTER 10

SIR JOHN DE SOUTHERAY

A great deal more is known about Alice's son, John, than about his sisters. He was probably born around 1364–5, and was given the surname 'de Southeray' (sometimes spelt 'Surrey'). This surname was also sometimes used by his sisters, although for what reason is unclear. John was brought up at court, and generously provided for by Edward III. In February 1374 the king made £100 a year available for his maintenance, and in 1375 a number of properties were made over to a group of Alice's associates who were to hold them in trust for him. Clothes from the king's great wardrobe were dispensed to him, as well as to the other young noblemen brought up at court. The attempt by the commons in the Good Parliament of 1376 to lessen his mother's influence over the king provided only a temporary interruption. By September 1376 Alice and her royal bastards were back at court. Further lands were granted to John, and in January 1377 he was married to Maud, sister of Henry Lord Percy. Percy was rising rapidly to political prominence. In November 1376 he had been created marshal of England, and in July 1377 he would be made earl of Northumberland. He was also at this time one of the foremost supporters of John of Gaunt (although later the two men would quarrel violently), and to marry into such a family clearly had its advantages. At the St George's Day festivities in April 1377 John de Southeray was knighted along with the future king, Richard II, Richard's cousin Henry Bolingbroke – also a future king – and several other scions of the English nobility. On 17 June the king gave John a gift of a coat of arms in satin. Four days later, Edward III died.

With the death of his royal father, John de Southeray's days of glory came to an abrupt end. His mother's position at court collapsed, and before long she had been subjected to a public trial in parliament, resulting in the confiscation of her goods and properties. Her son, however, who was after all a royal bastard, and who had not been formally indicted on any charge, was not treated ungenerously. Although he seems to have been deprived of some of his lands (probably because they had originally been granted to Alice, and were thus declared forfeit as a result of her conviction), his annuity of £100 at the exchequer was confirmed, and those moveable goods seized from Alice's properties which could be shown to belong to him rather than to her were soon returned to him. What became of him in the next few years is not clear. In 1378 he was said to be residing with the bishop of Exeter. Before long, however, he took the path trodden by most young noblemen in the Middle Ages, and embarked on a military

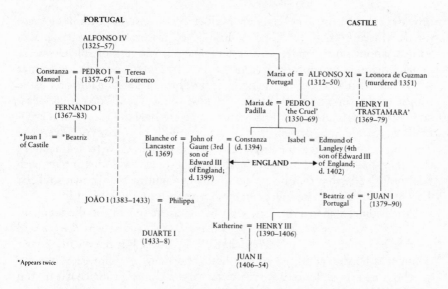

Table 9 Inter-relation of the English, Castilian and Portuguese
royal families (selective)

career. In doing so, he became involved in one of the most controversial English campaigns of the Hundred Years War, and one in which he himself was to play a prominent part. This was the Portuguese expedition of 1381–2, and the background to it requires some explanation.

The Hundred Years War (1337–1453) was more than an Anglo-French conflict. Although England and France were the two principal protagonists, around whom diplomatic alliances tended to be constructed, several other European rulers also became involved in the conflict, particularly those of the Low Countries and, in the second half of the fourteenth century, those of the Iberian peninsula. In the 1370s and '80s, at a time when the war was going badly for England, she found herself at war with Castile, France's ally. Edward III's third son, John of Gaunt, claimed the throne of Castile because he had married Constanza, daughter of the legitimate king, Pedro I, who had been murdered and supplanted on the throne by his illegitimate brother Henry of Trastamara (see Table 9). England's most constant ally against Castile in the peninsula was Portugal, and in 1381 Gaunt dispatched an English force under his brother Edmund of Langley (Edward III's fourth son) to lend much-needed aid to Portugal against her more powerful neighbour.

The campaign was an unmitigated disaster. Arriving too late, the English forces were rapidly dispersed from Lisbon by the Portuguese king, Fernando I, and billeted on a collection of frontier towns in the hope that they would provide a shield against Castilian raiding. The most important of these towns, where Edmund of Langley established his headquarters, was Vila Vicosa, about ninety miles due east of Lisbon. Months of idleness were punctuated only by sporadic raiding of the Portuguese countryside, so that what had been intended as a joint Anglo-Portuguese invasion of Castile turned into a running war between English soldiers and Portuguese peasants; Anglo-Portuguese relations were strained to breaking-point, and eventually Fernando was driven into an alliance with his Castilian adversary. To make matters worse, the English soldiers complained (with justification) that they had received no pay, and so widespread was discontent with Edmund's leadership that he ended up facing a mutiny by his own soldiers. The leader of this mutiny was none other than John de Southeray.

The chronicler Jean Froissart, who is our main source for the incident, calls him alternatively 'Soudŕee' or 'Soustŕee', and says he was the bastard brother of the king of England (Richard II, by now), but there can be little doubt that he was getting confused here, and that it is John de Southeray to whom he refers. Southeray was in fact bastard uncle to Richard II, and half-brother to Edmund of Langley. Matters came to a head in the summer of 1382. By this time the English army had been in Portugal for nearly a year, but still they had not apparently received any pay. Several of the knights held a conference, among them Southeray, 'who spoke more loudly than any of the others'. He openly accused Edmund of Langley of pocketing the wages of the soldiers, and suggested that the mutineers form themselves into a brotherhood under the flag of St George and make such a nuisance of themselves that their grievances would be listened to. The others agreed, and decided to appoint him as their leader, because – and the reasoning is of interest – he had more authority and power to make mischief than any of the others. So they raised the flag of St George and, with cries of 'For Southeray, the valiant bastard!', set off to make war on the king of Portugal.

Fortunately such a drastic solution was not required. On their way, Southeray and his band of hotheads were intercepted by some of the older and more experienced knights, led by Theodore (nicknamed 'the Canon') Robsart. Not without difficulty, 'the Canon' managed to persuade the mutineers to abandon their plan, and instead to go and present their grievances peaceably to Edmund of Langley. Once again Southeray was chosen as spokesman, and together they rode to the monastery where Edmund was lodged. They arrived – seven hundred in all, according to Froissart – just as Edmund was about to sit down to dinner, and demanded to speak with him. Southeray then put the case squarely to his commander, declaring:

My lord, you are our commander, and it was you who summoned us and brought us from England, both those who are here in your

140

presence, as well as many more waiting outside; it is to you we must look for our pay, and so far we have received no wages at all, for we should never have come to this country or entered the service of the king of Portugal if you had not been responsible for our pay. And if you say that the war is not yours but the king of Portugal's, we will simply take our own wages by overrunning the country, and let every man take what he can get.

Not surprisingly Edmund stalled, reminding Southeray of the dire consequences of mutiny, to say nothing of the dishonour which would fall on the head of the English king. Eventually a compromise was agreed: three knights were to be sent to treat with the king of Portugal at Lisbon, to do what they could to extract the soldiers' wages from him. The result of this was success for the mutineers. Fernando, faced with the threat of a hostile English army on his own soil as well as a war with Castile, promised to make payment within two weeks. When the three knights returned to inform their comrades of the success of their mission, Southeray is said to have remarked, 'Now see if this mutiny has not served its purpose? By being a little troublesome, we have secured our wages; he who is feared fares well.'

The English soldiers did indeed secure their wages, but they achieved precious little else during their remaining few weeks in Portugal. By the end of August, Fernando, despairing of the English alliance, had made a treaty with King Juan I of Castile, one of the terms of which was that the English army should leave the peninsula. Discredited and out of pocket, Edmund arrived back in England towards the end of the year, having severely damaged English interests in Iberia as well as brought dishonour upon the reputation of English arms. In an attempt to exculpate himself, he placed the blame on those who had mutinied against him, and a royal commission was issued to arrest nineteen of those who had been involved in the affair at Vila Vicosa. Amazingly, the name of John Southeray was not included on the list; it is pertinent to wonder whether his royal blood had anything to do with his exclusion from it.

What became of John de Southeray after this is not clear. He was still alive early in 1383, but he probably died soon after this. There is, however, one further point of interest connected with the affair at Vila Vicosa. Alice Perrers's affair with Edward III is usually said to have begun around 1364. If John was born in late 1364 or 1365, he would have been seventeen at the time he led the mutiny. This is not impossible: boys became men quickly in the Middle Ages, and perhaps his behaviour in 1382 smacks of youthful impetuosity. Yet it would be difficult to imagine that he was much younger than seventeen. Thus what we know of John's career suggests that Alice became the king's mistress not later than 1364, and possibly earlier. It is appropriate that John made a name for himself in Iberia, where royal bastards were strikingly more successful than in any other part of fourteenth-century Europe.

There is a tradition that Richard II (reigned 1377–99) had a bastard son, called Richard Maudeleyn, but it is almost certainly apocryphal. Maudeleyn was certainly a great favourite of Richard II's during the last few years of his reign. He was a clerk in the royal household, remained loyal to his king during the dark days of the 1399 revolution, and lost his life early in the following year when he joined a conspiracy aimed at restoring Richard to the throne. Thus he undoubtedly had a strong attachment to Richard, and he was said to resemble the king greatly. Yet he was already a scholar at Cambridge in 1386, when the king was only nineteen, which makes it virtually impossible that Richard II could have been his father. It is possible that Richard II's supplanter, Henry IV (reigned 1399–1413), had a bastard son called Edmund Labourde, said to have been born in 1401 and to have died in infancy. Henry's first wife had died in 1394, and he did not marry again until 1403, so it is far from impossible that he might have fathered a bastard during these years. On the other hand, there are no contemporary references to Labourde. Henry V (reigned 1413–22) and Henry VI (reigned 1422–61) have never been accused of taking mistresses, let alone of begetting bastards. This does not mean, however, that the question of bastardy in the royal family was a dead issue in fifteenth-century England. Far from it: in fact the problems which arose from actual or alleged bastardy in the royal family at this time were greater than at any other time in the Middle Ages. These problems were of two sorts. Firstly, there were the quasi-royal bastards of Edward III's sons, who, when the thorny problem of the succession raised its head, might be considered capable of either holding, or transmitting to their offspring, a claim to the throne. Secondly, allegations of bastardy became stock political smears in the fifteenth century, and within the royal family they could on occasion be used with devastating effect. Whether any of these allegations was true is quite another matter. Before investigating them, something must be said of the bastards fathered by Edward III's sons.

CHAPTER 11

SIR ROGER DE CLARENDON

According to the *Dictionary of National Biography*, Sir Roger de Clarendon

> was reputed a bastard son of the Black Prince and, being regarded as a possible pretender, was hanged by order of Henry IV in 1402. His execution was made the subject of one of the articles exhibited by Archbishop Scrope against the king in 1405.

This briefest of outlines can be expanded considerably, but before doing so it is important to make clear Roger's position in 1402. Edward the Black Prince, eldest son to Edward III, predeceased his father by a year, dying in June 1376. He left one legitimate son, Richard of Bordeaux, who became Richard II in 1377, and one (or possibly two) illegitimate ones. (Roger de Clarendon was undoubtedly the Black Prince's bastard, and the fact that he was the only bastard mentioned in the Black Prince's will strongly suggests that he was the only one. There was, however, a man called John de Galeis who was fighting in the service of the king of Navarre in 1392 and was called alternatively 'the bastard brother of the king of England' or 'the bastard of England'; a 'John Galeis' also received a gift of a tun of wine from the Black Prince in November 1360. It is possible that he was also a bastard of the Black Prince, but he was not acknowledged and brought up at court as Roger de Clarendon was, and he played no part in English politics.) Richard II had no legitimate issue, male or female. Thus after Richard's deposition and death in 1399–1400, Roger de Clarendon was probably the only, and certainly the only well-known, descendant of the Black Prince, the man who just a quarter of a century earlier had been the undisputed heir to the English throne. It is difficult to understand why historians have taken so little interest in Roger.

Roger's mother, Edith de Willesford, was the Black Prince's only known mistress. Who she was, and how their liaison occurred, is impossible to discover, but it seems likely that she was of relatively low birth, for in 1385 Roger's half-brother, Richard II, granted her an annuity of 10 marks (£6. 13s. 4d.) for life 'for her maintenance', which hardly suggests that she had any substantial resources of her own. The name given to him might indicate that he was born at the royal palace of Clarendon (Wiltshire), but his date of birth is unknown. The Black Prince married late by medieval standards. Born in 1330, he was offered several politically attractive matches in the 1340s and '50s, but when in 1360 he finally did decide to marry, it was for love. His bride was Joan, the 'Fair Maid of Kent', whose chequered marital career has already been discussed (pp. 15–17). This, together with what we know of Roger's career, suggests that he was the product of a premarital rather than an adulterous affair between his mother and the prince: he could have been born at any time between about 1345 and 1360.

Edward III treated his illegitimate grandson with his customary generosity. In January 1372 he granted Roger an annuity of £100 for life at the exchequer. It may well also have been King Edward who arranged Roger's favourable marriage to the youthful Margaret, heiress to the barony of La Roches, which brought him the prospect of considerable lands in Herefordshire, Pembrokeshire, and around Tipperary in Ireland. This marriage must have taken place between 1375 and 1381, but the unfortunate Margaret died in 1382, before she had even reached her own majority, and the greater part of her inheritance was divided between her three surviving cousins. Thus inopportunely deprived of a sizeable source of landed income, one might have expected Roger to marry again, but there is no evidence that he did so.

The Black Prince died in June 1376, leaving 'to Sir Roger de Clarendon a silk bed'. He was now a knight, then, and after his half-brother Richard II became king in the following year, he soon became a knight of the king's chamber, a highly privileged post normally reserved for the king's closest friends and relatives. In January 1378 Richard confirmed Roger's annuity of £100 'because he has retained the said Roger to stay with him'. He remained a knight of the king's chamber until at least 1396. There is also evidence for his military activity in the early years of Richard II's reign. In early 1378 he had indented with the king to take a retinue of soldiers abroad to fight in the French wars, but in June he was, without any explanation, released from this agreement. Two years later, in May 1380, he officially surrendered to the king the provostship of Entre-deux-Mers and the bailiwick of Craon, both in English-held Aquitaine, and both of which had originally been granted to Roger for life by his father, presumably during the time when the Black Prince was prince of Aquitaine in the 1360s. This surrender to the king was sealed with the official seal of the mayor of Bristol 'because the said Roger's seal is to many unknown'. When, in 1390, Roger exchanged his £100 annuity at the exchequer for a grant of £100 to be taken directly from the king's customs duties on cloth, it was from the customs officials at Bristol and the surrounding counties that he chose to take it. This suggests that when he was not at court, the West Country was his home, although there is no evidence of his having purchased or been granted property there.

144

Until the last years of his brother's reign, Roger's career seems on the whole to have been unexceptional. Presumably most of his time was spent at court or on his estates, although in October 1391 he was granted permission by the king to go abroad with £100 'for the expenses of his expedition'. In 1398, however, he got into serious trouble. He had brushed with the law once before: in 1379 he was outlawed by a London court for failing to honour a debt of £200 to Sir Peter de Veel. On this occasion he was pardoned by the king, but twenty years later he was not so fortunate. Some time in the summer of 1398 Roger wounded another knight, Sir William Drayton, in a brawl. The circumstances of the quarrel are not clear, but so severely was Drayton wounded that Roger was imprisoned in Wallingford castle, and only released on bail of £200 'in case the said William should die'. Drayton did die, and Roger was indicted for his murder, but promptly absconded. Those who had stood bail for him lost their £200, Roger himself was outlawed, and all his goods and chattels were forfeited to the king.

For the next three years, Roger seems to have remained on the run. The confused state of the country during these years – with the revolution which deposed Richard II in 1399 being rapidly followed by several attempted counter-revolutions, as well as a complete breakdown of law and order in Wales after 1400 – probably gave him an ideal opportunity to avoid capture. In November 1399 the new king, Henry IV (who was Richard II's cousin and therefore Roger's half-cousin), formally pardoned Roger's servant John Barbour, who had been indicted of Drayton's death but found not guilty, but no pardon ever seems to have been offered to Roger. His £100 annuity was granted to another man. Not until 1402 did he emerge from hiding, to join a desperate and pathetic adventure which was to cost him his life. On 19 May 1402 the mayor of London was ordered to arrest Roger and a clerk called John Calfe. His arrest had nothing to do with Drayton's death: his crime was that he had joined with several Franciscan friars, the prior of Launde priory in Leicestershire, and a few other hare-brained desperadoes in a conspiracy to overthrow Henry IV. By 23 May the ringleaders, including Roger, had been seized and sent to the Tower. Here they were indicted of treason. The friars admitted (under interrogation) that they had circulated letters saying that Richard II was still alive (in fact he had died early in 1400 in Pontefract castle, probably murdered on Henry IV's orders); convicted of treason, they were drawn on hurdles to Tyburn and hanged. Roger must have denied the charges, for the chronicler Thomas Walsingham states that he, his esquire, and his valet failed to prove their innocence. All three were found guilty of treason, and all three were hanged.

No contemporary source states that Roger was hanged because he aspired to the throne, nor even that Henry IV regarded him as a rival on account of his birth. The idea that he was eliminated because of his proximity to the royal family goes back no further than the nineteenth century. He had done quite enough to deserve a traitor's death without putting Henry IV to the inconvenience of inventing an excuse to remove him. On the other hand, it cannot be denied that he might have been seen by others as a more legitimate claimant to the throne than the usurper Henry IV. The arms which Roger bore proudly proclaimed his descent from the Black Prince (Plate 6a); the chroniclers referred to him as Richard II's brother. Nor was his death forgotten: three years later Henry IV faced another, and much more serious, rebellion, led this time by the earl of Northumberland and Richard Scrope, archbishop of York. As a prelude to the hoped-for rising, Archbishop Scrope issued a manifesto cataloguing the alleged crimes committed by Henry since 1399. The usurper, claimed Scrope, was gradually eliminating the ancient nobility of England, and the examples he gave were the earls of Huntingdon and Salisbury, Henry 'Hotspur', son of the earl of Northumberland, and 'Lord Roger Clarendon'. Royal blood did not pass unnoticed. One is left wondering whether Roger might have been a more serious candidate for the throne if his father had lived to become king of England.

CHAPTER 12

KATHERINE SWYNFORD AND THE BEAUFORTS

The Black Prince was not the only one of Edward III's sons to father illegitimate offspring. Deservedly more famous as a begetter of bastards was Edward's third son, John of Gaunt, one of the most fascinating and controversial figures of late medieval history. For fifteen years Gaunt styled himself 'king of Castile and León', and although he was never able to achieve more than nominal recognition for his own claim to a kingdom, he was destined, through three marriages, to become the ancestor of the kings of Scotland, Castile and León, and Portugal, as well as of the Lancastrian, Yorkist and Tudor kings of England (see Table 10). 'Thou shalt get kings, though thou be none' (Shakespeare, *Macbeth*). Gaunt's first marriage, in 1359, when he was aged nineteen, was to Blanche of Lancaster, who brought him the vast estates of the Duchy of Lancaster and bore him three children who survived infancy. The eldest of these, Philippa, married King João I of Portugal in 1387. The youngest, Henry Bolingbroke, the only son of this marriage, usurped the throne of England in 1399 and founded the Lancastrian dynasty which was to rule England for over sixty years. Blanche died of the plague in 1369, and in 1371 Gaunt married Constanza, daughter of the murdered King Pedro I of Castile. Thus he acquired his title to the Castilian throne (León was annexed to Castile), and in 1372 Constanza bore him a daughter, Katherine. In 1387 Katherine became the wife and queen of King Henry III of Castile and León, as part of a treaty whereby Gaunt agreed to abandon his claim to the Castilian crown. But the marriage with Constanza was never more than a political match. Gaunt never showed any sign of affection for his Spanish bride, and it was at about the same time that he married her that his celebrated affair with Katherine Swynford began.

Gaunt's infidelity was well known in his own day. One chronicler called him a *magnus fornicator*, and several remarked disapprovingly on the fact that he made little attempt to conceal his relationship with Katherine Swynford. Before, or possibly during, his first marriage, he had already had one affair, with a girl from Hainault called Marie de Saint-Hilaire, a lady-in-waiting to Edward III's queen, Philippa of Hainault. Marie bore Gaunt a daughter, Blanche, who married the English knight Sir Thomas Morieux. Katherine Swynford also came from Hainault. She was born in about 1350,

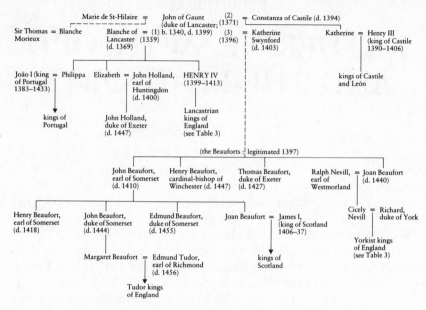

Table 10 The children of John of Gaunt

the younger daughter of Sir Payne Roelt, a knight of Hainault who had come to England in the service of Queen Philippa. Thus she was naturally associated with the English court, and this association was strengthened when her elder sister, Philippa, married the poet Geoffrey Chaucer, who was at that time an esquire in the household of Edward III. In 1367 Katherine married Sir Hugh Swynford, a knight from Lincolnshire who was retained by Gaunt. During the next four years she and Hugh had two children, firstly Thomas, who was born in 1368, and who later became a knight in Gaunt's household, and secondly Blanche, born about 1370, to whom Gaunt stood as godfather. In 1372, Sir Hugh Swynford was killed in battle in Aquitaine. By this time, Gaunt and Katherine were probably already lovers.

It seems to have been in 1371 or early 1372 that the liaison began. Katherine was already governess to Gaunt's two daughters by his first marriage, a post which she had taken up around the time of her marriage to Hugh Swynford. For the next ten years Katherine kept her post as governess to the two Lancastrian girls, and presumably Gaunt's 'visits to the nursery', as his biographer put it, took on added spice. During these ten years four illegitimate children were born to Gaunt and Katherine, the Beauforts, so named after the castle and lordship of Beaufort in Anjou, a former French possession of Gaunt's which he had lost to the French in

1369. Tradition had it that the four children were born there, but this has been shown to be false. It was simply a convenient name which did not jeopardise the right of Gaunt's legitimate children to any part of the inheritance which Gaunt still held. A wit at Richard II's court made a pun out of their name, translating it as 'Faerborn', which of course they were not.

Reputedly Katherine was beautiful. Froissart said she was 'a lady who knew much of all honours', but then he was always reluctant to criticise the wealthy and influential, especially if they came from his native Hainault. Other chroniclers were less generous, and when she eventually became duchess of Lancaster several of the fine ladies at Richard II's court were much put out at having to give precedence to the mere daughter of a knight. By 1375 her relationship with Gaunt was well known, and her own reputation was not enhanced by the increasing unpopularity of her lover. Gaunt at this time was the most hated man in England. His rumoured designs on the throne, his support of the 'heretic' John Wyclif, and his grandiose Continental ambitions all stirred up popular resentment: in 1377 there were riots against him in London, and in 1381 he figured at the top of a list of 'traitors' whose heads were demanded by the rebellious peasants. It was at about this time, in 1381 or early 1382, that Katherine left her post as governess to Gaunt's daughters. Thomas Walsingham asserted that this was because their affair was giving rise to too much scandal, so Gaunt repented of his conduct and withdrew from her company; it may also have been because of his claim to the Castilian throne, which he now began to pursue in earnest, and which perhaps demanded that he pay more attention to Constanza.

When she left her post as governess, Katherine went to live in the household of Mary de Bohun, the wife of Gaunt's son Henry Bolingbroke (later Henry IV), and here she seems to have resided, with her four Beaufort bastards, for the next seven or eight years. The accounts of Mary's household record that they received liveries of scarlet and white silk furred with miniver at Christmas, and presents such as diamonds, gold rings, and coral rosaries on New Year's Day and Egg-Friday. Between 1386 and 1389 Gaunt was abroad, but after his return he apparently began to live openly with Katherine again. The pitiful Constanza was given her own household and lived apart from her husband, while Gaunt and Katherine probably lived together while he was in England, and she on her Lincolnshire estates when he was abroad. On 24 March 1394 Constanza died. Soon after this Gaunt went to Aquitaine, and did not return until just before Christmas 1395. After spending a few days celebrating Christmas with the king at Langley (Hertfordshire), he rode straight on to Lincoln, and there at the beginning of January he and Katherine were quietly married.

After being his mistress for twenty-five years, Katherine was only to be Gaunt's wife for three years. On 3 February 1399 Gaunt, Shakespeare's 'time-honoured Lancaster', died at Leicester castle. In his will he left Katherine an enormous quantity of jewels, plate and rich clothes, as well as £2,000 in cash, an annuity of £1,000 to be taken from the revenues of the Duchy of Lancaster, and a life interest in all the lands which he had granted to her since their affair began. These bequests were confirmed by her stepson when he became King Henry IV in October 1399. The wealthy and widowed duchess of Lancaster retired from court to spend the last few years of her life in Lincoln. No doubt she felt at home here: her son by her first marriage, Sir Thomas Swynford, became sheriff of Lincolnshire in 1401, while her second son by Gaunt, Henry Beaufort, had been chosen as bishop of Lincoln in 1398. In her last years she presented the cathedral with numerous gifts of chasubles and other fine vestments, often embroidered with wheels in allusion to her paternal Roelt arms (French *roue* = wheel). She died on 10 May 1403, and was buried with monumental magnificence in the splendid Angel Choir of Lincoln cathedral. Her tomb bore the arms of England with those of Roelt, *gules*, three catherine wheels *or*.

From Katherine's marriage to John of Gaunt, much followed. Immediately after their marriage they petitioned the pope to confirm its legitimacy, since there were impediments which might render it invalid: these were firstly that they had committed adultery together, and secondly that Gaunt had stood godfather to Katherine's daughter by her first husband. In September the pope duly granted the dispensation, at the same time declaring all past and future offspring to be legitimate. This declaration by the pope of the legitimacy of the Beauforts was necessary because, having been conceived in adultery, they did not qualify as mantle-children. In the parliament of February 1397 the legitimacy of the Beauforts was confirmed by the king and the lords and commons of England in a ceremony unprecedented in English history. As a consequence of their new-found legitimacy, the four children and their offspring were declared to be capable of inheriting 'whatsoever dignities, honours, pre-eminencies, status, ranks and offices, public and private, perpetual and temporal, feudal and noble there may be ... as fully, freely and lawfully as if you were born in lawful wedlock. . . .'

The legitimated Beauforts prospered mightily – so mightily that one historian has described them as 'virtually a second royal family' in fifteenth-century England. After Henry Bolingbroke seized the throne in 1399, they became the half-brothers and -sister of the king, and as early as 1407 there seem to have been some misgivings as to what this might eventually lead to. In that year, King Henry confirmed the 1397 legitimation, but with one crucial difference: after the list of 'dignities, honours' and so forth which the Beauforts were said to be capable of inheriting, Henry inserted the words *excepta dignitate regali* – 'excepting the royal dignity'. In other words, the legitimation of the Beauforts left them free to inherit anything, with one exception: the crown of England. Whether Henry had the authority to qualify Richard II's letter of legitimation, which had after all been entered on the official record of parliament, is debatable. Certainly it has been the subject of much controversy, precisely because it was through his Beaufort ancestry that Henry Tudor justified his seizure of the throne in 1485.

It may well be that Henry IV in 1407 was merely confirming the commonly held opinion, namely that despite their legitimation, under no circumstances could the Beauforts be regarded as holding a place in the order of succession. And at that time, there was no hint of what was to come: the king had four healthy and active sons, upon whom, in turn, the crown had already been bestowed by act of parliament. Yet, as the ranks of the Lancastrian royal family gradually thinned out over the next sixty or so years, the claim of the Beaufort branch to represent it was a factor in English politics which could never quite be forgotten. And when, in the 1450s, and again in the 1480s, uncertainty over the succession and political instability flared into civil war, the claim re-emerged as a potent and divisive force. This is not to argue that the 'Wars of the Roses' were in essence a dynastic struggle: this view is unfashionable now, and rightly so. Nowadays most historians would argue that the real causes of the Wars of the Roses are to be found in the incompetence and incapacity of Henry VI, his inability to balance the interests of his magnates, and his disastrous foreign policy. The dynastic element certainly became important as the struggle progressed, but it was more of a rallying-cry for those discontented with Henry VI's and later Richard III's rule than a primary cause of civil war. By briefly tracing the descent of John of Gaunt's bastards through the fifteenth century, the singular importance of the Beauforts becomes apparent.

The children that Katherine Swynford bore John of Gaunt were: (1) John Beaufort, born *circa* 1372; (2) Henry Beaufort, born *circa* 1375; (3) Thomas Beaufort, born *circa* 1377; (4) Joan Beaufort, born *circa* 1379. The three younger children can be discussed relatively briefly. Henry, the ablest of the brood, became bishop of Lincoln in 1398, and then of Winchester in 1404. For over forty years, until his death in 1447, he was one of the foremost politicians in England. First appointed chancellor of England in 1403, he was to hold that post under three successive kings, and after Henry V's death in 1422 he was one of the leading figures on the council which governed England during Henry VI's long minority. His wealth was legendary, and the sums which he loaned to the crown were staggering by medieval standards. In 1421 he stood godfather to Henry VI, and in 1426 he became a cardinal (there were even rumours that he might be elected pope). His death in 1447 deprived England of its wisest and most experienced administrator at a time when his guiding hand was sorely needed. Thomas Beaufort also rose high. Like his brother, he became chancellor of England (1410–12), the only lay chancellor of Henry IV's reign. Created earl of Dorset in 1412, and duke of Exeter in 1416, he served as Henry V's lieutenant in Normandy and was a Knight of the Garter. Although married, he had no children. Joan, the youngest of John of Gaunt and Katherine Swynford's children, was married twice. By her second marriage, to Ralph Nevill, earl of Westmorland, she had a daughter, Cicely, who married the greatest of all fifteenth-century English magnates, Richard duke of York. Richard and Cicely had four sons, Edward, Edmund, George and Richard. The first and last of these became the 'Yorkist' kings of England, Edward IV and Richard III. Thus in 1485, when Henry Tudor and Richard III met at Bosworth Field, the descendant of one Beaufort line was challenging the descendant of another Beaufort line for the crown.

Dynastically speaking, the most interesting of the Beauforts was the eldest, John. Created earl of Somerset in 1397, he too was a Knight of the Garter (see his coats of arms, Plate 6b, c). His daughter, also called Joan, married King James I of Scotland (for their romance, see p. 41). Through his second son, John, he had a granddaughter called Margaret, born in 1443, and it soon became apparent that Margaret had a crucial role to play. The problem was that the Lancastrian line had failed to propagate itself in sufficient numbers. Of Henry IV's four sons, only the eldest, Henry V, had a legitimate child, and this was the feeble Henry VI. Thus when the last of Henry IV's sons, Humphrey duke of Gloucester, died in 1447, and Henry VI's marriage to Margaret of Anjou was still childless, there was no obvious successor to the throne, and the whole question of the Beaufort claim once again came to the fore. On the other hand Richard duke of York, who was descended from the second son of Edward III, also had a good claim to be recognised as Henry VI's successor. Initially it was the rivalry between York and Edmund Beaufort (John Beaufort's son) which set the scene for the disastrous confrontations of the 1450s. The central role accorded to young Margaret Beaufort in this contest is demonstrated by events in 1450. In that year Henry VI's favourite and chief minister, and York's deadly enemy, William de la Pole, duke of Suffolk, was impeached in parliament. Although allowed by Henry to flee, he was intercepted by pirates off the Kentish coast and summarily beheaded at sea. What is interesting is that at the time of his impeachment one of the charges against Suffolk was that he had conspired to make his son John king of England, by, firstly, murdering Henry VI, and secondly, marrying his son to Margaret Beaufort (who was in Suffolk's wardship) and presenting her as the heiress of England. That Suffolk was planning Henry VI's death is most improbable – nothing would have suited York better in 1450. Yet clearly the place of the Beauforts in the line of succession was still an open question.

When Henry VI's queen, Margaret of Anjou, gave birth to a son, Edward, in October 1453, it seemed that fears about the succession had been quieted, and Margaret Beaufort's proximity to the throne became a less pressing issue. In 1455 she married Edmund Tudor, earl of Richmond, and in January 1457 their son, Henry Tudor, was born. Yet the battle for the throne was not over. In 1460, with Henry VI now chronically insane, York publicly set forth his claim to the throne in parliament, based on the fact that while Henry VI was descended from Edward III's third son (Gaunt), he, York, was descended from Edward III's second son (Lionel of Clarence). Although York was defeated and killed at the battle of Wakefield later that same year, in the following year his eighteen-year-old son, Edward of Rouen, earl of March, made good his father's claim and became Edward IV. Ten years later, the Lancastrian royal line was extinguished when both Henry VI and his son, Prince Edward, died within a few days of each other, the former murdered in the Tower of London, the latter killed by Edward IV's soldiers at the battle of Tewkesbury. This left only one possible 'Lancastrian' claimant: Henry Tudor. Fourteen years later the house of York came to grief, and Margaret Beaufort's son became Henry VII.

To illustrate the dynastic importance of the Beauforts it has been necessary almost to provide an outline of English political history in the fifteenth century – and this of course is a measure of their importance. Several factors, including their royal blood and their personal ability, contributed to their rise, but what cannot be doubted is that their official legitimation was crucial. This is amply demonstrated by the number of other high-born bastards in fifteenth-century England, many of whom had royal blood in their veins, but who never cut a figure on the political stage. Two of Henry IV's sons, John duke of Bedford and Humphrey duke of Gloucester, left bastard children; so did the duke of Exeter, the duke of Suffolk, the earl of Kent, the earl of Salisbury, the earl of Pembroke (Jasper Tudor, Henry VII's uncle), Lord Herbert and Lord Dynham, to name only the most obvious. So did Edward IV and Richard III. It was only after their legitimation in 1397 that John Beaufort and Henry Beaufort were granted an earldom and a bishopric respectively. Without that legitimation, it is impossible to imagine that they would ever have come near to the throne, and here one can see a clear difference between twelfth-century attitudes and fifteenth-century attitudes, in England at least. In the twelfth century, there had been no need to legitimate Robert of Gloucester or Geoffrey 'Plantagenet' or William Longsword. Yet it is instructive to remember why it was that the Beauforts were legitimated in 1397. It had nothing to do with potential claims to the throne in the distant future: it was because John of Gaunt decided to marry his mistress.

CHAPTER 13

ALLEGATIONS OF BASTARDY IN THE FIFTEENTH-CENTURY ROYAL FAMILY

The impression that bastardy, unless legitimated, was considered to be a more serious defect in late medieval England than it had been before then is reinforced by the number of allegations of bastardy in the royal family that were put around. Henry VI's son Prince Edward, King Edward IV, his sons Edward V and Richard of York, and Henry Tudor all found that slurs were cast on either their own birth or that of their ancestors. The object in each case was the same: to try to provide justification for denying their right to the throne. Henry Bolingbroke is said to have used the same argument against Richard II in 1399 (although the accusation was never made publicly), and as the question of the succession grew increasingly complex from about 1450 onwards, so the allegations of illegitimate birth multiplied.

Henry VI's wife, Margaret of Anjou, was one of the most unpopular queens of medieval England. Born in 1430, the daughter of René of Anjou the titular king of Sicily, she married Henry in 1445 at the age of fifteen, and soon found herself plunged into an English political scene strewn with pitfalls:

> The queen is a great and strong-laboured woman, for she spareth no pain to sue her things to an intent and conclusion to her power,

remarked one contemporary. The rivalry between, on the one hand, York and his followers and, on the other hand, Edmund Beaufort and Suffolk, was growing ever more intense, and, like the king himself, Margaret found herself forced to take sides: York was her enemy, and Suffolk and Beaufort her friends. As her unpopularity increased, rumours began to be spread around: some said that Margaret herself was illegitimate, and no true daughter of the king of Sicily, while others hinted at the intimacy of her relationships with Suffolk and Beaufort. Yet it is very difficult to believe that her son, Prince Edward, was illegitimate. He was born on 13 October 1453. Two months earlier Henry VI had been struck by his first bout of

154

insanity, but in January 1453 he had been quite sane and had spent most of that month with Margaret at Greenwich. In the following year the infant prince was proclaimed prince of Wales, and it was over two years before the first whisper of his illegitimacy was heard. In February 1456 a London apprentice was hanged, drawn, and quartered for making the allegation. By this time Henry VI was sporadically insane, and the first battle of the Wars of the Roses had been fought. In the next few years the rumours became more persistent: a popular ballad set up on the town gate of Canterbury repeated the allegation, and Margaret was said to be terrified at the prospect of her son's right to the throne not being recognised. French chroniclers knew the rumours too, and said that it had been spread abroad by Richard Nevill, earl of Warwick ('the Kingmaker'). Apparently Warwick had it preached publicly that Prince Edward 'was a child of fornication, conceived in sin with a base man, a mountebank, which rendered him unworthy to succeed to the crown'.

In 1460, Margaret's worst fears were confirmed. Richard duke of York publicly claimed the throne, and Henry VI, in a position of political and military weakness, was persuaded to agree to a compromise: he would remain king until his death, after which he would be succeeded, not by his son Prince Edward, but by the duke of York and his heirs in perpetuity. Henry VI, like Stephen three hundred years earlier, had publicly disinherited his own child, and no doubt this lent credence to the rumours of Prince Edward's bastardy. Yet this was not the reason why the prince was disinherited: the argument used by York had nothing whatsoever to do with the rumours of bastardy, but was founded on the fact that whereas Henry VI was descended from Edward III's third son, York was descended from his second son. Neither York nor his son Edward IV ever impugned Prince Edward's birth.

Before long Edward IV was to face the same problem himself, and the allegation of bastardy made against him reveals a point of considerable interest. Royal births, like royal marriages, were best accompanied by as much publicity as possible. If they occurred secretly, or at distant places, there was always a chance that people would begin to question them. This was particularly true of members of the royal family born abroad, who were always liable to be called changelings or bastards. The point is clearly illustrated by a statute passed in the parliament of 1351. By this time Edward III had four sons: Edward the Black Prince (born 1330), Lionel of Clarence (born 1338), John of Gaunt (born 1340), and Edmund of Langley (born 1341). The second and third of these had been born abroad, at Antwerp and Ghent (hence 'Gaunt') respectively. The statute of 1351 declared that

because some people be in doubt if the children born in parts beyond the sea and out of the ligeance of England should be able to demand any inheritance within the same ligeance or not . . . our lord the king . . . hath charged the said prelates, earls, barons and other wise men of his council assembled in parliament to deliberate upon this point; all which of one assent have said, that the law of the crown of England is, and always hath been such, that the children of the kings of England, in whatsoever parts they be born, in England or elsewhere, be able and ought to bear the inheritance after the death of their ancestors; which law our said lord the king, the said prelates, earls, barons and other great men, and all the commons assembled in this parliament do approve and affirm for ever.

This statute deals specifically with inheritance, but when malicious gossipers proceeded from there to an accusation of spurious birth, they seem to have found a ready audience. At the height of his unpopularity in the 1370s, when it was suspected that he had designs on the throne, the rumour that John of Gaunt was a changeling gained widespread currency in London. Richard II was born at Bordeaux, and one story current in 1399 was that his mother, Princess Joan, had conceived him in adultery with a canon or clerk there. The only other king of late medieval England to be born abroad was Edward IV, who was born at Rouen, and several of his political opponents accused him of being a bastard.

It is difficult to say when the allegation of bastardy was first used against Edward IV. After Edward's death, it was asserted that his own mother had told him he was illegitimate in 1464, and threatened to reveal the fact if he persisted in his intention to marry Elizabeth Woodville. This story is almost certainly spurious. In 1469, however, Edward's brother George, duke of Clarence, and Warwick the Kingmaker, who were then in rebellion against Edward, spread the story abroad that he was the son of an archer from Calais named Blaybourne. Louis XI of France and Charles the Rash, duke of Burgundy, both picked up and used the story; Duke Charles is said to have repeated it to Edward's face. When Clarence was eventually attainted and executed in 1478, after yet another rebellion against his brother, Edward specifically accused him of spreading 'the falsest and most unnatural coloured pretence that man might imagine, falsely and untruly noised, published and said, that the king our sovereign lord was a bastard and not begotten to reign upon us'. Doubtless it was Clarence's hope that if he could make the charge of illegitimacy stick, then he, as the next surviving son of Richard duke of York, would succeed to the throne. Again, it is difficult to see the allegation of Edward IV's bastardy as anything more than an unpleasant political smear.

After Edward's death in 1483, however, the smear was revived, and this time with much more serious consequences: it was one half of the two-pronged attack used by Edward's youngest brother, Richard III, to declare Edward IV's two sons, 'the princes in the Tower', incapable of inheriting the throne, and thus to justify Richard's own usurpation. The Italian historian Dominic Mancini, who was in London during the fateful months of May and June 1483, said that preachers were going around saying that Edward IV was illegitimate, and it may be that Dr Ralph Shaw, in his celebrated speech at St Paul's Cross on 22 June, made the same accusation. The petition submitted to Richard a few days later, and incorporated in the parliamentary act by which he claimed the throne in the following year, raised the old question of Edward's foreign birth, if only by implication. Richard, it said, was 'the undoubted son and heir of Richard, late duke of York . . . and how that ye be born within this land, by reason whereof . . . all the three estates of the land have, and may have, more certain knowledge of your birth and filiation'. Yet the revival of doubts about Edward IV's birth was much the shorter and less lethal prong of Richard III's attack: more deadly by far was the charge of bastardy which he laid on his brother's children.

The main point of the Act (the *Titulus Regis*) by which Richard III formally claimed the throne in January 1484 was that Edward IV's marriage to Elizabeth Woodville had been invalid, partly because it was made secretly, and partly because at the time he married Elizabeth, he had already made a 'precontract of matrimony' with another lady, Dame Eleanor Butler: hence all issue of Edward and Elizabeth's marriage was illegitimate, and incapable of inheriting anything, least of all the throne. This was the 'precontract story' in its final version. Not surprisingly it has been the subject of ceaseless speculation, and to rehearse all the arguments and counter-arguments here would be tedious in the extreme. There are, however, three points which should be stressed.

Firstly, Eleanor Butler did exist, and Edward IV's reputation as a woman-iser, combined with the fact that his marriage to Elizabeth Woodville had been a clandestine affair, must have lent some credence to the story. Eleanor was the daughter of John Talbot, earl of Shrewsbury, and soon after 1450 she married Thomas Butler, Lord Sudeley. She died in 1468. That is practically all that is known about her. It has been suggested that she and Edward IV had a bastard son, Edward de Wigmore, but nothing is known of this boy, and the information is derived from a late and unreliable source.

Secondly, there has been much confusion as to who the lady involved in the precontract story was. Mancini said that the lady to whom Edward was precontracted was the French princess Bona of Savoy, to whom the earl of Warwick had married him by proxy; Warwick was indeed trying to negotiate a French marriage for Edward at the time he married Elizabeth, and Bona of Savoy was apparently the intended bride, but there is no evidence that a contract of matrimony had already been concluded. Thomas More and his followers, on the other hand, said that it was Edward's well-known mistress Elizabeth Lucy to whom he was precontracted. This raised a major problem, however, for Elizabeth was almost certainly the mother of Edward's bastard Arthur Plantagenet: if her 'marriage' to Edward was to be declared valid in order to invalidate the Woodville marriage, was not Arthur the heir to the throne? The contemporary Croyland chronicler agreed that the lady in question was Eleanor Butler, but stated flatly that the whole story was false; he added, quite correctly, that parliament, being a lay court, had no right to pass judgment on the validity of any marriage, but 'it presumed to do so, and did so'.

Thirdly, there is little evidence that contemporaries believed the story. Apparently Ralph Shaw won few cheers for his bastardisation of the princes: Richard was supposed to arrive at St Paul's Cross in the middle of the sermon, just as Shaw got to the point of declaring him the only lawful candidate for the throne, but apparently the timing went wrong, Richard arrived late (or Shaw spoke too fast), and the hoped-for triumphal acclamation fell flat. The archbishop of Canterbury was said to be very unwilling to crown Richard, and would not attend the coronation banquet. Edward and Elizabeth had been married for nineteen years, and, despite early misgivings about the advisability of the match, its validity had never been questioned. The man who is said to have told Richard about the precontract was Robert Stillington, bishop of Bath and Wells, who claimed to have celebrated the marriage between Eleanor and Edward and then have been sworn to secrecy about it. Stillington's motives have often been questioned (he had been imprisoned in the Tower for a while by Edward IV); if it was true that Richard first heard the story from Stillington, then presumably he believed it because he wanted to believe it. Richard may well have reckoned that the parlous state of the country demanded a grown man, rather than a twelve-year-old boy, as king, but if he thought that the end justified the means, he miscalculated badly.

Henry VII suppressed all official documents relating to the precontract story, but this is hardly surprising, for one of his first acts after coming to the throne was to marry Elizabeth of York, eldest daughter of Edward IV and Elizabeth Woodville. Any precontract bastardised her as much as it did her brothers.

It is difficult to disagree with the verdict of the great majority of historians, namely, that the precontract of Edward IV and Eleanor Butler (or Elizabeth Lucy, or Bona of Savoy) was invented in 1483 to suit the ambition of Richard III, and that it had no foundation in truth. Nevertheless, it served its purpose. The twelve-year-old Edward V and his ten-year-old brother were incarcerated in the Tower. On 25 June Richard formally 'accepted' the throne, and on 6 July he was crowned. By the time Dominic

Mancini left London in mid-July, it was already being suggested that the boys had been done away with; by early December, rumours of their death had reached the south of France. Despite valiant efforts to shift the blame, the overwhelming mass of evidence still points to Richard III as their murderer.

Two years later, in June 1485, Richard nervously roamed the Midlands waiting for Henry Tudor to invade. At Nottingam he issued a proclamation declaring that Henry

> is descended of bastard blood both of the father's side and of the
> mother's side, for the said Owen the grandfather was bastard born,
> and his mother was daughter unto John duke of Somerset, son unto
> John earl of Somerset, son unto Dame Katherine Swynford, and of
> her in double adultery begotten, whereby it evidently appeareth that
> no title can nor may be in him, who fully intendeth to enter this realm
> purposing a conquest.

On the Beaufort side, Richard was quite right, although he forgot to mention the official legitimation of 1397. Owen Tudor's birth, however, has not usually been questioned; what was much more questionable was the secret marriage, the true facts of which will probably never be discovered, which he and Queen Katherine de Valois entered into (see p. 18). Considering Richard's fondness for bastardising his rivals, it is surprising that he did not make more of this. Not that it would have made any difference, of course. In fifteenth-century English politics, an allegation of bastardy was never more than a makeweight. Political and military power were the factors which tipped the scales. Thus it was that against two child-princes, charges of bastardy could be used successfully to justify an act of gross opportunism. Against men like Edward IV and Henry Tudor, they were shots in the dark.

CHAPTER 14

YORKIST ROYAL BASTARDS

It is time to turn again from imaginary bastards to real ones. With the advent of the Yorkists in 1461, England was once again ruled by men who, like the Angevins, seem to have regarded adultery as a routine kingly occupation. Richard III has been credited with as many as seven bastards, but only three of them are known by name, and one of these is questionable. The other two – both of whom were probably born before his marriage to Anne Nevill in 1472 – he openly acknowledged. His illegitimate daughter Katherine was married in 1484 to William Herbert, earl of Huntingdon, at which time Richard settled property worth 1,000 marks (£666), as well as a cash annuity of £150, on the couple. This was generosity indeed. Richard's illegitimate son, John of Gloucester (or John of Pomfret as he is sometimes known, suggesting that he may have been born at Richard's Yorkshire castle of Pontefract), seems to have been a favourite of his father's. He was probably born around 1470, for he was knighted in 1483, and in 1485 he was still under-age. Nevertheless on 11 March 1485, Richard appointed 'our dear son, our bastard John of Gloucester, whose quickness of mind, agility of body, and inclination to all good customs, give us great hope of his good service for the future' to be captain of Calais. The future, unfortunately, was to be short-lived. After Bosworth, John apparently fell into the hands of Henry Tudor, and was imprisoned along with any other potential Yorkist pretenders. In 1499 Henry finally decided that his security on the throne necessitated the elimination of any rivals, and both the pretender Perkin Warbeck and the earl of Warwick (son of George duke of Clarence) were executed. According to a seventeenth-century writer,

It happened about the same time that these unhappy gentlemen suffered, there was a base son of King Richard III made away, and secretly, having been kept long before in prison. And the occasion whereof (as it seemeth) was to prevent a practice of certain Irishmen of the west and south parts of Ireland who sought and attempted to get him into their hands, and with a purpose to make him their chief or prince, for they would have been glad of any noble gentleman of the house of York, were he legitimate or natural, for the love which they bore to Richard duke of York.

That John was imprisoned by Henry VII is confirmed by other chroniclers, but this is the only mention of his death, and it can hardly be regarded as a totally reliable source. It is, however, quite possible that Henry VII would have had a bastard of Richard III's murdered. Another of Richard's bastards may have been called Richard 'Plantagenet'. There is a tradition (unsubstantiated by any contemporary source) that he was born in 1469, but only told of his true identity on the eve of the battle of Bosworth Field, and that he spent the rest of his life working as a bricklayer in Eastwell (Kent), dying there on 22 December 1550. A fanciful story, but it may be true.

There is abundant evidence for Edward IV's over-healthy sexual appetite (e.g., see p. 11). Only three of his bastards are known by name, a son called Arthur, and two daughters called Grace and Elizabeth. There is only one known reference to Grace: she was said to have been on the funeral barge of the dowager Queen Elizabeth Woodville in 1492 (which suggests, rather surprisingly, that she might have been brought up in Elizabeth Woodville's household). Little more is known about Elizabeth. In the sixteenth century it was said that she married Sir Thomas Lumley, and that 'the advancement of Lumley to be Lord was by marriage of a bastard daughter of King Edward IV'. While this is an interesting comment on the advantage to be had from marrying a royal bastard, it is incorrect, for the Sir Thomas Lumley who became Lord Lumley had a wife with a different name. It is possible that she was betrothed to his infant grandson, another Thomas, but otherwise nothing is known of Elizabeth. She is often said to have been the daughter of Edward's mistress Elizabeth Lucy, and to have been born at about the time of Edward's marriage to Elizabeth Woodville in 1464, and while there is nothing to contradict this, nor is there any contemporary evidence to substantiate it.

CHAPTER 15

ARTHUR PLANTAGENET

Arthur is much better known than Grace and Elizabeth. Indeed, he has recently become one of the best-known characters in sixteenth-century England. Although his early life is shrouded in obscurity, he rose to prominence in middle age, becoming one of the favourites of his nephew King Henry VIII, and serving as one of that king's most trusted officials in the 1520s and '30s. In 1523 he was created Viscount Lisle, in 1525 vice-admiral of England, and in 1533 lord deputy of Calais. At the court of Henry VIII, however, no man was safe. The harmless, elderly Arthur – Henry once called him 'the gentlest heart living' – was arrested in May 1540 on a charge of treason and imprisoned in the Tower of London. At the time of his arrest, some 3,000 private letters were seized from his house in Calais for examination by royal officials. They have remained in crown custody ever since, and recently a selection of more than half of them has been published, in six volumes, entitled *The Lisle Letters*. Through his letters, Arthur Plantagenet comes alive like few other sixteenth-century Englishmen.

The date of Arthur's birth is problematic. His mother was almost certainly Elizabeth Lucy (née Wayte), and he was called Arthur Wayte in his youth. He was probably born sometime between 1461 and 1464, for tradition has it that this was the period of Edward IV's affair with Elizabeth Lucy. 'He loved her well,' said Sir George Buck, 'and she was his witty concubine, for she was a wanton wench, and willing and ready to yield herself to the king and to his pleasures without any conditions'. She was of undistinguished birth, the daughter of one Thomas Wayte whose family had lived near Southampton for generations; her affair with the king was more than a casual encounter, however, for she was probably the mother of his bastard daughter Elizabeth too.

Arthur's boyhood was spent at the easy-going, slightly decadent court of Edward IV. In 1472, the king's tailor was ordered to make various robes for 'my lord the bastard', residing in the royal household – almost certainly Arthur. What became of him after Edward's death in 1483, however, is a mystery. He may well have been sent down to his mother or her relations in Hampshire. Not until 1501 does he re-emerge from the shadows. By this time the Tudor monarchy was well established, and Henry VII could afford to be more generous to his illegitimate brother-in-law. In 1501 Arthur became a member of the household of the queen, his half-sister Elizabeth of York. After her death in 1503, he transferred to the king's household, and when Henry VIII became king in 1509 he was appointed as one of the new king's esquires of the body. By this time he was known as Arthur Plantagenet: since the Plantagenets no longer ruled England, there was presumably no objection to his use of the name. The coat of arms which he bore, on which the arms of England and France were quartered with those of March and Ulster, traversed by the *bendlet sinister* signifying illegitimate birth, clearly proclaimed his royal descent (see Plate 8).

From the beginning of Henry VIII's reign it is clear that Arthur was a close and trusted companion to the young king, and for thirty years he prospered in the royal service. Apart from their kinship, it is difficult to see what uncle and nephew had in common. At the time of his accession in 1509, Henry was not yet twenty, a robust, ostentatious, and splendidly self-confident young man: everyone's idea of what a new king should be. Arthur, on the other hand, was approaching fifty, and had already seen plenty of the changing fortunes of the world. He was apparently tall and slender, but no portrait of him survives and we have no real clue as to his physical appearance. A mild-mannered, gentle, rather easy-going and perhaps slightly dull character, he would not have cut much ice in the slippery world of Tudor politics had he not had the advantage of birth. His faithful proctor, John Husee, more of a friend than a servant of the family, once had to remind him to seal his letters properly in case they fell into the wrong hands.

It was almost certainly the king who arranged Arthur's first marriage, in 1511, to the Lady Elizabeth, daughter of Edward Grey, Viscount Lisle, and widow of Henry VII's notorious minister Edmund Lord Dudley. Elizabeth bore him three daughters, and it was through her that he acquired his title of Viscount Lisle in 1523, which elevated him to the English peerage. With the title came also a vast landed estate: in 1527 his estates were valued at £800 *per annum*, placing him in the top rank of English landowners. In 1524 he was further honoured by being installed as a Knight of the Garter, and in 1525 came his appointment as vice-admiral of England. He was also a member of the king's privy council, and in 1533 he acted as 'chief panter' (technically, the head of the pantry, but really an honorary court office) at the banquet celebrating Henry VIII's second marriage, to Anne Boleyn.

By this time Arthur too had embarked on a second marriage. Elizabeth Dudley died in 1525–6, and early in 1529 Arthur married Honor Grenville, widow of Sir John Basset. Honor was much younger than Arthur: she was born between 1493 and 1495, so there was probably a disparity of some thirty years in their ages. Despite this disparity, and despite the great differences in their characters which are revealed in their letters, there is no doubt that their marriage was an extremely happy one. The letters which they exchanged are full of expressions of affection: 'mine own sweetheart' was the usual opening, but Arthur's letters to Honor sometimes began 'my very heart root, and entirely beloved bedfellow'. One of Honor's letters to Arthur concluded with 'her that is more yours than her own, which had much rather die with you there than live here'. It is against this background of an extremely happy family life that one must view the tragedy that overtook them at the hands of Henry VIII.

In March 1533, barely a month after attending the king's marriage to Anne Boleyn, Arthur relinquished his post as vice-admiral of England to take up his last and most demanding responsibility, as the king's lord deputy – governor, in effect – of Calais. It is from the period 1533–40 that almost all the Lisle correspondence dates, over 3,000 letters, an average of more than one per day. Their residence in Calais enforced upon them both the continual chore of letter-writing in order to manage their affairs in England, to keep in touch with their children, friends and relatives, and to keep the king and his ministers in touch with affairs at Calais. The most regular correspondent with both Arthur and Honor was their splendid factotum, John Husee. Husee was the perfect servant. A shrewd bargainer, a very energetic and capable businessman on his employer's behalf, he was at the same time a man of compassion and loyalty, and clearly revelled, a little self-importantly, in being known as 'Lord Lisle's man'. Each New Year he went personally to the king to deliver the Lisles' New Year's gift, and each year he wrote with glowing pride and immense detail of his conversation with 'the King's Majesty'. Once he declared himself to be sure that the king had spoken more words to him than to anyone else that day. His capacity for letter-writing was remarkable, and the range of duties which he performed on the Lisles' behalf almost endless. Sometimes he wrote two or three letters in one day, always trying to be first with the news and to keep Arthur and Honor closely in touch with English affairs. In return, he was treated with the utmost confidence by both his employers. If Honor – a much more demanding task-master than her husband – was sometimes a little testy with him, it is clear that her moods never lasted long and that John Husee was soon restored to full confidence.

Honor seems to have been prone to emotional instability: in 1537 she experienced a phantom pregnancy, and after Arthur's death she apparently went out of her mind – although the circumstances of his death probably had a lot to do with this. She was also more hard-headed than her husband, more outspoken, shrewder in business matters, and eager to win influential friends. Those who requested office or favour from Arthur were well aware that if Honor could be persuaded to put in a good word for them, more than half the battle was won. At the same time she behaved in public with all the deference to her husband – 'my lord, my governor' – that was expected of her. Yet despite the outward show of submission to her husband's will, Husee was not the only friend of the Lisles to recognise that Arthur had both a formidable and a rather highly-strung wife. Writing to Arthur, friends could afford to be slightly less than formal on occasions; writing to Honor, they recognised that the due formalities had to be observed.

Honor also had strong views on religion, and in the strife-torn England of the 1530s, these were a dangerous liability. Early in 1534, England's breach with Rome had been finalised: papal authority over the English church was denied, and the monarch instead became the head of the English church. What was equally difficult to decide, however, was just how far down the road to Lutheran doctrines the English church should go. Throughout the 1530s – and indeed for many decades following – there was fierce controversy in England between those who wished to retain as many as possible of the beliefs and practices of the Roman Catholic church, and those who wished to turn England into a fully fledged Protestant state. And of course it was not merely a matter of religion. The pope endeavoured by any means at his disposal, including military ones, to regain England for the Catholic cause. Catholic France was persuaded – if any persuasion were necessary – to wage war on the excommunicated English king. To declare oneself a 'papist', therefore, was to be guilty not only of heresy, but also of treason. Even to be suspected of 'papistical' sympathies was highly dangerous. There is no doubt that Honor had strong papist sympathies. In 1537 she wrote to Archbishop Cranmer to intercede on behalf of two 'papist' priests who had been arrested in Calais, and received a warning from Thomas Cromwell to stop meddling. In 1538 Husee advised her 'to leave part of such ceremonies as you do use, as long prayers and offering of candles, and at some time refrain you and not speak, though your ladyship have cause, when you hear things spoken that liketh you not, it should sound highly to your honour and cause less speech'. Clearly rumours about Honor's religious sympathies had reached England.

What made Honor's indiscretions doubly indiscreet was the situation in Calais. For nearly a hundred years Calais had been the sole English outpost in a hostile France. Permanently garrisoned under the command of the lord deputy, it was not only constantly vulnerable to French attack, but also more exposed than England to the tide of both reforming and reactionary ideas which swept over Europe in the 1520s and '30s. Religious dissension flourished in Calais: it was known at one and the same time as both a nest of papists and a hotbed of reformers. If the lord deputy's wife was a secret papist, might not the lord deputy be a secret papist too? And if he was, surely it was not impossible that he might use his power to deliver Calais over to the French? There were few things that the French coveted more than to be rid of this last vestige of English occupation in France. In fact, there was no such danger. On the religious question, as on most questions,

Arthur bent with the wind: in attempting to deal with religious dissidents in Calais, he constantly sought advice from Cromwell as to what was the orthodox line of the moment, and enforced it to the best of his ability. He would not have dreamt of betraying Calais to the French. It is not difficult to see, however, why Honor's views should have caused some consternation in England. Moreover, it was Arthur's misfortune to become caught up in a conspiracy in which, as it appears, he was entirely innocent, but which appeared at the time to cast grave doubts upon his loyalty to the English crown.

The train of events which was to lead to Arthur's and Honor's arrest in the early summer of 1540 really began in the spring of 1538. In April of that year, two young men arrived from England to take up new appointments in Arthur's household at Calais. One was Gregory Botolf, a vain, smooth-talking young priest from Lincolnshire who soon became known among the Calais community as 'Gregory Sweet-lips'. Botolf had come to take up his post as one of Arthur's three personal chaplains. Unbeknown to Arthur, he was a vehement papist. He was also reckless, ambitious, and able to bend other men to his will. It was Botolf who was to play the leading part in the conspiracy which proved Arthur's downfall – usually known as 'the Botolf plot'. The second man was Clement Philpot, a young Hampshire gentleman who had been recommended to Arthur by a mutual acquaintance and who was now to become an esquire in the lord deputy's household. Philpot was ambitious too, but he was as indecisive as Botolf was decisive, and he seems soon to have fallen under the sway of 'Gregory Sweet-lips'. They were not a pair whom Arthur would knowingly have welcomed into his household.

A month after the arrival of Botolf and Philpot, a new outburst of religious fever was sparked off in Calais by the arrival there of a preacher called Adam Damplip. Damplip was as strongly reformist as Sweet-Lips was papist, and his sermons soon gained great popularity among the reformist section of the community. There was at this time confusion both in England and in Calais as to which way the king was going to turn on religious matters. Cromwell, who carried more authority than anyone except the king in matters of state, was pressing for more clear-cut Lutheran reforms, but there was a strong party in both church and state which argued for a return to more conservative (i.e., Catholic) practices, and public opinion generally seemed to favour this party. Until the king made up his mind, however, it might be fatal to go too far in either direction. Arthur, somewhat naively, welcomed Damplip to Calais and licensed him to preach. When the contents of his sermons became known in England, however, orders were sent to Arthur to arrest him and send him across the water for examination by the English bishops. As it turned out, Damplip was eventually executed for his overzealous reformist views, but in Calais the damage had already been done. The unwitting lord deputy, by trying to follow what he thought to be the orthodox line, had stirred up religious dissension in Calais to a new pitch of fervour, and raised grave doubts at home about his ability to handle the situation.

Throughout the rest of 1538 and all through 1539 Calais remained in a state of ferment. In the spring of 1539 the king finally made up his mind on the religious question. The Act of Six Articles, which became a statute in June 1539, was an undoubted victory for the 'conservatives', led by Cromwell's arch-foe the duke of Norfolk. Although it did not question the king's supremacy over the English church, and thus unequivocally confirmed the breach with Rome, it was in many ways more 'Catholic' than 'Protestant' in outlook, and thus put the reformist Cromwell in a very difficult position. His reaction to the Act was ambiguous. Officially, he had no option but to trim his sails to the wind, to support the Act and to be seen to be supporting it, but unofficially he continued to try to protect his reformist friends – including those at Calais. Cromwell's attitude thus put Arthur in almost as difficult a position as Cromwell himself. He was almost entirely dependent on Cromwell for guidance in his handling of affairs at Calais: Cromwell intercepted all his letters to the king, and it was Cromwell who wrote back to him telling him how to enforce this and all other laws. It is clear that Arthur was in awe of Henry's devious and forceful chief minister. What was Arthur to do? The council over which he presided at Calais was divided on religious matters, and while the king's new Act declared that the hard-line reformers on the council were heretics, Cromwell himself sent only evasive replies and was clearly doing his utmost to protect them from the rigours of the law. Meanwhile the trouble among the community was increasing. At one point Arthur claimed that he dared not go to bed at night without his armour on because of the warring factions. And as the religious problem increased, so did the problem of security, for the garrison was as split on the question as the council and the people, and Arthur found it increasingly difficult to maintain order among his own soldiers. It was surely only a matter of time before the French realised that Calais had become a soft target. Affairs at Calais were coming to a climax.

At the beginning of 1540 the king decided that enough was enough. Urged on by the duke of Norfolk, who saw clearly the double game that Cromwell was trying to play over the question of the reformers, and needed no second bidding to strike a blow at his opponent, Henry appointed a commission, headed by the earl of Sussex, with a mandate to investigate all the problems associated with the government of Calais, and particularly to try to stamp out the religious dissension. At the same time, Arthur was informed that he was to be relieved of his post as lord deputy. There was not at this time any suggestion that he might be arrested, nor even that he was being dismissed for incompetence: indeed, friends wrote to Arthur

167

congratulating him on his recall, and expressing the hope that he would be granted an earldom. On the other hand it is difficult not to believe that Henry now considered that matters at Calais had become too hot for his septuagenarian uncle to handle. Although Arthur was later to be accused of incompetence, and even of petty corruption, it is impossible not to feel some sympathy with him in the immensely difficult position in which he found himself. He had not been given enough money to pay the garrison in full; his authority had always been limited by the fact that men could appeal straight over his head to Cromwell – and naturally Cromwell did not discourage them from doing so. All in all, Calais needed firmer handling than Arthur was capable of, but the state of affairs there in the late 1530s would have tested the ability of men much younger and abler than himself. Had King Henry known what Gregory Botolf was doing in the early months of 1540, he would have been doubly convinced of this fact.

Towards the end of January, Gregory Botolf, Clement Philpot and another man in Arthur's household called John Woller, who was later also accused of complicity in the 'Botolf plot', were granted permission by Arthur to go to England on business. On the night of 5 February they left the town by the main gate and went to a tavern in the suburbs, ostensibly to await the boat to England which left with the 2 a.m. tide. Here they spent the evening drinking and gambling rowdily, informing all those around them of their intention to go to England and trying to ensure that their presence would not go unnoticed. When the time came for them to leave, they left the tavern and began to walk towards the boat. Philpot and Woller duly took the boat. Botolf, however, never went to England. In the darkness he simply slipped off from his companions and crossed the frontier into France. His destination was Rome; his mission, to secure an interview with the pope and the English Catholic exile Cardinal Pole, to offer to betray Calais to England's Catholic enemies.

Initially all went according to plan for Botolf. He made his way safely through France and arrived at Rome in good time. Here he had little trouble in arranging interviews with both the pope and Cardinal Pole, and to them he unveiled his plan. Philpot, he said, would remain within the walls of the town, while Botolf himself would gather a force of some five hundred men to mount the assault. At a given time, Philpot, with a dozen or so co-conspirators, would overcome the watch at the weakest point on the walls, and allow Botolf's men to scale the twenty-foot-high wall with ladders. Once Botolf's men were inside the town, they would quickly overpower the English soldiers guarding the main gate and allow a small army of Frenchmen, ready and waiting, to seize the town and expel the English. Calais would be French once more, and the pope would have struck a devastating blow at the 'arch-heretic' king of England. The pope was apparently so pleased with the plan that he gave Gregory Botolf 200 crowns with which to start making preparations.

Having secured papal backing for his plan, Botolf promptly returned to Calais. He arrived back there on 17 March, one day after the king's commissioners, led by the earl of Sussex, had arrived in the town. The presence of the commissioners must have been something of a blow to Botolf. Charged with rooting out heresy and setting the town's defences on a proper footing, they struck fear into the hearts of all those whose religious beliefs were open to question, and no doubt Botolf thought it better to be out of Calais at such a time. On 18 March he obtained permission from Arthur to go to Louvain university to study privately there, and on the following day he left. But he did not go to Louvain. He went instead to a nunnery just outside Gravelines, in Flanders, a few miles up the coast from Calais, to await the return of Clement Philpot.

Philpot returned from England five days later, on 24 March, and at once set off to Gravelines to find Botolf. He arrived there on the following day, where, he said, Botolf welcomed him warmly and suggested that they take a walk somewhere where they would not be overheard. They agreed to walk along the walls of Gravelines, and as they did so, Philpot later claimed, Botolf unfolded to him for the first time the details of his plan. Up to this time, Philpot said, he had known that Botolf had strong papist sympathies and that when he slipped off into the darkness on the night of 5 February he had been intending to make his way to Rome, but he had had no idea of the full extent of Botolf's treachery. Nevertheless he agreed to the plan – in order not to rouse Botolf's suspicions, he claimed later – and on the following day, 26 March, which was Good Friday, Philpot returned to Calais. Two or three days later, Botolf left Gravelines for Ghent to meet his papal contacts.

So far it must have seemed to Botolf that everything was going well, but it was at this point that Philpot's resolution began to waver. How much he had known, or guessed, of Botolf's real plans is impossible to say. Knowing Botolf's character, his religious sympathies, and his intention to travel to Rome, he must have been either naïve or dim-witted not to suspect that something more than a good-will visit to the pope was afoot, but it is possible that he was telling the truth when he declared that, until that afternoon spent walking on the walls of Gravelines, he had been unaware of the enormity of the conspiracy in which he was implicated. It may be that Botolf, cunning manipulator of other men that he was, had gradually sucked the unwitting Philpot into the plot, telling him only as much as he needed to know for the moment until the time came when the truth had to be revealed, by which time he judged that his unfortunate friend would be too deeply implicated to back out. For a week Philpot agonised – a week that for him was to prove fatal. Then, on 2 April, when Botolf was still at Ghent discussing the details of the plan with the pope's agents, Philpot took fright. Requesting an interview with the Calais commissioners, he blurted out all that he knew about the plot to them, implicating not only himself and Botolf but several other members of Arthur's household. In doing so, Philpot not only forfeited his own life and the lives of several of his companions, but he also placed his employer under strong suspicion of treason.

The king was informed immediately, and on 19 April he sent a letter to the Calais commissioners ordering that Arthur be sent back to England immediately, and that Philpot be used to try to lure Botolf back to Calais. Meanwhile, however, Botolf himself had been less than cautious. While in Ghent he had mislaid various letters of an incriminating nature, which had found their way into the hands of Sir Thomas Wyat, the English ambassador to Flanders. These were forwarded to the commissioners at Calais, and gave further evidence of the scope of the conspiracy. By now it must have been evident that it would not be possible to lure Botolf back to Calais, so a royal sergeant was sent to Flanders to find him. The sergeant found him at Louvain and succeeded in having him committed to prison there on a charge of theft. Within a few weeks he had been extradited to England and imprisoned in the Tower, where by mid-May he had been joined by some half a dozen members of Arthur's household. It remained to be seen what would become of the former lord deputy himself.

When Arthur arrived back in England on 22 April, there seemed little reason to believe that within a month he would be joining his former servants in the Tower. On 9 May he attended the installation ceremony of new Knights of the Garter at Windsor, where he sat on the king's left, next to Thomas Cromwell, who had been newly created earl of Essex on 18 April. On 17 May Arthur attended the royal court at Greenwich. There were rumours that he too was about to be made an earl, but instead he found himself summoned before the king's council to be questioned about his knowledge of the Botolf conspiracy. Clearly the council was not satisfied with his explanation. On the following day he was personally interrogated by the king. On 19 May he was arrested on a charge of treason, on suspicion of being involved in the conspiracy, and committed to the Tower. The French ambassador Marillac wrote to his master that 'Lord Lisle is in a very strait prison, and from which none escape save by miracle'.

When treason was involved, the king's officials moved with speed. By the evening of the following day messengers had arrived at Calais to arrest Honor and her two daughters at the Staple Inn, the lord deputy's residence. They were dispersed to different prisons in the town. Honor was said to be distraught, almost to have taken leave of her senses, and it is hardly surprising. Their house was broken up and searched, and the Lisles' entire personal correspondence of seven years seized – which, if it was a tragedy for Arthur and Honor, has proved a goldmine for historians. Meanwhile, Arthur languished in the Tower, confined apparently in 'one small chamber, very narrow'. Initially rumours abounded that he was about to be executed any day: at one point his name was removed from an Act of Attainder at the last moment by the king. The execution of Botolf and his fellow conspirators, a foregone conclusion since their removal to the Tower in May, came and went without any further attempt to implicate Arthur. So did Cromwell's: Cromwell, the king's chief minister for half a decade and more, had made too many enemies. At 3 p.m. on 10 June 1540, as he entered the council chamber at Westminster for a meeting, he was suddenly arrested. Within seven weeks he was dead. For all his ambition and cunning, he had been an administrator of genius, and King Henry was later to rue this execution of 'the most faithful servant he had ever had'.

As time passed, Arthur's position seemed to become more hopeful. According to Ambassador Marillac, Henry declared that he thought Arthur had erred in ignorance rather than malice; in other words, he might have been guilty of serious neglect in allowing a treasonable plot to be hatched within his own household, but not even the ever-suspicious Henry could believe that his kindly, doddering uncle might have master-minded a plan to betray Calais to the king's enemies. Moreover, hard evidence on which to convict Arthur was conspicuously lacking.

Yet both Arthur and Honor remained in prison for almost two years. Apart from the fact that for most of this time he was kept in close and solitary confinement, we know virtually nothing about this period of his life. With Arthur's arrest on 19 May 1540, the Lisle letters come to an abrupt end. For an old man approaching eighty, accustomed to the comforts of a nobleman's life, a man who had spent most of his life in devoted service to the crown and who knew himself to be innocent of the charges laid against him, it must have been a bitter and humiliating experience. 'Never was captain better welcome to Calais', they had said when he first arrived there in June 1533. He might have taken some comfort from the fact, if he ever got to hear of it, that the new deputy at Calais, Lord Maltravers, was no more successful at quelling the disturbances there than Arthur had been.

In the spring of 1541 Henry VIII declared his intention to empty the Tower of all its prisoners by the end of the summer – which meant either that they would be released or that they would be executed. The king's meaning soon became clear. The new reign of terror began on 28 May with the execution of Margaret Pole, countess of Salisbury, Arthur's cousin, who was aged sixty-seven and whose only crimes were that she was the daughter of George duke of Clarence, and that she had married into the family which Henry most feared, the Poles. Eustace Chapuys, the imperial ambassador in England, described her death in grim detail: 'as the ordinary executioner of justice was absent, doing his work in the north, a wretched and blundering youth was chosen, who literally hacked her head and shoulders to pieces in the most pitiful manner'. During the next few months others followed rapidly: in mid-June Marillac wrote that 'it is also said that lords Lisle and my lord Leonard Grey are in great danger to die this week or the next'. Grey was the son of Thomas Grey, marquis of Dorset, and was accused of treasonable dealings with the Irish following his appointment as deputy-governor of Ireland. He was executed on 28 June, but still Arthur remained in the Tower, and by the middle of July Marillac had heard that he had been moved out of solitary confinement and been granted the freedom to walk on the walls of the Tower. From now on, his position became ever more hopeful. In January 1542 Marillac thought that he was 'at a point to have his pardon'. By the end of the month his arms had been restored to the Chapel of the Garter at Windsor – a sure sign that he was about to be freed. Yet at this time Henry was busy with other matters. His fifth wife, Katherine Howard, was found guilty of committing adultery with a member of the king's household, Thomas Culpeper. On 13 February 1542, she was executed. Four days later, as Henry was being rowed down the Thames from Westminster to Greenwich, passing by the Tower, Arthur caught his first glimpse of the king for almost two years, and he

> raised his hands high, and shouted hoarsely from the Tower where he was imprisoned for mercy and release from prison. The king took it graciously, and sent his secretary to the Tower to the lord to show him the king had given him his pardon, and that he would have his freedom and release from prison two or three days later, and that he would get back his possessions and offices.

Arthur was indeed to be released, with a full pardon, and with full restoration to his titles and dignities. But Arthur never did leave the Tower. The man whom Henry had sent to inform him of his pardon was Thomas Wriothesley, the king's new-found successor to Cromwell. When Wriothesley brought him the news, Arthur became so excited that 'his heart was overcharged therewith', and he promptly collapsed with a heart attack. Two days later, on 3 March, having never left the Tower, he died. 'Which makes it observable', remarked one eighteenth-century historian, 'that this king's mercy was as fatal as his judgments'.

A few days later, they brought the news to Honor at Calais. It was hardly a month since she had been told that Arthur was about to be released. Of the rest of her life we know very little, but it takes little imagination to believe that Foxe was telling the truth when he said that she 'fell distraught of mind' at the news, 'and so continued many years after'. 'I never heard', remarked another contemporary, 'that God gave her back her senses.' Honor and her two daughters were released on 15 March 1542, and returned to England a few days later. She soon retired to her West Country estates to live out the remaining twenty-four years of her life. In an age when widows older than herself often embarked on third and fourth marriages, Honor never remarried. She died on her estate of Tehidy, in Cornwall, aged about seventy-two, and was buried at neighbouring Logan on 30 April 1566.

Thus, somewhat pathetically, perished the last of the bastards of the medieval monarchs of England (unless, that is, Richard 'Plantagenet' was still laying bricks at Eastwell). Arthur was probably buried in the parish church of his Hampshire manor of Soberton, but a wooden floor now covers the medieval paving-stones of the church and it would require a major upheaval to try to discover the exact position of his tomb. Arthur was not a great man, but he was a kind man. The letters which he and Honor wrote are marvellously human, always readable, always illuminating character and motive. To read two or three letters by an individual might well tell us next to nothing about his or her personality. To read several hundred is gradually to build up a sure understanding of the author, his joys and sorrows, his hopes and fears, and his private tragedies. In the end, for Arthur and Honor, tragedy dominated all. What he was like as a young man we do not know, but by the time he presents himself to us in his letters – and he was probably seventy when the full flow of them begins – he seems somehow to be rather out of place, in a world dominated by younger and more thrusting men than himself. If Henry VIII was suspicious of all men, Arthur seems to have suspected no man. The enduring memory of the Lisle letters is of the happiness found by two people, one approaching middle age, the other already well past it, in what was for both of them a second marriage, and of the pitiful destruction of that happiness in the cynical machinations of Tudor politics.

POSTSCRIPT:
THE TUDORS

Towards the end of the fifteenth century, the status accorded to royal bastards was once again beginning to rise. In some ways this was simply a question of numbers, for between 1216 and 1461 England had been ruled by an unusually high proportion of 'clean and faultless' kings. Yet there was more to it than this. Arthur Plantagenet was the first royal bastard to enter the peerage since the twelfth century; John of Gloucester seems to have been intended for similarly high rank, while the marriage of Richard III's daughter, Katherine, to an earl provides a telling contrast to the marriages made by Alice Perrers's daughters. However, it is the remarkable career of Henry FitzRoy, bastard son of Henry VIII, which best illuminates this trend.

Of Henry VIII's six wives, only the third, Jane Seymour, was able to provide him with a son, and she died giving birth to the prince, on 12 October 1537. Yet the inability of Katharine of Aragon and Anne Boleyn to produce healthy male children was not entirely Henry's fault, for he fathered at least one, and probably two, illegitimate sons by other women. The most famous of these was Henry FitzRoy, and he is the supreme example of the prominence which a king's bastard could achieve at a time of uncertainty over the succession. He was born in 1519, the product of a royal liaison with Elizabeth Blount, lady-in-waiting to Katharine of Aragon. By 1525, after fifteen years of marriage, Queen Katharine still had not managed to provide Henry with a male heir: the only one of her children to survive infancy was Mary, born in 1516. In 1525, Henry began to heap honours upon his illegitimate son. On 7 June, the six-year-old boy was made a Knight of the Garter. A few days later, on 18 June, he was created earl of Nottingham, duke of Somerset, and duke of Richmond, with precedence over all other lords in the realm; on 16 July he was appointed lord high admiral of England (with Arthur Plantagenet as his deputy), and on 22 July warden-general of the Scottish Marches; lands amounting to the enormous sum of £4,000 *per annum* were granted him. There were rumours that the king, despairing of Katharine's ability to bear a son, was grooming FitzRoy for the succession, and surely there must have been some truth in the rumours.

Within two years, however, Henry had embarked on a different scheme for securing a male heir: this was the king's 'great matter', his divorce from Katharine of Aragon and remarriage to a new wife, which it took six years and a political and religious upheaval of immense proportions to accomplish. Yet even when the negotiations for the divorce were at their height, the royal bastard was not forgotten. In October 1528 Cardinal Campeggio, who had been appointed by the pope to try the divorce case, wrote that Henry and Wolsey were trying to persuade Queen Katharine to enter a nunnery, on condition that the succession should 'for the present' be established in Princess Mary. 'They have thought', he continued,

> of marrying the princess, by dispensation from his Holiness [the pope], to the king's natural son, if it can be done. At first I myself had thought of this as a means of establishing the succession, but I do not believe that this design would suffice to satisfy the king's desires.

Any marriage between Henry FitzRoy and Princess Mary would have been manifest incest. Yet Henry was prepared to go to almost any lengths to secure the succession in a male heir. A month later he sent ambassadors to the pope to ask if he might be allowed two wives, the offspring of both to be regarded as legitimate, 'whereof some great reasons and precedents, especially of the Old Testament, appear'. He even ordered a copy of the Talmud (the standard collection of texts and commentaries on Jewish religious law) from the Venetian printer Daniel Bomberg, to see if it contained any passages which might justify his proposal. But it was all to no avail. The pope was not his own master. A few months earlier Rome had been occupied by the troops of the Emperor Charles V, Katharine of Aragon's nephew. The pope refused to grant the divorce, Henry had to go it alone, and England broke with Rome.

In 1529 the rumours that the succession was to be vested in FitzRoy were stronger than ever. In that year he was created lord-lieutenant of Ireland, constable of Dover castle, and warden of the Cinque Ports. It was said that Henry intended to make him king of Ireland in preparation for his eventual succession to the throne of England. A French princess, a Danish princess, and a Portuguese princess were all put forward as possible brides for him, but when, in November 1533, he did marry, his bride was Mary, daughter of the duke of Norfolk. By this time the king's divorce had been accomplished, Anne Boleyn was queen of England, and Henry, doubtless confident that it would not be long before Anne bore him a son to set beside the baby Elizabeth (of whom she had been delivered on 7 September), no longer seems to have regarded his bastard as a future king. When the first Act of Succession was passed in the following year, there was no mention of Henry FitzRoy. By the time of the second Act of Succession (1536), FitzRoy was dying. His health had been poor for several years now, and he died, aged seventeen, on 22 July 1536, at St James's

Palace. There were rumours that he had been poisoned by the relatives of Anne Boleyn, or even by Anne herself, but since she had been executed in May 1536, it hardly seems possible that she could have had a hand in it.

Fifteen months after FitzRoy's death, Henry's long-hoped-for legitimate son was born. A frail, sickly child, Edward VI became king of England at the age of nine, and died aged fifteen. Henry's daughters Mary and Elizabeth were both longer-lived. Mary, who was queen from 1553 to 1558, died at the age of forty-two, while Elizabeth, born in 1533, became queen in 1558, and reigned over England until her death in 1603. Given that both Katharine of Aragon and Anne Boleyn also gave birth to stillborn male infants, it seems probable that it was some genetic defect which prevented Henry from producing healthy male heirs. His inability to do so created the classic succession problem, and raised Henry FitzRoy to an eminence unrivalled by any royal bastard since the Conquest. Perhaps it is idle to speculate, but if Henry VIII had died in the late 1520s or early 1530s, it is difficult to believe that FitzRoy would not have been a strong candidate for his father's throne. As it was, Henry was succeeded first by a nine-year-old boy, and then successively by the two daughters whom he had bastardised by Act of Parliament in 1536.

In 1035, the royal bastard Harold Harefoot became king of England. Exactly 450 years later Henry Tudor, the great-grandson of the legitimated bastard of Edward III's son, also became king of England. It may seem as if nothing had changed in the meantime, but in fact a great deal had changed. We might call Harold Harefoot a bastard, but it was not nearly so obvious to contemporaries either that he was one, or, if he was, that this should prejudice his right to be his father's heir, even in preference to his 'legitimate' brother Harthacnut. Before a clear line could be drawn between the legitimate and illegitimate children of any man, kings included, a revolution in attitudes towards marriage and the family had to take place. This revolution was essentially the work of the twelfth century, and its effects on both the political and social history of Western Europe were profound.

Once the line between legitimacy and illegitimacy had been brought more sharply into focus, the royal bastard was in a more equivocal position. As the son of his father he had automatic status within the privileged elite of the nobility, as well as a certain inherent authority, yet his ability to convert these natural advantages into something more, to cut a real figure on the political stage, perhaps even to challenge for the throne, depended on two things: firstly, his own merits, and secondly, a combination of fortuitous circumstances. Both Robert of Gloucester and Henry Tudor had talents in abundance, which is why they became such dominating figures on the English political scene, but without the combinations of circumstances occurring in 1135 and 1485 neither would have had the opportunity to thrust himself to the fore. It is worth recalling finally that such situations were not confined to the Middle Ages. When King Charles II died on 6 February 1685, he left no legitimate children to succeed him. His heir was his brother, crowned as James II, but Charles had also fathered at least sixteen illegitimate children, of whom the most distinguished and ambitious was James duke of Monmouth, the son of Lucy Walters. Monmouth had gained a considerable following among the Protestants who opposed James II's Catholic sympathies, and even before Charles II's death it had been suggested on several occasions that the king should name Monmouth as his heir. With his father dead, Monmouth decided to take matters into his own hands. On 11 June 1685 he landed at Lyme Regis on the Dorset coast, claiming a 'legitimate and legal' right to the crown. On 20 June he was proclaimed king of England by several thousand followers at Taunton. His moment of glory, however, was a brief one. In the early morning of 6 July his army was massacred by royalist troops at Sedgemoor (near Bridgwater), and two days later he was discovered hiding in a ditch near Ringwood (Hampshire), taken to London, and there beheaded on 15 July. He was the last royal bastard in England to entertain such ambitions. It is one of those perverse ironies of our history that neither Henry I, who fathered more bastards than any other English king, nor Charles II, who ran him a close second, was able to pass his crown to a legitimate son.

APPENDIX:
THE BASTARDS
OF THE ENGLISH KINGS
1066–1485

No definitive list of the bastards of the English kings could ever be drawn up, but below is a list of (i) the forty-one who can be identified with a fair degree of certainty; (ii) those for whom the evidence is rather less conclusive; (iii) those who have sometimes been described as royal bastards but whose attribution seems doubtful.

KING	BASTARDS		
	Identifiable	Possible	Doubtful
William II			Berstrand
Henry I	Robert of Gloucester	daughter to be	
	Sybil	betrothed	
	William	to William de	
		Warenne	
	Rainald of Dunstanville	daughter to be	
	Rohese	betrothed	
	Gundred	to Hugh Fitz Gervais	
	Robert	daughter married to	
	Richard	Fergus of Galloway	
	Juliane		
	Maud	Sybil of Falaise	
	Alice		
	Constance	Emma, wife of	
	Maud	Guy de Laval	
	Isabel		
	Fulk		
	Maud		
	Gilbert		
	William de Tracy		
	Henry		
	unnamed daughter		

178

| KING | BASTARDS | | |
	Identifiable	Possible	Doubtful
Stephen	Gervais of Blois	Almaric Ralph daughter married to Hervey le Breton	William
Henry II	Geoffrey 'Plantagenet' William Longsword Morgan		Peter, brother of Geoffrey Hugh bishop of Lincoln daughter by Alice of France child by Alice de Porhoët Richard
Richard I	Philip de Cognac		
John	Joan Oliver Geoffrey Richard de Dover Osbert Giffard John Henry	Richard Eudo (or Ivo)	Isabel la Blanche
Edward I			John de Botetourt
Edward II	Adam		
Edward III	John de Southeray Joan Skerne Jane Northland		Nicholas Litlyngton
Richard II			Richard Maudeleyn
Henry IV		Edmund Labourde	
Edward IV	Arthur Plantagenet Elizabeth Grace		Edward de Wigmore
Richard III	John de Gloucester Katherine Plantagenet	Richard Plantagenet	Stephen Hawes

NOTE ON SOURCES

Considerable parts of this book are based on research in primary sources, but it has not been possible to provide footnotes. Below is a list of the most important secondary sources consulted.

PART I: INTRODUCTION

Chapter 1 The English Royal Family in the Middle Ages

Short biographies of many of the characters mentioned in this and subsequent chapters may be found in the *Dictionary of National Biography* and/or *The Complete Peerage*. Two articles which discuss similar themes to those discussed here are, firstly, C. T. Wood, 'Queens, Queans and Kingship: An Inquiry into Theories of Royal Legitimacy in Late Medieval England and France', in *Essays Presented to J. R. Strayer* (1976); secondly, Pauline Stafford, 'Sons and Mothers: Family Politics in the early Middle Ages', in *Medieval Women*, ed. D. Baker (1978). Joan of Kent's marital career is discussed in M. Galway, 'Joan of Kent and the Order of the Garter', *University of Birmingham Historical Journal*, 1947, and K. P. Wentersdorf, 'The Clandestine Marriages of The Fair Maid of Kent', *Journal of Medieval History*, 1979.

Chapter 2 Marriage and Divorce

The two books which have been most useful are G. Duby, *Medieval Marriage* (1978), and R. H. Helmholz, *Marriage Litigation in Medieval England* (1975). F. Pollock and F. W. Maitland, *The History of English Law* (2nd edn 1969), vol. ii, deals succinctly with the law of both marriage and illegitimacy. See also a series of articles edited by J. Leyerle headed 'Marriage in the Middle Ages' in *Viator*, 1973; and three articles by M. M. Sheehan, in *Medieval Studies*, 1971 and 1978, and *Studies in Medieval and Renaissance History*, 1978.

Chapter 3 Sex, Love and Illegitimacy

Particularly useful are W. Hooper, *The Law of Illegitimacy* (1911), and R. H. Helmholz, 'Bastardy Litigation in Medieval England', *American Journal of Legal History*, 1969. See also P. Laslett (ed.), *Bastardy and its Comparative History* (1980); Sir H. Nicolas, *A Treatise on the Law of Adulterine Bastardy* (1836); J. L. Barton, 'Nullity of Marriage and Illegitimacy in the England of the Middle Ages', in D. Jenkins (ed.), *Legal History Studies* (1972); and I. Pinchbeck, 'Social Attitudes to the Problem of Illegitimacy', *British Journal of Sociology*, 1954. For heraldry and bastardy, see especially G. R. Gayre, *Heraldic Cadency* (1961). There are numerous works on attitudes to sex and love in the Middle Ages.

Note on sources

PART II: ROYAL BASTARDS 1066–1216

The royal bastards whose careers have been the subject of detailed study already are: Robert of Gloucester, in R. B. Patterson, 'William of Malmesbury's Robert of Gloucester: a revaluation of the *Historia Novella*', *American Historical Review*, 1964–5; Gervais of Blois, in H. G. Richardson and G. O. Sayles, 'Gervase of Blois, abbot of Westminster', in *The Governance of Medieval England from the Conquest to Magna Carta* (1963), Appendix II, and B. F. Harvey, 'Abbot Gervase of Blois and the fee-farms of Westminster Abbey', *Bulletin of the Institute of Historical Research*, 1967; and Geoffrey 'Plantagenet', in W. Stubbs's introduction to *Chronica Rogeri de Hoveden*, vol. iv (1871). G. H. White's notes on Henry I's bastards in *Complete Peerage*, vol. xi, Appendix D, were very useful.

PART III: ROYAL BASTARDS IN LATE MEDIEVAL ENGLAND

For Edward II's son Adam, see F. D. Blackley, 'Adam, Bastard son of Edward II', *Bulletin of the Institute of Historical Research*, 1964; details of Nicholas Litlyngton's career are in E. H. Pearce, *The Monks of Westminster* (1916); for Sir John de Southeray, see M. Galway, 'Alice Perrers's son John', *English Historical Review*, 1951. The best account of Richard III's usurpation is in C. D. Ross, *Richard III* (1982), and for Henry Tudor's ancestry see S. B. Chrimes, *Henry VII* (1972) and T. Artemus Jones, 'Owen Tudor's Marriage', *Bulletin of the Board of Celtic Studies*, 1943. For Arthur Plantagenet, see Muriel St Clare Byrne, *The Lisle Letters*, 6 vols (1981). Some of the themes discussed in this chapter are also dealt with in Mortimer Levine, *Tudor Dynastic Problems 1460–1571* (1973).

INDEX OF NAMES AND PLACES

Numbers in **bold** refer to principal references

Abingdon (Oxon), abbey 71

Adam, bastard of Edward II, 8, 136

Adela, wife of Count Stephen of Blois, 69

Aelfgifu of Northampton, 17

Aeneas, 53

Agincourt (Normandy), battle of (1415), 11

Akeny, Roger of, 100

Alan IV Fergant, duke of Brittany (1084–1112), 68–9

Albertus Magnus, on contraception, 41–2

Alençon (Normandy), 58

Alexander I, king of Scots (1107–24), marries Sybil, bastard of Henry I, 17, 61, 64, 71

Alexander II, king of Scots (1214–49), 72

Alexander III, pope (1159–81), 26, 108

Alexander, bishop of Lincoln, 80–1

Alice, bastard of Henry I, wife of the constable of France, 70

Alice, bastard of Henry I, wife of William, 64

Alice, daughter of Louis VII, king of France, seduced by Henry II? 10, 12, 98

Alice, daughter of Richard Fitzalan, earl of Arundel, marriage contract, 22

Almaric, brother of Gervais of Blois, 94

Alnwick (Northumberland), 106

Alpesia, 'the queen's damoiselle', 127

Amélie, daughter of the lord of Cognac, 126

Amice, daughter of Ralph de Gael, betrothed to Richard, Henry I's bastard, 67, 69

Angharad, mother of Gerald of Wales, 62

Anglesey, invasion of (1157), 71, 72

Anjou, 69, 97, 108, 110; count of, see Geoffrey

Ansfride, mistress of Henry I, 9, 13, 64; her bastards, 61, 66–8, 71

Anthony, the 'Great Bastard of Burgundy', 18, 50

Antwerp (Belgium), 155

Apulia, Simon of, dean of York cathedral, 118–22

Aquitaine, 97, 144, 148, 149; see Eleanor of

Arthur, prince of Wales (d. 1502), 35

Arthur 'of Brittany' (d. c.1203), 6, 121, 127

Arthur 'Plantagenet' (or Wayte), Viscount Lisle (d. 1542), bastard of King Edward IV, 158, **161–73**, 174; arms of, 53, 163, plate 8

Arundel (Sussex), 81, 82, 83, 88, 89; earl of, see Fitzalan

Aumâle, countess of, see Hawise

Avranches (Normandy), 70

Ballan (nr Tours), conference at (1189), 110

Balmerino (Fife), abbey, 72

Barbour, John, servant of Roger de Clarendon, 145

Barfleur (Normandy), 74

Baron Hill, Beaumaris (Anglesey), 129

Basset, John, 163

Bath (Somerset), 84

Bath and Wells, bishop of, see Stillington

Beatrice, wife of Rainald, earl of Cornwall, 65

Beaufort, family of, 53, **147–53**; arms of, 53, plate 6b, c; legitimation of, 49, 150; why so called, 148–9

Beaufort, Edmund, duke of Somerset (d. 1455), 148, 152, 154

Beaufort, Henry, bishop of Lincoln, cardinal-bishop of Winchester, 150–1, 153

Beaufort, Joan, queen of Scotland, 41, 53, 152

Beaufort, Joan, countess of Westmorland, 152; her daughter Cicely, 152

Beaufort, John, earl of Somerset (d. 1410), 18, 152–3, 159; arms of, 52–3, plate 6b, c; descendants of, 152

Beaufort, John, duke of Somerset (d. 1444), 148, 152, 159

Beaufort, Margaret (b. 1443), 18, 152–3

Beaufort, Thomas, Duke of Exeter, earl of Dorset, chancellor of England, 152

Beaumont, Robert, earl of Leicester, 73; adviser to King Stephen, 80

Beaumont, Roscelin de, vicomte of Maine, marriage to a bastard of Henry I, 70, 71

Beaumont, Waleran, count of Meulan, earl of Worcester, 73; adviser to King Stephen, 80, 83

Becket, Thomas, archbishop of Canterbury (d. 1170), 97, 116, 124–5

Bedford, duke of, see John

182

Bellebelle, ?mistress of King Henry II, 99–100

Bellême (Normandy), 68; Robert of, 68, 70, 71

Benevento (Italy), battle of (1266), 54

Berengaria of Navarre, wife of King Richard I, 126

Beverley (Humberside): provost of, see Morgan; townspeople of, 122

Berkeley (Glos), castle, 7

Berkely, Henry, his bastard becomes his heir, 48

Berstrand, ?bastard of William II, 59

Bigod, Hugh, 77

Biset, Henry, wife of, 127–8

Blanche, daughter of John of Gaunt, 147–8

'Blaybourne', archer of Calais, 156

Bloet, Nest, mistress of Henry II, 9, 13, 99–100

Bloet, Ralph, 13, 99

Blois, 69; counts of, see Stephen, Theobald

Blois, Henry of, bishop of Winchester, 95; besieged, 86–7; and Stephen 76, 77, 79–80, 81, 82, 88, 90; supports Matilda, 85

Blount, Elizabeth, mistress of King Henry VIII, 174

Bohun, Mary de, wife of King Henry IV, 149

Boleyn, Anne, wife of King Henry VIII, 13–14, 47, 163–4, 174–6

Bomberg, Daniel, 175

Bona of Savoy, 157–8

Boniface IX, pope (1389–1404), legitimates the Beauforts (1397), 18, 150

Bordeaux (Aquitaine), birthplace of King Richard II, 17, 156

Bosworth Field, battle of (1485), 4, 6, 152, 160, 161

Botetourt, Sir John, ?bastard of King Edward I, 135–6

Botolf, Gregory, conspiracy of, 166–71

Boullers, Baldwin de, 71

Boulogne, count of, see Eustace

Bouvines (Belgium), battle of (1214), 100

Bowes (Durham), castle, 106

Bracton, Henry, on bastardy, 45

Brantingham, Thomas, bishop of Exeter, 138

Braose, William de, 129

Brémule (Eure), battle of (1119), 70, 75

Bréteuil (Normandy), 66, 68; William of, 66

Bristol, 82–3, 84, 85, 86, 88, 90, 91; mayor of, 144; priory of St James at, 91

British Library, chronicle in, 136

Brittany, 61, 67, 68, 69, 97; duchess of, see

Joan; dukes of, see Alan IV Fergant, Conan III, Conan IV, Porhöet

Buck, George, Master of the King's Revels (17th c.), 53, 162

Buckingham, duke of, see Henry

Burgundy: Chief King of Arms to the duke of, 51, 52; dukes of, see Charles, Philip

Bury St Edmunds (Suffolk), abbey, chronicler of, 136

Butler, Eleanor: precontract of marriage to King Edward IV, 4, 12, 29, 157–8

Butler, Thomas, lord Sudeley, 157

Caen (Normandy), 61, 75, 80, 97

Calais, 21, 160, 162, 164–72

Calfe, John, clerk, arrested (1402), 145

Calle, Richard, marriage to Margery Paston, 27

Cambridge, university of, 142

Camden, William, antiquarian, 130

Campeggio, Cardinal, 175

Canterbury (Kent), 113, 119, 155; archbishop of, see Becket, Cranmer, Islip, Walter

Cardiff (Glam), constable of, 62

Carolingian kings of Frankia, 25

Castelbon, will of the vicomte de, 51

Castile: and Hundred Years War, 139; kings of, 54, 139, 140, 141, 147–8; and León, throne of, 147, 149

Celestine III, pope (d. 1198), 120

Cenarth Bychan (Dyfed), castle of, 62

Ceredigion (Dyfed), 62

Chalus-Chabrol (Limousin), death of King Richard I at, 120, 126–7

Chapuys, Eustace, imperial ambassador to England (1541), 171–2

Charlemagne, king of Frankia (768–814), 25

Charles II, king of England (1660–85), 9, 14, 54, 61, 135; grants titles etc. to his mistresses, 13; succession to, 177

Charles V, Holy Roman Emperor (1519–56), 35, 175

Charles VI, king of France (1380–1422), 18, 21; disinherits his son, 46

Charles VII, king of France (1422–61), 50; disinherited as Dauphin, 46

Charles, 'the Rash', duke of Burgundy (1467–77), 156

Chaucer, Geoffrey, poet (d. 1400), 148; Canterbury Tales, 40; his wife Philippa, sister of Katherine Swynford, 148

Chelsea, manor of, 95

Chester, earl of, see Ranulf, Scot

Chilham, Richard de, see Dover

Chinon (Touraine), 105, 110–11

Cinque Ports, warden of, 100, 175
Clare, Gilbert de, earl of Pembroke, 71
Clare, Gilbert de, earl of Gloucester, his wife, 62, 136
Clare, Richard de, 'Strongbow', 72
Clare, Roger de, earl of Hertford, his sister, 98
Clarence, dukes of, see George, Lionel
Clarendon (Wilts), 143
Clarendon, Roger de, bastard of Edward, the Black Prince: arms of, 52, plate 6a; his career, 143–6
Clement VI, pope (1342–52), annuls marriage of Joan, countess of Kent, and William Montacute, 16, 28
Clementia, mistress of King John, 128
Clementhorpe (Lincs), prioress of, 118
Cleveland, archdeaconry of, 122
Clifford, Rosamund, 'Fair Rosamund', mistress of King Henry II (d. c.1176), 9, 10, 13, 14, 100; Matilda, great-niece of, 102; Walter, father of, 9, 13, 14
Clito, William, son of Robert Curthose, (d. 1128), 100
Cnut, king of England (1016–35), 17
Cognac (Charente), 126
Conan III, duke of Brittany (1112–48), 61, 68
Conan IV, duke of Brittany (1156–70), 69
Conrad IV, Holy Roman Emperor (d. 1254), 54
Constance, bastard of King Henry I, 71; marriage, 70
Constance, daughter of Conan IV, duke of Brittany, marriage to Geoffrey, son of King Henry II, 69
Constance, daughter of King William I, 68–9
Constanza, daughter of King Pedro I of Castile, 139; married to John of Gaunt, 139, 147, 149
Corbet, Sybil, mistress of King Henry I, 9, 13, 74; bastards of, 62, 64–6; marriage arranged by Henry, 14, 62; Robert, father of, 13, 62
Cornwall, 64, 65, 66, 72–3, 130; earl of, see Rainald, Richard; sheriff of, 72
Coutances, Walter, archbishop of Rouen, 116–17
Cranmer, Thomas, archbishop of Canterbury, 165
Craon (Aquitaine), 144
Cromwell, Thomas, earl of Essex (d. 1540), 165–8, 170, 172; arrest and execution of, 171
Croyland (Lincs), abbey, chronicler of, 158
Culpeper, Thomas, 172

Dameta, mistress of King Stephen, 8, 94–5
Damietta, crusade to, 130
Damplip, Adam, 166
David, grandson of King John, 129
David I, king of Scots (1124–53), 64, 75, 78
de la Pole, Margaret, countess of Salisbury (d. 1541), 171–2
de la Pole, Reginald, Cardinal, 168
de la Pole, William, duke of Suffolk (d. 1450), 40, 152, 153, 154; his son, William, 152
de la Pomerai, Henry, husband of Rohese, 65
Despenser, Hugh (d. 1326), 136
Devizes (Wilts), castle, 81, 83, 86
Devon, 64, 65, 70
Domfort (Normandy), 68
Dorset, 177; earl of, see Beaufort; marquis of, see Grey
Dover, 113, 129; abbey of St Radegund at, 101; castle, 100, 116, 136, 175; priory of St Martin at, 116
Dover, Richard de, bastard of King John, 130
Drayton, William, killed by Roger de Clarendon, 145
Dreux, son of the count of, 100
Duby, Georges, on medieval marriage, 20, 26
Dudley, Edmund Lord, 163
Dudley, Elizabeth, see Grey
Dunois, Jean de, 'the bastard of Orleans', 50
Dunstable (Beds), 101
Durham, bishop of, see Morgan, Poitiers, Puiset
Dynham, Lord, 153

Eastwell (Kent), 161, 173
Edith, mistress of King Henry I, her bastard, 61, 68
Edith of Greystoke, mistress of King Henry I, 13, 65–6, 70; marriage arranged by Henry, 14, 62
Edith, wife of King Harold, 21
Edith 'Swan's Neck', mistress of King Harold, repudiated, 21
Edmund, earl of Kent, father of Joan 'Fair Maid of Kent', 15
Edmund 'of Langley', duke of York, son of King Edward III, 155; his campaign to Portugal (1381), 139–41
Edmund, earl of March (d. 1381), 152; marriage contract of (1354), 22
Edward I, king of England (1272–1307), 5, 6, 8, 54, 57; possible bastard, 135; possible mistresses, 136

Edward II, king of England (1307–27), 5, 7, 8, 15, 135; his bastard, 136; considers divorce, 34; deposition of, 22; marriage of, 21

Edward III, king of England (1327–77), 5, 6, 7, 15, 37, 40, 46, 49, 135, 138, 139, 142, 143, 144, 147, 148, 152–3, 155, 176; and Alice Perrers, 10, 11; arranges marriage for Alice Perrers, 14; his bastards, 136–7; disapproves of son's marriage, 16; makes overtures to the countess of Salisbury, 12; marriage contract of, 22

Edward IV, king of England (1461–83), 15, 18, 28, 37, 53, 135, 152–3, 154; affair with Eleanor Butler, 4, 12, 33; alleged bastardy of, 46, 155–7, 159; bastards of, 161–73; and Elizabeth Shore, 10–11, 13, 14; notorious womaniser, 4, 5, 6, 8, 14, 40; secret marriage to Elizabeth Woodville, 7, 23, 29, 36; succession problem following death of, 3–4

Edward V, king of England (1483), 36, 54, 154; alleged illegitimacy of, 4; deposition and death of, 3, 4, 5, 157–9

Edward VI, King of England (1547–53), 47, 176

Edward, 'the Black Prince', son of King Edward III, 52, 155; bastards of, 143; marriage of, 16–7, 144, 146, 147; papal dispensation in order to marry, 30

Edward, prince of Wales, son of King Henry VI, 152–3, 154; death of, 153; rumoured illegitimacy of, 46, 154–5

Edwin, earl of Mercia, 21

Ela, wife of William Longsword, 100

Eleanor of Aquitaine, wife of King Henry II, 7, 118; ?adulteress before marriage to Henry, 15; children of, 104; divorce from Louis VII (1152), 23; rebels against Henry II, 105–7; relations with her husband, 97–8; release of by Richard I, 113; and Rosamund Clifford, 9

Elizabeth, bastard of King Edward IV, 161–2

Elizabeth I, queen of England (1558–1603), 54, 176; bastardisation reversed, 47; birth of, 175; declared illegitimate, 47

Elizabeth of York, wife of King Henry VII, 158, 162

Ellen, granddaughter of King John, 129

Ely, bishop of, see Nigel

Entre-deux-Mers (Aquitaine), 144

Ermengard, wife of William the Lion, marriage, 71–2, 73

Essex, earl of, see Cromwell

Eudo (or Ivo), bastard of King John, 130

Eustace, son of King Stephen, 88, 89

Eustace, count of Boulogne, 94

Evreux, siege of (1119), 68

Exeter: bishop of, see Brantingham; duke of, see Beaufort, Holand

Eye (Suffolk), castle of, 101

Falaise, family of, 71

Falaise, Sybil of, ?bastard of King Henry I, 71

Faulconbridge, Philip de, 126

Fergus, lord of Galloway, marriage to a bastard of Henry I?, 71

Fernando I, king of Portugal (1367–83), 139–41

Fitzalan, Richard, earl of Arundel (1330–76); daughter's marriage contract, 22; granted land by King Edward III, 49

FitzGerald, David, bishop of St Davids, 62

FitzGervais, Hugh, seigneur of Châteauneuf-en-Thimerais, attempted betrothal to bastard of Henry I, 70

FitzGilbert, Baldwin, on Robert of Gloucester, 93

FitzHerbert, Herbert, husband of Sybil Corbet, 14, 62

FitzHubert, Robert, 83

FitzRichard, William, father of Beatrice, wife of Rainald, earl of Cornwall, 65

FitzWalter, Robert, 128; Matilda, daughter of, 128

Flanders, 100, 117

Flete, c.15th historian, 95

Fontevrault: abbey of, 68; Henry II buried at, 112

Fortibus, William de, 128

Foxe, John, 172

France, 61, 159, 165; adherence to canon law on adultery in, 45–6; constable of, 69–70; and Hundred Years War, 139; status of bastards in, 50

Franciscan friars, 145

Frederick II, Holy Roman Emperor (d. 1250), 54

Froissart, Jean, chronicler of Hainault, 140, 149

Fulk, bastard of King Henry I, 71

Gael (Brittany), 67; Ralph de, 67; William de, 66, 67

Gaines-in-Upminster (Middx), Alice Perrers's manor of, 137

Galeis, John de, ?bastard of the Black Prince, 143

Gascony, 100

Geoffrey, bastard of King John, 130

Geoffrey 'of Brittany', son of King Henry II (d. 1186), 69, 104, 127, 130; death of, 109; rebels against Henry II, 105–7

Geoffrey 'Plantagenet', archbishop of York (?1151–1212), bastard of King Henry II, 10, 13, 42, 57–8, 94, 98, 99, 100, 102, 103–25, 135, 153

Geoffrey, count of Anjou, 69, 89, 90, 97; marriage to Matilda, 81

George, duke of Clarence (d. 1478), 152; his daughter Margaret, 171; rebels against Edward IV, accuses Edward IV of bastardy, 156; his son, 160

Gerald of Wales, 35, 72

Germany, 81; bastards legally unfree, 50; emperor of, see Conrad IV, Frederick II, Henry V, Otto IV

Gervais 'of Blois', bastard of King Stephen, 8, 94–6

Ghent (Flanders), 169–70; birthplace of John of Gaunt, 155

Giffard, Osbert, bastard of King John, 130

Gilbert, bastard of King Henry I, 71

Gladys, step-daughter of Joan, princess of North Wales, 129

Glamorgan, lordship of, 75

Glanville, Ranulf, chief justiciar to King Henry II, Glanville, on bastardy, 43, 44

Gloucester: abbey of, 91; dukes of, see Humphrey; earls of, see Robert; honour of, 75

Gloucester (or Pomfret), John of, bastard of King Richard III, 8, 160–1, 174

Godstow (Oxon), nunnery of, burial place of Rosamund Clifford, 9

Gouet, William III, lord of Montmirail, marriage to a bastard of King Henry I, 69

Grace, bastard of King Edward IV, 161–2

Gravelines (Flanders), 169

Grancey, Reginald de, 66

Grandmont, monastic order of, 124

Gratian, Master (of Bologna), 28; Decretum of, 26, 27

Greenwich, 155, 170, 172

Gregory IX, pope (1227–41), Decretals of, 26

Grenville, Honor, wife of Arthur 'Plantagenet', 163–73

Grey, Edward, Viscount Lisle, 163

Grey, Elizabeth, wife of Arthur 'Plantagenet', widow of Edmund lord Dudley, 163

Grey, Leonard, marquis of Dorset, his execution (1541), 172

Grey, Thomas, marquis of Dorset, 172

Grosmont, Henry of, duke of Lancaster, 39

Grosseteste, Robert, bishop of Lincoln, on mantle-children, 44

Gruffydd ap Cynan, prince of South Wales (d. 1137), father of Nest, 62

Guildhall, 4

Gundred, bastard of King Henry I, 64, 65

Hailes abbey (Glos), chronicle of, 136

Hainault, 147–9

Hait, sheriff of Pembroke, 62

Halesowen (Worcs), occurrence of bastardy in, 49–50

Harenc, Ralph, 66–7

Harold, king of England (1066), repudiates mistress, 21

Harold 'Harefoot', king of England (1035–40), a bastard, 17, 42, 176

Harthacnut, king of England (1040–42), 42, 176

Hastings, battle of (1066), 11, 58

Hastings, William Lord, beheaded, 3

Hawise, countess of Aumâle, 128

Hawise, mistress of King John, 128

Henry, son of King Henry II (d. 1183), 104; death of, 109; rebels against Henry II, 105–7

Henry, bastard of King John, 57, 130

Henry I, king of England (1100–35), 5, 6, 39, 53, 59, 94, 130, 135, 177; appearance and character of, 60–1; arranges marriages for his mistresses, 14; bastards of, 8, 17, 37, 60–73, 74–93, 98; coronation charter, 24; death of heir (1120), 58, 74; mistresses of, 9, 10, 11, 13

Henry II, king of England (1154–89), 5, 6, 7, 8, 14, 15, 17, 43, 44, 57, 58, 61, 65, 68–9, 72, 73, 94–5, 126–7; during the Anarchy, 88–9, 90, 91, 93; bastards of, 97–124, 130; birth of, 82; considers divorce, 34; mistresses of, 9–10, 11, 12, 13, 98–9; last years and death of, 109–11

Henry III, king of England (1216–72), 5, 6, 57, 73, 100–2, 129; birth of, 127; no recorded bastards or mistresses, 135

Henry IV, king of England (1399–1414), 5, 6, 57, 143, 145–7, 149, 150, 152, 154; alleges that Richard II was a bastard 17; ?bastard of, 142; betrothed (1402), 21; knighted (1377), 138; qualifies legitimation of Beauforts (1407), 18, 150–1

Henry V, king of England (1413–22), 5, 6, 11, 18, 57, 151, 152; no recorded mistresses or bastards, 142

Henry VI, king of England (1422–61 and 1470–71), 5, 15, 18, 46; death of, 153;

incapacity of, 151, 154–5; minority of, 151; no recorded mistresses or bastards, 142

Henry VII, king of England (1485–1509), 6, 152–4, 158–9, 160–3; his ancestry, 4–5, 18, 151

Henry VIII, king of England (1509–47), 13–14, 135, 162–73, 176; children of, 174–6; divorce from Katharine of Aragon, 35

Henry II 'Trastamara', king of Castile (1369–79), murdered his legitimate brother Pedro, 54, 139

Henry III, king of Castile, 147–8

Henry V, Holy Roman Emperor (d. 1125), marriage to Matilda, 74, 81

Henry FitzCount, bastard of Rainald, earl of Cornwall, 72–3

Henry 'FitzHenry', bastard of King Henry I, 62, 71, 72

Henry 'FitzRoy', bastard of King Henry VIII, earl of Nottingham, duke of Somerset and duke of Richmond (d. 1536), 174–6

Henry, duke of Buckingham, 3, 4, 13

Henry the Lion, duke of Saxony, 72

Herbert, chamberlain to Henry I, 62

Herbert, Lord, 153

Herbert, William, earl of Huntingdon, marriage to a bastard of Richard III, 8, 160

Hercules, 53

Herefordshire, 144

Herleva, mother of William I, 58

Hertford, earl of, see Clare

Hervey, viscount of Léon (Brittany), 94

Heythrop, Carthusian monastery at, 101

Hikenai (or Ykenai), mother of Geoffrey 'Plantagenet', 57, 100, 103–4

Holand, John, duke of Exeter, 153

Holand, John, earl of Huntingdon (d. 1400), 146

Holand, Thomas, husband of Joan, countess of Kent, marriage of, 15–16, 28, 29, 30

Holy Land, 90

Hommet, Richard du, 97

Honorius III, pope (1216–27), 129–30

Howard, Katherine, wife of King Henry VIII, 172

Howard, Mary, wife of Henry 'FitzRoy', 175

Howard, Thomas, duke of Norfolk, 167, 175

Howden, Roger of, chronicler, 126

Hugh, bishop of Lincoln, 116; orders Rosamund Clifford's tomb to be moved

from church, 9; said to be the son of King Henry II, 99

Humphrey, duke of Gloucester, son of King Henry IV, 152, 153

Hundred Years War, 139

Huntingdon, 107; earls of, see Holand, Herbert; honour of, 72

Husee, John, servant of Arthur 'Plantagenet', 163–5

Iberia: and Hundred Years War, 139–41; royal bastards in, 142

Innocent III, pope (1198–1216), 26, 28, 31, 38, 54, 99, 120–1, 123–4, 130; excommunicates King John, 101

Ireland, 61, 97, 144, 160, 172, 175; Norman invasion of, 72; status of bastards in, 50

Isabel, bastard of King Henry I, 71

Isabel of Angoulême, wife of King John, 73, 127

Isabel of Gloucester, wife of King John: divorce of 34–5, 127, 129; marriage of, 53, 71

Isabella, wife of King Edward II; adulteress, 15; leads revolution against Edward II, 7; marriage of, 21; treaty with count of Hainault, 22

Isabella, wife of King Richard II, marriage of, 21

Isabella of Bavaria, wife of Charles VI, king of France, adulteress, 46

Islip, Simon, archbishop of Canterbury (1349–66), and marriage of the Black Prince, 16

Ivo, see Eudo

Ivry (Normandy), castle of, 66

James I, king of Scots (1406–34), 152; and Joan Beaufort, 41, 53; The King's Quair, 41

James II, king of England (1685–8), succession of, 177

James, duke of Monmouth, bastard of King Charles II (d. 1685), bids for the throne, 177

Jerusalem, fall of (1187), 109

Jesus Christ, 53

Joan, bastard of King John, wife of Llewelyn, prince of North Wales: legitimation of, 42, 130–1; marriage of, 17, 128–30

Joan of Arc, 50

Joan, duchess of Brittany, betrothal to Henry IV, 21

Joan, countess of Kent, 'the Fair Maid of Kent (d. 1385), 46; divorce of, 32–3; her

INDEX OF NAMES AND PLACES

marriages, 15–17, 28, 29, 30, 144; rumoured infidelity of, 156

João I, king of Portugal (1383–1433), 54, 139, 147–8

John, impotence of, 33–4

John, bastard of King John, 130

John, king of England (1199–1216), 5, 6, 7, 8, 10, 11, 12, 17, 43, 53, 57, 58, 71, 72, 73, 99, 103–5, 109–10, 114–15; bastards of, 126–31; becomes regent, 117; character of, 121; divorce of, 34; and Magna Carta, 24; mistresses of, 14, 127–8; rebels against his father 111; relations with Geoffrey 'Plantagenet', 120–5; relations with William Longsword, 100–2; succession of, disputed, 127

John, duke of Bedford (d. 1435), son of King Henry IV, 153

John de Botetourt, ?bastard of King Edward I, 8

John 'of Gaunt', duke of Lancaster, son of King Edward III (d. 1399), 18, 40, 41, 49, 138, 155; alleged to be a changeling, 156; his bastards and descendants, 147–53, 176; claims throne of Castile, 139; his mistresses, 147–8

Johnson, Dr Samuel, on chastity of women, 20

Juan I, king of Castile (1379–90), 139, 141

Juliane, bastard of King Henry I: dispute with Henry I, 67–8; marriage of, 66, 69, 71

Katharine of Aragon, wife of King Henry VIII, 13, 47; divorce of, 35, 174–5

Katherine, daughter of John of Gaunt, 147–8

Katherine 'Plantagenet', bastard of King Richard III, 8, 160, 174

Katherine de Valois, wife of King Henry V, secret marriage to Owen Tudor, 18, 159

Kemp, Thomas, bishop of London (1450–89), 38

Kent, 152; countess of, see Joan; earl of, see Edmund

Kinardferry (Isle of Axholme), 106

Kingston-upon-Thames (Surrey): church of All Saints at, 137; Down Hall at, 137

Kirby Malzeard (Yorks), 106

Labourde, Edmund, ?bastard of King Henry IV, 142

Lacock (Wilts), abbey, 101

Lancaster, Blanche of, wife of John of Gaunt, 147–8; duchess of, see Swynford;

duchy of, 147, 150; dukes of, see Grosmont, John of Gaunt

Lancastrian kings, 147, 151, 152, 153; claimants to throne, 6

Langley (Herts), 149

La Roches, Margaret de, married to Roger de Clarendon, 144

Lateran Council, Fourth (1215), 28, 31

Launceston (Cornwall), castle and constable of, 72

Launde (Leics), prior of, 145

Leicester: castle, 150; earls of, see Beaumont, Montfort

Léon (Brittany), viscount of, see Hervey

León (Iberia), king of, 147

Limoges, Adhemar, vicomte of (1199), 126

Lincoln, 150; bishops of, 95 and see Alexander, Beaufort, Grosseteste, Hugh; cathedral, 105–8, 130, Angel Choir of, 150; diocese of, 104; siege and battle of (1141), 84–5, 88

Lincolnshire, 148, 149; men of, 106; sheriff of, 150

Lionel, duke of Clarence (d. 1368), son of King Edward III, 155; descendants of, 153

Lisbon (Portugal), 139, 140, 141

Lisieux (Normandy), 78

Lisle, viscount, see Arthur 'Plantagenet', Grey

Lisle Letters, 162, 164, 170–1

Litlyngton, Nicholas, abbot of Westminster (1362–86), his parents, 136

Llanvaes (Anglesey), 129

Llewelyn, prince of North Wales, marries Joan, bastard of King John, 17, 128–9

Loch Tay, island of, 64

Logan (Cornwall), 173

London, 3, 39, 50, 77, 89, 117, 119, 145, 156, 157, 159, 177; apprentice of, 155; bishop of, see Kemp; citizens of, 85–6; mayor of, 145; riots in, 149; Temple in, 118

Longchamp, William, justiciar of England, 115–17, 120

Longsword, William, duke of Normandy, 100

Longsword, William, earl of Salisbury, bastard of King Henry II, 11, 98–102, 130, 153; tomb and seal of, plate 3a, b; William, son of, 102

Louis VI, king of France (1108–37), 67, 68, 70, 75

Louis VII, king of France (1137–80), 7, 105, 109; divorced from Eleanor (1152), 23, 97–8

Louis VIII, king of France (1223–6), 54, 101, 130
Louis XI, king of France (1461–83), 46, 156
Louvain, university of, 169, 170
Low Countries, and Hundred Years War, 139
Lucy, Elizabeth (née Wayte), mistress of Edward IV, 13, 158, 161–2
Lumley, Thomas Lord, 161
Lyme Regis (Dorset), 177
Lyons-la-Forêt (Normandy), 75, 77

Mabel, wife of Robert, earl of Gloucester, 75; holds Stephen captive, 87–8
Magna Carta (1215), 24, 101, 121
Maine, 69, 97; vicomte of, see Beaumont
Maitland, Frederick, 29–30; on bastardy, 53–4
Malmesbury (Wilts), 90
Malmesbury, William of, chronicler; on the Anarchy, 83; Gesta Regum, 93; on Henry I's affairs, 60–1, 62, 69; Historia Novella, 93; on Robert of Gloucester, 78–9, 87, 92, 93
Maltravers, Lord, 171
Malvern (Worcs), priory, 95
Mancini, Dominic, historian, 157–9
Mandeville, Geoffrey de, 128
Map, Walter, chronicler, 92, 108
March, earl of, see Edmund, Edward, Roger
Margam (Glam), abbey, 91
Margaret, stepdaughter of Joan princess of North Wales, 129
Margaret of Anjou, wife of King Henry VI, 153; adulteress?, 15, 46; unpopularity of, 154–5
Marillac, French ambassador to England (1540), 170–2
Marisco, William de, ?brother of Rainald earl of Cornwall, 64
Marlborough (Wilts), 108–9
Marseilles, 115
Martel, William, steward to King Stephen, 90
Mary, queen of England (1553–8), 54, 174–6; bastardisation reversed, 47; declared illegitimate, 47
Matilda, wife of King William I, 59
Matilda, daughter of King Henry I, 6, 61, 65, 66, 69, 94, 98; and Robert of Gloucester, 74–93
Matilda, wife of King Stephen (d. 1152), 94; capture of Robert of Gloucester, 87; demands husband's release, 85–6; negotiates exchange of prisoners, 87–8

Matilda, daughter of Robert, earl of Gloucester, 84
Maud, bastard of King Henry I, wife of Conan III, duke of Brittany (1112–48), 68, 69, 72, 98
Maud, bastard of King Henry I, wife of Rotrou count of Perche: drowned, 74; marriage of, 61, 68, 69, 71; mother of, 61
Maud, abbess of Montivilliers, bastard of King Henry I, 71
Maud, wife of Robert 'FitzRoy', 70
Maud, daughter of Henry the Lion, duke of Saxony, 72
Maudeleyn, Richard, ?bastard of King Richard II, 142
Meaux (Yorks), abbey, chronicler of, 127–8
Meiler, son of Henry 'FitzHenry', 72
Mendlesham (Suffolk), 135
Mercia, earl of, see Edwin
Merovingian kings of Gaul, 25
Merton: council of (1236), 44; Statute of (1236), 27
Meulan, Isabel of, mistress of King Henry I, 62, 71, 73
Meulan, Waleran of, see Beaumont
Meulles (Normandy), 70
Milan, duke of, see Sforza
Monmouth, duke of, see James
Monmouth, Geoffrey of, chronicler, on Robert of Gloucester, 93
Montacute (or Montague), William, earl of Salisbury (d. 1397), 15, 28; leaves money to his bastard, 49; marriage annulled, 16
Montague, John, earl of Salisbury (d. 1400), 146
Montague, Thomas, earl of Salisbury (d. 1428), 153
Montfort (Brittany), 67
Montfort, Simon de, earl of Leicester (d. 1265), 136
Montivilliers (Normandy), 71
Montmorenci, Burchard de, 70
Montmorenci, Matthew de, constable of France, marriage to a bastard of King Henry I, 69–70
Morcar, earl of Northumbria, 21
More, Thomas, 158; on King Edward IV's mistresses, 12
Morgan, bastard of King Henry II, provost of Beverley, 9, 130; tries to secure see of Durham, 99
Morieux, Thomas, 147–8
Mowbray, Roger of, 106
Murdac, Hugh, canon of York cathedral, 120, 122

Navarre, king of, 143; *see also* Berengaria of

Neath (Glam), abbey, 91

Nest, mistress of King Henry I, **62**, 71, 72

Nevill, Anne, wife of King Richard III, 160

Nevill, Cicely, countess of Westmorland, 152; mother of King Edward IV, 25

Nevill, Ralph, earl of Westmorland, 152

Nevill, Richard, earl of Warwick ('the Kingmaker'), 155, 156, 157

Neville, Hugh de, his wife, 128

Newburgh, William of, chronicler, 98

New Forest (Hants), 60

Nigel, bishop of Ely, 80–1

Norfolk, duke of, *see* Howard

Normandy, 42, 58, 61, 65, 66, 68, 69, 71, 74, 76, 78, 80, 82, 89, 91, 97, 110, 124, 152; dukes of, *see* Longsword, Robert, Robert Curthose, William I; left to Robert Curthose, 6, 23, 60; lost by King John, 123

Northampton, 106

Northamptonshire, 65

Northland, Jane, daughter of King Edward III and Alice Perrers, 136–7

Northland, Richard, 137

Northumberland, earl of, *see* Percy

Northumbria, earl of, *see* Morcar

Norwich, Geoffrey of, clerk (d. 1212), 101

Notre-Dame-du-Parc (Normandy), Grandmontine monastery of, 124

Nottingham, 159; castle, 106; earl of, *see* Henry 'FitzRoy'

d'Oilli, Robert, constable of Oxford castle, 14, 62, 65

Oliver, bastard of King John, 128–30

Orleans, 'the bastard of', *see* Dunois

Otto IV, Holy Roman Emperor (dep. 1214), 100

Owain, son of Cadwgan ap Bleddyn, 62

Oxford, 62, 78, 86, 88, 89, 92, 117; constable of, 14

Pacy (Normandy), 67, 68; Eustace de, husband of Juliane, 66–8

Paris, 105; treaty of (1303), 21

Paston, family of, *Letters* of, 27

Paston, Elizabeth, successfully rejects marriage, 27

Paston, Margery, marriage of, 27

Pedro I 'the Cruel', king of Castile (1350–69), murdered by his brother, 54, 139, 147

Pembroke: castle, 62; earls of, *see* Clare, Tudor; sheriff of, 62

Pembrokeshire, 144

Perche, lordship of, 68, 130; *see also* Rotrou, count of

Percy, Henry, earl of Northumberland (d. 1408): rebellion of, 146; his sister Maud, 138

Percy, Henry (Hotspur), son of the earl of Northumberland, death of (1403), 146

Perrers, Alice, mistress of King Edward III, 10, 11, 12, 13, 15, 37; marriage arranged by King Edward III, 14; Richard, father of, 13; her royal bastards, 136–8, 141–2, 174

Peter, brother of Geoffrey 'Plantagenet', 118

Peter the Lombard, 28; *Liber Sententiarum*, 26

Phares, 53

Philip, son of Robert earl of Gloucester, 90

Philip 'de Cognac', bastard of King Richard I, 8, 126–7

Philip II 'Augustus', king of France (1180–1223), 54, 100, 109–10, 123

Philip IV, king of France (1285–1314), treatment of adulterous daughters-in-law, 39

Philip the Good, duke of Burgundy (1419–67), 51, 52; many mistresses and bastards, 18, 50

Philippa, daughter of John of Gaunt, 147–8

Philippa of Hainault (d. 1369), wife of King Edward III, 13, 147–8; marriage contract, 22

Philpot, Clement, and the 'Botolf plot', 166–71

Plantagenet, *see* Arthur, Geoffrey, Katherine, Richard

Poitiers, Philip de, bishop of Durham, 123

Poitou, 130

Pomfret, John of, *see* Gloucester

Pontefract castle (Yorks), 160; death of King Richard II in, 145

Pontorson (Normandy), castle, 101

Porchester (Hants), castle, 72, 100

Porhöet, Eudo de, count of Brittany (dep. 1156), 69, 98; Bertha, wife of, 98

Portugal: English campaign to (1381), 139–41; kings of, 18, 139, 147

Puiset, Hugh de, bishop of Durham, and Geoffrey 'Plantagenet', 106, 112–25

Quinci, Robert de, 129

Radcliffe, Robert, earl of Sussex (d. 1542), 167, 169

Rainald de Dunstanville, earl of Cornwall, bastard of King Henry I, 64, **65**, 66, 72

Ralph, brother of Gervais of Blois, 94

Ranulf, earl of Chester, besieged at Lincoln (1141), 84–5
Reading (Berks), 77, 117
René of Anjou, titular king of Sicily, father of Margaret of Anjou, 154
Richard, bastard of King Henry I, 58, 66–8, 69
Richard, bastard of King John, 130
Richard I 'the Lionheart', king of England (1189–99), 5, 6, 8, 10, 58, 98, 100, 102, 130, 136; bastard of, 126–7; rebels against his father, 105–7, 109–11; relationship with Geoffrey 'Plantagenet', 103–4, 111–21; treatment of mistresses, 14
Richard II, king of England (1377–99), 5, 6, 28, 140, 142–6, 149, 150; ?bastardy of, 16–7, 46, 154, 156; knighted in 1377, 138; legitimates the Beauforts (1397), 18, 49, 150; marriage of, 21
Richard III, king of England (1483–5), 5, 6, 135, 151, 152, 153, 174; bastards of, 8, 160–1; imposes penance on Elizabeth Shore, 11, 38; usurpation of (1483), 3–4, 29, 157–9
Richard 'Plantagenet', ?bastard of King Richard III, 161, 173
Richard, earl of Cornwall, son of King John, 73
Richard, duke of York (d. 1460), 152–3, 154, 156, 157, 160; claims the throne (1460), 155
Richard, duke of York, son of Edward IV (d. 1483), 154; alleged illegitimacy of, 4; imprisoned in Tower, 3; murdered, 4, 157–9
Richmond, duke of, see Henry 'FitzRoy'
Ricze, Anthony, 21
Ringwood (Hants), 177
Robert, son of Henry 'FitzHenry', 72
Robert Curthose, son of King William I, 71, 100; inherits Normandy, 6, 23, 60
Robert 'FitzRoy', bastard of King Henry I, 65, 70
Robert, earl of Gloucester (1090–1147), 42, 53, 61, 65, 66, 71, 73, 127, 135, 153, 176; career of, 74–93
Robert, duke of Normandy (d. 1035), 58
Robsart, Theodore 'the Canon', on campaign of 1381–2, 140
Rochester (Kent), castle, 87
Roelt, Payne, father of Katherine Swynford, 148
Roger, earl of March (1354–60), son's marriage contract, 22
Roger, bishop of Salisbury, 80–1
Rohese, bastard of King Henry I, 64, 65, 66

Rohese, daughter of the lord of Dover, 130
Rome, 29, 40, 165, 168–9, 175
Romulus, 53
Roseworthy (Cornwall), manor of, 66
Rotrou, count of Perche, 73; marriage to Maud, bastard of King Henry I, 68, 70, 71
Rouen (Normandy), 74, 121, 124; archbishop of, see Coutances; archdeacon of, 108; birthplace of King Edward IV, 156

St Augustine, views on sex, 37
St Davids, bishop of, see FitzGerald
St George, brotherhood of, 140
Saint-Hilaire, Marie de, mistress of John of Gaunt, 147–8
St James's Palace (London), 175
St Jerome, on sex, 37
St Paul's: cathedral, 117; Cross, 3, 157
Saladin, 109
Salisbury: bishop of, see Roger; cathedral of, 101–2; countess of, see de la Pole; earls of, see Longsword, Montacute, Montague; John of, 97
le Sap (Normandy), 70
Saxony, duke of, see Henry the Lion
Scot, John, earl of Chester (d. 1237), 129
Scotland, 61, 97; bastards of Henry I in, 64, 72; English campaign to (1322), 136; kings of, 53–4, 84, 147, 152, see also Alexander I, Alexander II, David I, James I, William the Lion; status of bastards in, 50
Scrope, Richard, archbishop of York, executed (1405), 143, 146
Scrope, Stephen, 27
Sedgemoor (Somerset), battle of (1685), 177
Seymour, Jane, wife of King Henry VIII, 47, 174
Sforza, Francesco, duke of Milan (1450–66), bastards of, 18
Shakespeare, William, 58, 147, 149; King John, 47, 126; Macbeth, 147
Shaw (or Shaa), Dr Ralph, his speech in 1483, 3–4, 157–8
Shore, Elizabeth, mistress of Edward IV, 10–12, 13–5; marriage annulled, 33; public penance, 38
Shrewsbury, earl of, see Talbot
Sicily, 115; kings of, 54; royal bastards in, 18, 54
Skerne, Joan, daughter of Edward III and Alice Perrers, 136–7, plate 5; Robert, husband of, 137
Soberton (Hants), 173

Somerset, dukes of, *see* Beaufort, Henry Fitzroy; earl of, *see* Beaufort
Sotheby's, 22
Southampton (Hants), castle, 100
Southeray, John de, son of Edward III and Alice Perrers, 136, **138–42**
South Tawton (Devon), manor of, 70
Southwark (London), 39
Spain, royal bastards in, 18; *see* Iberia
Spigurnell, Justice, 48
Stephen, king of England (1135–54), 5, 6, 8, 65, 97, 155; bastards of, 94–6; reign of, 74–93
Stephen, count of Blois, father of King Stephen, 69
Stephen, constable of Cardiff, 62
Stillington, Robert, bishop of Bath and Wells, and Edward IV's marriages, 158
Stockbridge (Hants), 87
Succession, Acts of, 175–6
Sudely, John de, of Sudely and Toddington, 73
Suffolk, duke of, *see* de la Pole
Surrey, 49; earls of, *see* Warenne
Susanna, mistress of King John, 14, 127
Sussex, 49; earl of, *see* Radcliffe
Swynford, Katherine, mistress and wife of John of Gaunt, 18, 49, **147–53**; duchess of Lancaster, 149, 159; Blanche, her daughter, 148; Hugh, her husband, 148; Thomas, her son, sheriff of Lincs, 148, 150
Sybil, bastard of King Henry I, wife of Alexander I king of Scots, 72; marriage of, 62, **64**, 71

Talbot, John, earl of Shrewsbury, 157
Tancred, king of Sicily (1189–94), 54
Taunton (Somerset), 177
Tehidy (Cornwall), 173
Test, river, 87
Tewkesbury (Gloucs), battle of (1471), 153
Themistocles, 53
Theobald, count of Blois, 78, 92, 94
Theseus, 53
Thirsk (Yorks), 106
Tinchebrai (Normandy), battle of (1106), 60
Tipperary (Ireland), 144
Titulus Regis, 46, 157
Toddington (Gloucs), family of Tracy of, 73
Topcliffe (Yorks), 106
Touraine, 69, 97
Tours (Touraine), 105, 110; archbishop of, 116; cathedral school of, 107, 115
Tower of London, 117, 145, 170; imprisonment of Arthur Plantagenet in, 162, 170–2; murder of Henry VI in

(1471), 153; murder of the princes in, 3, 158–9
Tracy, family of, 128
Tracy, Grace de, 71, 73
Tracy, Henry 8th Viscount (d. 1797), 73
Tracy, William de, bastard of King Henry I, 71, 73
Trent, council of, 26, 29
Trent, river, 85
Tudor, Edmund, earl of Richmond (d. 1456), 18, 153
Tudor, Henry, *see* Henry VII
Tudor, Jasper, earl of Pembroke, 18, 153
Tudor, kings, 147, 162
Tudor, Owen: alleged bastardy of, 159; secret marriage of, 18
Tyburn (London), executions at, 145

Uhtred, son of Fergus lord of Galloway, 71

Veel, Peter de, 145
Vesci, Eustace de, 128
Vikings, 25
Vila Vicosa (Portugal), 140–1
Vitalis, Orderic, chronicler, 58, 67–8
von Poppelau, Nicolas, imperial ambassador to England, 41

Wakefield (Yorks), battle of (1460), 153
Wales, 49, 50, 61, 62, 64; Marches of, 100; rebellion in (1400), 145
Wallingford (Berks), castle, 89, 130, 145
Walsingham, Thomas, chronicler, 145, 149
Walter, Hubert, archbishop of Canterbury (1193–1205), 28; relations with Geoffrey 'Plantagenet', 112–25
Walters, Lucy, mistress of King Charles II, 177
Warbeck, Perkin, death of, 160
Wareham (Dorset), 89, 91
Warenne, John de, earl of Surrey (d. 1347), refused permission to make a bastard his heir, 49
Warenne, William de, earl of Surrey (12th c.), 73; attempted betrothal to a bastard of King Henry I, 71
Warenne, William de, earl of Surrey (13th c.), 128, 130
Wars of the Roses, 6, 151, 155
Warwick, earl of, 160; *see also* Nevill
Wayte, Arthur, *see* Arthur Plantagenet
Wayte, Elizabeth, *see* Lucy
Wayte, Thomas, 162
Westminster, 3, 4, 172; abbey, 3, 94–6; abbots of, Gervais of Blois, 94–6, Herbert, 95, Lawrence, 96, Nicholas

Litlyngton, 136; palace, 86; royal council at, 171

Westmorland: countess of, *see* Beaufort, Nevill; earl of, *see* Nevill

White Ship, wrecked (1120), 6, 23, 58, 67, 68, 74, 81, 96

Wigmore, Edward de, ?bastard of King Edward IV, 157

Willesford, Edith de, mistress of Edward the Black Prince, 143–4

William, bastard of King Henry I, 64–5

William, 'brother of the chamberlain', 64

William, son of King Stephen, 89

William, ?bastard of King Stephen, 94

William, son of King Henry II, died in infancy, 104

William I 'the Conqueror', king of England (1066–87), 5, 42, 53–4, 68; a bastard, 17, 58–9; divides lands, 6, 11, 23, 60

William II 'Rufus', king of England (1087–1100), 5, 6, 23, 36, 60, 61

William 'the Lion', king of Scotland (1165–1214), 97, 113; joins rebellion against Henry II (1173–4), 106; marriage of, 71–2

William II, king of Sicily (d. 1189), 54

William Audelin, son of King Henry I, 75; drowned (1120), 6, 58, 68, 74, 81

William, count of Hainault, 22

Wilton (Wilts), 90

Wiltshire, 65

Winchester (Hants), 21, 77, 89; bishops of, 40, *see also* Beaufort, Blois; castle, 100; council at (1139), 81; Eleanor of

Aquitaine imprisoned at, 107; 'geese', 39; siege and sack of, 86–7

Windsor (Berks), 170, 172

Windsor, Gerald of, marriage to Henry I's mistress, 62

Windsor, John de, nephew of Alice Perrers, 137

Windsor, William de, husband of Alice Perrers, 14

Woller, John, 168

Wolsey, Thomas, cardinal-archbishop of York (d. 1530), 175

Woodstock (Oxon), 9, 72

Woodville, Elizabeth, wife of King Edward IV, 3, 7, 23, 156, 161; her marriage questioned, 4, 29, 157–8

Worcester, 123; earl of, *see* Beaumont

Wriothesley, Thomas, secretary of King Henry VIII, 172

Wyat, Thomas, English ambassador to Flanders, 170

Wyclif, John, supported by John of Gaunt, 149

Ykenai, *see* Hikenai

York: archbishop of, *see* Geoffrey Plantagenet, Wolsey; cathedral and canons of, 108, 111–24; citizens of, 114; diocese of, 33; duke of, *see* Edmund, Richard

Yorkist kings, 6, 147, 152–3; bastards of, 160–73

Yorkshire, sheriff of, 106, 122

SUBJECT INDEX

Adultery: as grounds for divorce, 32; punishment for, 38–9
Affinity, see Marriage
Annulment of marriage; grounds for, 31–6; see also Divorce
Aphrodisiacs, 38

Banns, 28
Bastardy: adulterine, 45–6; allegations of, 51, 77, 154–9; divorce and, 32, 46–8, 129, 176; in English royal family, 17–19, 46–7, 54, 57–8, 61, 69–70, 73, 77–8, 104–5, 130, 135, 153, 174–7, and *passim*; in European law, 50, 53; in European royal families, 54; in French royal family, 45–6, 54; 'general', 47–8; heraldry and, 51–3; inheritance and, 43–53; law of, 42–8, 53–4; social attitudes to, 48–51; 'special', 47–8; see also Legitimation, Mantle-children, Precontract
Betrothal, 21, 29
Bigamy, 28, 35, 175; not listed in Roman law, 25
Born abroad, members of the royal family, 155–7

Cadency, heraldic, 51–2
Canon law, of bastardy, 42–8; dissemination of, 36; of marriage, 26–31, 33
Changelings, 155–6
Church: attitude to marriage, 7–8, 26–31, 35–6, 38; attitude to sex, 37–9, courts, and marriage, 26–9, 31, 36, 38; treatment of bastards by, 43–8
Common law: of bastardy, 42–8, 53–4; of marriage, 29, 158
Concubines, 25, 35
Consanguinity: bastardy and, 46–7; divorce and, 31–4, 97–8, 127; marriage and, 30–1, 36
Consent of marriage partners, 25, 27–30, 35, 37; lack of, as grounds for annulment, 34
Contraception, 41–2
Cruelty, as grounds for divorce, 32

Divorce, 31–6; *a mensa et thoro*, 32; bastardy and, 32, 46–8, 129, 176; in English royal family, 7, 15–17, 34–5, 127, 175; in French royal family, 23; lay attitudes to, 25, 32; political implications of, 35; upper classes and, 34; see also Annulment
Dower, 24, 29
Dowry, 22, 24

Endogamy, 25, 30–1

Family, ideas on, 21–4
Feudalism, 23–4; see also Marriage

Heraldry, bastardy and, 51–3, 146, 163; see also Plates 6a, b, c, 8
Heresy, as grounds for divorce, 32
Homosexuality: of King Edward II, 8; of King Richard I, alleged, 126

Impotence, 45; as grounds for annulment, 33–4
Incest, 175; see also Consanguinity
Indissolubility, of marriage, 32–3, 35
Inheritance, see Bastardy, Marriage, Primogeniture

Legitimation of bastards, 18, 43, 49–50, 52–3, 94, 107, 129, 150–1, 153, 176; refused, 99
Love, attitudes to, 40–2

Mantle-children, 44–5, 49–50
Maritagium, 22
Marriage, 20–36; affinity and, 30, 35; attitude of church to, 7–8, 20, 26–36, 176; of children, 21–2, 25, 34, 36; clandestine, 28–30, 34–5; clerical, 35, 38, 50; consanguinity and, 30–1, 36; consent of partners to, 25, 27–30; consummation of, 29; contracts of, 21–2, 34; in English royal family, 7, 36; in feudal society, 23–5, 27–8; indissolubility of, 32–3, 35–6; inheritance and, 25, 29; lay attitudes to, 21–6, 36; love and, 20, 36; political implications of, 17, 21; property and, 21–2; reproduction and, 23, 36

Marriage-portion, 22, 24
Men, adultery and fornication by, 25
Mistresses: royal, 8–15, 40; of Edward III, 10; of Edward IV, 10–12, 162; of Henry I, 9, 61–4; of Henry II, 9–10, 98–100, 103–4; of John of Gaunt, 147–50; of King John, 127–8
Monogamy, 'serial', 25

Parliament: Beauforts legitimated in (1397), 49, 150; 'Good' (1376), 138; impeachment in (1450), 152; Legitimacy Act (1920) passed in, 44; statutes in, 155, 157, 167, 175; trial of Alice Perrers in (1377), 138

Polygamy, 25
Precontract, bastardisation and divorce by, 4, 16–17, 32–4, 46–7, 157–8
Primogeniture, 6, 23, 26, 42, 51–2, 127
Prostitutes, 39–40

Queens, adultery by, 7, 15, 46, 172

Sex: attitudes to, 37–42; in literature, 40–1

Wedding, as exchange of 'weds', 22
Women: adultery by, 25, 39; status of, 25–6, 35; see also Queens